The Royal Marriages

Also by Lady Colin Campbell

Diana in Private

The Royal Marriages

What really goes on in the private world of the Queen and her family

Lady Colin Campbell

St. Martin's Press
New York

Library of Congress Cataloging-in-Publication Data

Campbell, Colin, Lady.
The royal marriages / Lady Colin Campbell.
p.   cm.
ISBN 0-312-09377-2
1. Elizabeth II, Queen of Great Britain, 1926–   —Family.
2. Marriages of royalty and nobility—Great Britain—
History—20th century.   3. Great Britain—Princes and
princesses—Biography.   4. Great Britain—Kings and rulers—
Biography.   I. Title.   DA590.C244   1993
941.085′092′2—dc20   [B]   93-695   CIP

First published in Great Britain by Smith Gryphon Limited.

First U.S. Edition: July 1993
10   9   8   7   6   5   4   3   2   1

CONTENTS

CHAPTER ONE

Empty Vessels?

*T*he intimate lives of the leading members of the British Royal Family have an abiding fascination for people all over the world. Every day tens of thousands of column inches are dedicated to that small handful of human beings who form the nucleus of the universe's most famous family.

There used to be constant speculation about the state of the Queen's marriage, but a dearth of information and the coming of age of her children put paid to that. Since then, the personal lives and private vicissitudes of the Prince of Wales, the Duke of York and the Princess Royal have kept everyone agape. Who played what part in the erosion of each of the Queen's children's marriages has accounted for the felling of several rain forests. But, even well-informed journalists seldom know a fraction of what is really going on. For those who do possess a wealth of information you have to look to the upper reaches of British society. It is they who surround the Royal Family, and, in their world, which is so incestuous that everyone somehow seems to be interconnected with everyone else, it is never possible to keep anything secret for long.

The way the system works is simple. If you are staying with friends who had a member of the Royal Family to stay the week before, and that royal was overheard making noisy and passionate love with someone to whom he or she is not married, you are obviously going to get a blow by blow description of all the oohs, aahs, squeaks and creaks. Very few people are so compulsively secretive that they will not share a good story with close friends, especially if it involves someone of great fame or rank, in whose reflected glory they can then bask.

As a result, if you and your friends and relations are members of any of the many circles surrounding the Royal Family, you very quickly learn what is going on, even if you do not want to. It is not a case of seeking gossip or

1

rumour, so much as being inundated by a welter of information from so many different sources, and in so many different forms, that you soon cannot avoid hearing the truth bells ring.

The real question that absorbs everyone is: who is sleeping with whom. All roads inexorably lead to or from the royal bedchamber. Is the Duke of Edinburgh faithful? Has the Queen ever known another man? Do the Prince of Wales and Camilla still share a friendship? Does he have other female interests and, if so, whom? What about Diana? Does she only blow kisses down the telephone line? What's her true story, and Andrew's, Fergie's and Anne's?

Royal marriages are not like ordinary marriages. They are affairs of state as much as unions between two human beings, and, in recent years especially, this has produced a host of conflicts, which have seldom resulted in happy marriages.

It should hardly be surprising that this is so. If you stop to think, now that royalty no longer looks to other royal families for the provision of its spouses, more than just availability has been thrown open. So, too, has a Pandora's box of possibilities, for you now have the situation where any ambitious person with a good line in chatter and a good seduction technique stands a chance of sweet-talking and screwing his or her way into a royal bed and, from there, into a royal marriage. Indeed, at least two women spring to mind who have used those precise means to acquire their coronets.

In both instances, these princesses have ended up with marriages that they did not find personally fulfilling. But this should not have come as a surprise to either of them. It is stretching things somewhat to marry a man you would not have wanted, had he not been a prince, then expect him to transmogrify into an entirely different person, more in keeping with what your ideal of a man should be like. Princes, after all, are first and foremost men, and more than one ambitious woman throughout the ages has married royalty, then found that she bitterly resents the man taking satisfaction in intimacies, which she cannot enjoy, and which she soon comes to resent.

Until 21 March 1871, when Queen Victoria's artist daughter Princess Louise married the Marquis of Lorne (later 9th Duke of Argyll), things were different. Royals only ever married other royals, at least in Britain, where the last marriage with a commoner had been that of the seventeenth-century Duke of York, later King James II, and the Earl of Clarendon's daughter, Lady Anne Hyde.

There were two overriding advantages to excluding from the selection of royal spouses those outside royal families. The first, and most obvious, was that the person selected would share a similar background, with all that implied. They would therefore know that their marriage was essentially for the purpose of providing future successors to the throne and for the

2

fulfilment of the social expectations attached to their great rank. No one expected to attain gratification of their romantic sensibilities, and, indeed, in a day and age when the fantasy worlds of the film, television and the print media had not yet coloured everyone's expectations with often unattainable dreams, people of all ranks, from royalty downwards, simply did not expect as much personal gratification from marriage as they do now.

If they were lucky enough to find the crock at the end of the rainbow, they counted themselves most fortunate in having stumbled upon so rare and unexpected a treasure. But marriage and children and family life, not necessarily a happy marriage in the modern understanding of that word, were the order of the day, and, at a time when status devolved upon women through their husbands, all married women, whether happily, blandly or unhappily married counted themselves privileged to have been spared the ignominy of spinsterhood.

Out of the shared values of royalty grew the second advantage of limiting the choice of a spouse to those of the same rank. Ambition was curtailed in such a way that its more dangerous and detrimental effects, which have become only too visible recently, were minimized. That is not to say ambition or the means for implementing it did not exist. There were many princes and princesses who plotted and schemed to marry their progeny off well, but at a time when the world was more stable and those in positions of power felt that they occupied these due to the wisdom of the Almighty, there was a franker appreciation of the merits of position than exists nowadays. The ambition of a lesser royal to marry into a greater royal house was therefore not a failing but a quality to be appreciated by all.

Quite another matter was the misplaced ambition of non-royals wishing to crash the hallowed and exclusive royal circle. This was frowned upon by all and sundry, until an exceedingly open-minded queen in the shape of Victoria ascended the throne and threw open her arms to all comers. So acutely did she feel the loss of her daughters, when they married foreign princes and moved away, that she actually changed the rules governing royal marriages. She actively sought husbands for her younger daughters from two hitherto unacceptable strata of society: the sons of morganatic and aristocratic houses.

It is difficult with hindsight to appreciate the full extent of Queen Victoria's revolution in opening up the spheres of selection for potential royal spouses. But up until 1870, when she broke the mould in her decision that Princess Louise's husband could be non-royal, only fellow royals had been deemed good enough. This caused terrible problems for members of any royal family who fell in love with non-royals. On the Continent, things had been managed with greater pragmatism than in Britain, for there was the institution of the morganatic marriage. This was a union whereby the royal husband retained his rank, style, title and privileges, while his wife remained a commoner. Queen Mary and the Duke of Edinburgh's mother, Princess Alice of Battenberg, were both products of morganatic houses, but the whole

3

thing was fraught with difficulties. Until Queen Victoria came along and made them all right, the descendants of these marriages were not regarded as suitable candidates for marriages with real royals and usually regarded themselves as too grand for marriages with mere aristocrats.

Queen Victoria, however, was a lady with a very practical turn of mind. Exceedingly passionate, with an unabashed appreciation of the pleasures of the flesh, and wearing one of the two most splendid crowns of the day (the other was the Russian), she saw no reason to let prejudice about the quality of royal blood prevent royal women who might otherwise remain spinsters from enjoying the pleasures of the marriage bed. Even before she had to consider husbands for her younger daughters, she had the problem of her cousin, Princess Mary Adelaide of Cambridge.

Mary Adelaide was pretty, charming, erudite and grotesquely fat, and when the morganatic Duke of Teck showed an interest in her, she moved mountains to marry him. Cousin Victoria obliged her, more out of compassion than from fear of being crushed by this human steamroller, and the Queen's reward was to see the Tecks' eminently sensible and truly regal daughter Mary marry her grandson George, Duke of York, later King George V.

From then until now, the field of acceptability has widened with the passage of the years. Morganatic, aristocratic or commoner, all comers from well-born families have been welcomed into the British Royal Family. Usually the neophyte has been incorporated into the fold without the loss of rank and privilege to the royal partner, but this has not invariably been so. Upon her marriage to Captain the Hon. Alexander Ramsay in 1919, Princess Patricia of Connaught had to relinquish her royal rank, and when Prince Michael of Kent married the divorced, Roman Catholic Marie-Christine Troubridge in 1978, he lost his place in the line of succession, though not his rank. Admittedly, this loss could not be reckoned a tremendous sacrifice, as there was more prospect of pigs flying to Mars than of him ascending the throne.

Aside from Lady Patricia Ramsay and Prince Michael, all the other royals who married commoners have done so with impunity. Not all of them, however, have upgraded their spouses without the dream turning sour. Royal Families are traditionally difficult to marry into. Whether one is talking about the British, the Japanese or one of the Continental versions, the courtiers who effectively run the institution of monarchy seldom make life easy for newcomers. Nor does it matter if the addition to the family is a royal or a commoner. All newcomers are given, to a lesser or greater degree, a hard time, as the courtiers jealously guard their privileges and bamboozle or steamroller their charges into performing in a way that suits them, the courtiers, whether it suits the royals or not.

It is often said, as so many of the marriages between royals and commoners have come to grief, that possibly royals should revert to the old system and marry each other exclusively. Yet it only takes a moment's pause for thought to realize that this is not a solution and is based on the fallacy that in-marriages only can be successful. In an older generation, four of the five children of King George V married commoners, and the marriages were successes as far as all sets of partners were concerned.

Admittedly the two subsequent generations have not fared so well, but it is debatable whether that signifies a lack of staying power of the commoner spouses, or merely the fact that contemporary values have changed to such an extent that divorce is now more acceptable than it ever was. Even for royalty.

But the failed marriages of Princess Margaret, Prince Charles, Prince Andrew and the Princess Royal are not the whole story. There have been successful marriages among their contemporaries. The Duke of Kent is solidly and securely under the thumb of his frail-looking, publicly charming but privately waspish (only to him) Duchess. Prince and Princess Michael of Kent have a civilized arrangement, which is a testament to old-world values. Princess Alexandra and the Hon. Sir Angus Ogilvy have a secure marital base, though the shining royal beacon is the glowingly happy marriage of the Duke and Duchess of Gloucester.

'Happy people have no story to tell,' says the eminent psychologist Dr Gloria Litman, formerly senior lecturer at the Institute of Psychiatry, and no aphorism more accurately encapsulates the joyous family life of Richard and Birgitte Gloucester. Born into a middle-class family in Denmark, Britain's lowest-profile royal Duchess is a charming, attractive, down-to-earth woman who should be every putative princess's role model. She not only looks good and behaves well, she is good. And, like the person of depth she is, she does not play to the gallery. The reason why she is quiet is not that she is boring or uninteresting or uninterested. She is simply a full vessel. And empty vessels make the most noise.

CHAPTER TWO

A Prince of
the Blood
Royal

*T*o a certain extent, we are all prisoners of our heritage. That is as true of commoners as it is of royalty. It is therefore futile to attempt to understand the Queen and her marriage without first looking at the environment in which she was raised and the family into which she was born.

The infant Elizabeth Alexandra Mary, born at 17 Bruton Street in London's smart West End district at 2.40 a.m. on 21 April 1926, was the first child of a relatively, in royal terms, unimportant couple. Her father was the second and shambling son of the King, George V, her mother a Scots noblewoman who might never have been allowed to marry into the Royal Family had the prospective bridegroom not been such an unpromising wreck and the First World War not swept away most of the Continental thrones from which royal brides emanated.

The generally accepted view of the couple who became King George VI and Queen Elizabeth has been glamorized considerably. But, if we are to arrive at anything akin to an accurate appreciation of individuals as they were when particular events in their lives were unfolding, we must view them instead with the harsh light of contemporaneousness. The soft blur of hindsight might be kinder and more flattering, but it gets us no nearer the truth.

Bertie, as the Duke of York was known, was and had always been a figure of pathos. His elder brother was the glorious David, the then Prince of Wales. Generally acknowledged to be the most glamorous and desirable

6

man of his time, David seemed incapable of putting a foot wrong; Bertie, of putting one right. From the moment of their respective births, in 1894 and 1895, these seemed to be the roles nature allotted them. David, born Prince Edward of York, was a bright and beautiful child, with the face of an angel. From the word go, Prince Albert of York, on the other hand, was a duller and coarser version of his elder brother. As they grew into boyhood, David was charming and graceful while Bertie stuttered and was clumsy. Everyone loved the enchanting David; everyone ignored the unappealing Bertie.

Lord Esher's opinion of the brothers was typical of the way they struck those surrounding them. 'He found David clever and composed. He had thought of a riddle in bed, and it was really quite witty for a child. Prince Edward develops every day fresh qualities, and is a most charming boy: very direct, dignified, and clever.' About Bertie he could find nothing complimentary to say, so he said nothing.

The boys' childhoods finished off what nature started. In her excellent biography of King Edward VIII, who David became in 1936, Frances Donaldson paints a grim picture of their youthful lives. They seldom saw their parents, and, when they did, the experience was one of anguish rather than of pleasure. King George V quite deliberately brought up his children to be in terror of him. And Queen Mary, who had grave communication difficulties with everyone, found it impossible either to shield her children from their father's cruelty or to provide them with a mother's love and warmth. According to her aunt, the German Empress Frederick, Mary was 'very cold and stiff and very unmaternal'.

As if that were not enough, the little boys' difficulties with their parents were exacerbated by their nanny, who was a seriously unbalanced woman with a pathological love for David. Whenever she took her charges to see their parents, she ensured that the aloof and unmaternal mother would have them removed from her presence by pinching them just before being shown into the room. As Queen Mary, then the Duchess of York, could not abide crying children, the nanny's objectives were realized, with the result that the boys had no relationship with either parent until their demented nanny had a complete breakdown. Then the grim truth emerged, not only of her sick adoration of David but also of her neglect of Bertie. So contemptuous was she of this unfortunate little boy that she paid him no attention at all and never even bothered to feed him properly. The result was that Bertie had serious digestive problems and a speech impediment, which would stay with him, in varying degrees of severity, all his life.

Caught up in a downward spiral not of his own making, this spare to the throne continued to be subjected to an abusive upbringing, which was deemed to be for his own good. When he and his elder brother were old enough to begin lessons, Madame Bricka, their mother's former governess, joined Mrs Bill, their nurse, in the nursery. Then, at the age of six, Bertie and his elder brother David were turned over to the care of Mr Hansell, their tutor, and Frederick Finch, their valet. Bertie was found to be left-handed, a serious failing in those days, and the regimen that would intensify his stammer began in earnest. Day in, day out, Mr Hansell drummed into him how severe a moral failing left-handedness was. This only had the effect of increasing the eager-to-please little boy's stammer, which became yet another failing for which his tutor castigated him. It is hardly surprising that Mr Hansell had cause to complain about Bertie's lack of concentration, or about the stress-induced rages, which the frustration he instilled caused.

To add to his woes, Bertie had terrible knock knees. Part of most days and all of most nights were spent subjected to the restriction of splints specially constructed by Sir Francis Laking, Bt, GCVO, KCB, MD. This the good-natured little boy accepted with a stoicism that would later on, during the Second World War when he was King and Britain's back was against Hitler's wall, earn his country's admiration. 'I am sitting in an armchair with my legs in the new splints,' he wrote to his mother. 'I have got an invalid table, which is splendid for reading but rather awkward for writing at present. I expect I shall get used to it.'

What Bertie could not get used to, however, was the unremitting pressure, which increased daily with Mr Hansell's demands. Arithmetic induced heartfelt tears, which persisted until the advent of adolescence, causing his concerned father to write a letter that came as close to a display of understanding as that admonitory personality could summon. 'You must really give up losing your temper when you make a mistake in a sum. We all make mistakes sometimes, remember you are now nearly 12 years old & ought no longer to behave like a little child of 6.'

Life would have been intolerable but for two reasons. The first was that Bertie's parents were essentially decent people with noble ideals, and while they were undoubtedly inadequately skilled as parents, the surrogates to whom they turned over responsibility, and the regimen they created, left the children in no doubt that they did care about their welfare. Abstract though this sense of love was, it was nevertheless real. But it was the second reason that brought real joy and warmth into the children's lives. Their grandparents, the Prince and Princess of Wales, later King Edward VII and Queen Alexandra, adored children. Whenever their grandchildren came to stay, they encouraged them to tear about the house 'romping' and, far from abiding by the Victorian dictum that children should be seen and not heard, encouraged them to mingle with and show off in front of their adult guests. Such spectacular freedom, such unusual attention was almost too much for the overly restricted, hyperdisciplined York children. Bertie, especially, was prone to over-excitement and would sometimes have to be sent off to bed to quieten down.

In 1901 when their great-grandmother Queen Victoria died, and Grandpapa succeeded to the throne as Edward VII, the York princes moved up the pecking order. Their father and mother became Prince and Princess of Wales, and they, in turn, became Princes Edward and Albert of Wales. The pressure upon both boys increased. Although they were treated as a unit, Bertie continued to have the worst of all worlds, with David reaping all the praise, attention and affection. Even Finch, their valet, preferred the captivating David.

According to Penelope Mortimer in her acclaimed biography of Queen Elizabeth the Queen Mother, the 'handsome, stalwart, muscular' Finch was the nearest thing the boys had to a natural parent, and they were both devoted to him. His duties involved waking them up in the morning, hearing their prayers, bathing them, dressing them and tucking them into bed last thing at night. During the day, he took care of their clothes when he was not taking care of their needs. But it was nevertheless clear to everyone, Bertie included, that David was his favourite, and indeed Finch went on to serve him in adult life firstly as his valet and latterly as his butler when he became Prince of Wales.

It would have defied the laws of natural justice for Bertie to have lacked any virtues. But, in this, as in so much else, he was unexceptional. His mother's lady-in-waiting was the redoubtable Mabell, Countess of Airlie, and she became an object of veneration for this affection-starved royal waif. However, she recounts in her memoirs how he waylaid her at Easter 1902 with a card he had made for her. Intending to present it to her, he lost his courage, so silently thrust it into her hands and darted off without a word. 'When I succeeded later in gaining his confidence he talked to me quite normally, without stammering, and then I found that far from being backward he was an intelligent child with more force of character than anyone suspected in those days.' The card was also well and imaginatively made.

The course of Bertie's life was laid down by his father, who had served in the navy. He would have to join his brother David and head for the sea. A less suitable career for the pathologically shy, perpetually seasick youngster was unimaginable. Nevertheless, he was made to sit his Osborne entrance examinations to the Royal Naval College for Cadets, then established in the grounds of Osborne House on the Isle of Wight. Being royal, there was no question of failing these, so any hopes Bertie had on that score would have been dashed, though he was so desperate for his parents' approval that it is inconceivable that he would have put his personal feelings before a chance to gain George and Mary's approbation.

In January 1909, Bertie began his stint at the Royal Naval College. David was in his final term, but this was scant comfort to the dreadfully homesick younger brother. The rules forbade communication between the older and newer cadets, and as a result the shy, stammering Bertie was left to sink or swim on his own.

Bertie's solution was to get sick. Thereafter, whenever the weight of an unbearable burden became too heavy for him, he would avoid it, not by refusing to shoulder it but by allowing it to erode his health to the point of breakdown. Six months into his naval course, Bertie developed whooping cough. In yet another display of how inconsequential he was, he was treated, not by the chief medical officer, as his brother David would undoubtedly have been had he taken ill, but by a lowly assistant, Surgeon-Lieutenant Louis Greig.

Unimportant though Bertie was, he was still a member of the Royal Family, and once the doctors had him on his feet, they decided to take the cautious course and order a long period of rest. He was despatched to an estate ten miles from Balmoral in the Scottish Highlands with the loyal Finch and a tutor, Mr Watt, in attendance. Free of the relentless pressure, his health improved. So, too, did his stammer. He fished, he shot, he stalked, he walked. As he enjoyed the serenity of country life and a more relaxed pace, he even stopped drooling, a disconcerting habit to which he was prone. Soon he was so fit and well that his other nervous habits such as twitching and squinting, all but disappeared. There was the occasional hesitation in his speech, but he no longer even lost his temper the way he had done all his life.

Resuming his naval career brought back his nervous ailments as well as his constant seasickness. Once more, however, Bertie displayed a dogged determination to live up to his duty. Illnesses such as measles did afford him the occasional break from a way of life to which he was unsuited, but his colours were firmly nailed to the naval mast, especially after 1910, when his grandfather King Edward VII died, and his father succeeded to the throne as King George V.

Ill health did not afford Bertie a proper release until the Great War began in 1914. Within three weeks of its declaration, his ship, the *Rohilla*, had to return to port in Aberdeen to discharge the prince. Bertie, having been seized by crippling stomach pains, was diagnosed as suffering from appendicitis. Once more, the standard recuperative period of three months was prescribed, at the end of which yet more crippling stomach pains came to Bertie's rescue and spared him being sent back to sea.

For the next two years, Bertie's life became a round of illness and recovery. Throughout this period, the King's advisers were aware that his son must be returned to active service at the earliest moment, otherwise the press, which had hounded his cousin Prince Louis of Battenberg out of a job, might round on the second in line to the throne and accuse him of cowardice.

Posted to the Admiralty with a desk job, as soon as Bertie was deemed fit enough to return to active service, he was sent back to sea. This time the doctors took the precaution of forbidding any undue physical exertion. To someone as intensely active and *sportif* as Bertie, being denied the release that football and hockey or even ordinary calisthenic exercises provided was yet another pressure, which resulted in yet another deterioration in his health. This time he was diagnosed as having stomach problems, and, after toing and froing between his own ship and a hospital ship, he was sent back to Balmoral, to recover.

No sooner did his health improve than he was back at sea, on HMS *Collingwood*, though he did precious little fighting, spending most of his time in the sick-bay, with what was diagnosed as 'acute depression'. Within months he was back on dry land, this time at Windsor, ill with a duodenal ulcer. He took one last stab at seafaring, with the inevitable result, and, writing to his father from his sick-bed, asked to be relieved of his duties at sea. In November of that year, 1917, he was operated upon for ulcers, and early in the new year he was transferred to the Royal Naval Air Services.

Despite chronic ill health, Bertie's career at sea had not been a completely inglorious affair. In May 1916, when he was serving on the *Collingwood*, he darted from his sick-bed to man his post on top of the turret for a fight, which has gone down in history as the battle of Jutland. He acquitted himself courageously, which should hardly have been surprising to anyone who stopped to think that his whole life had been a fight against adversity.

After the war, Bertie's health remained as uncertain as it had always been. Louis Greig, who had been pulled from his post as second surgeon of the *Malaya* in 1917 and transferred to Bertie's staff as his permanent doctor-in-situ, abandoned the physical restrictions placed upon the energetic Bertie. When he was not shooting and hunting or fishing and stalking, he was playing tennis. A born sportsman, he excelled in all outdoor activities, even winning the RAF Doubles Competition at Wimbledon with Louis Greig as his partner.

It was just as well that Bertie shone out of doors, for within the civilized confines of the drawing-room he remained as much a disaster as ever. His stammer had returned in force. He drooled and twitched and squinted in a disconcerting and embarrassing way. To make matters worse, he had developed an affinity with the bottle in an attempt to soothe his troubled nerves. This Queen Mary found distressing, especially as it soon became apparent that the habit was exacerbating rather than lessening his ungainliness and the uncontrollable rages to which he had been prone since childhood.

Whatever his personal inadequacies, Bertie was still a Prince of the Blood Royal. He therefore had to be seen to be functioning usefully. As the decade drew to a close, he undertook an ever increasing load of public engagements, was made a Squadron Leader in the Royal Air Force, into which the Royal Naval Air Service was incorporated, and also became an undergraduate at Trinity College, Cambridge. There was no question of his

11

merits being tested, however, so he was not allowed to sit exams. Indeed, in so artificial and protective an environment did he function, that he did not even study or live with the other students.

CHAPTER THREE

The Ivory Tower

*T*o say that Bertie's prospects looked bleak would be to understate a future that seemed assured of nothing but embarrassment and discomfort. It would be charming to be able to say, as many other writers have claimed, that Lady Elizabeth Bowes-Lyon walked into this wasteland of dissatisfaction and, bowled over by his many attributes, gave way to the inclinations of her heart and agreed to marry him after a decorous period of playing hard-to-get. That, however, could not be further from the truth. Elizabeth came into Bertie's life through his equerry. Captain James Stuart, later Viscount Stuart of Findhorn, was the third and youngest son of the 17th Earl of Moray, and Elizabeth was in love with him, not with Bertie.

Jamie Stuart was a witty, attractive and articulate bachelor, the archetypal charmer for whom all the girls fell. His path crossed Bertie's in November 1918, in Brussels, where he was detailed to the visiting prince's staff. Bertie was there to represent his father as he rode beside the King and Queen of the Belgians in their victory march into their capital city. In his autobiography, Jamie Stuart wrote that he and Bertie 'had a great deal of fun'. Despite the war, Brussels still had fine restaurants and a full night life, and Bertie, for all his failings, liked nothing better than enjoying himself.

In 1920, just as Bertie was due to come down from Cambridge, Jamie Stuart was invited to become his equerry. Although he was in Scotland reading Law, he accepted and was soon installed at Buckingham Palace, where the Windsor children were now coming into their own. David had already begun to dedicate his off-duty hours to pleasure, and his younger siblings, Bertie, Princess Mary (later the Princess Royal), Prince Henry (the Duke of Gloucester) and Prince George (the Duke of Kent) followed suit.

Social life had already picked up to the point where it was as if there had been no Great War, and the Royal Family embarked on a round of official and private entertainment, attending the balls, galas, levees and parties that were so much a feature of the great age of the aristocracy. Every evening during the season there was a ball at one of the mansions of the nobility, unless a State Ball at Buckingham Palace was taking place, in which case *everyone* could be found there.

One of the young ladies who was seen everywhere, north and south of the Border, was Elizabeth Bowes-Lyon. The youngest daughter of the Earl and Countess of Strathmore and Kinghorne, she had tremendous charm, a pretty face and that indefinable something that is star quality. Already fêted by a plethora of swains, she and her younger brother David had been born to a middle-aged couple who spoilt them rotten. 'The Princess', they had called her since early childhood, and she lived for the adulation over-indulged children often need, the way morphine addicts need their opiate.

Elizabeth, however, was more than just a sucker for praise. The Duke of Windsor told Michael Thornton, author of the acclaimed book on the feud of Queen Elizabeth the Queen Mother and the Duchess of Windsor, 'She was bright and fun and very, very good company.' Twinkling like the star she was about to become, she brightened every room she entered with her lilting laugh, her witticisms, her beguiling flirtatiousness. She was already a past mistress at the art of enchantment, having spent the war entertaining and amusing a succession of grateful wounded soldiers who had been billeted on her family home in Scotland, Glamis Castle, which had been turned into a hospital for the duration. Elizabeth had a lot going for her, not the least of which was that she was 'dainty', a quality much in fashion in those days and seen as the pinnacle of femininity. This was something she capitalized upon, melding daintiness and femininity into a potent force, so that when daintiness deserted her, she retained all the brittleness of captivation and steeliness of the consciously feminine creature that she is.

For all her appeal, Elizabeth lacked what the Duke of Windsor called 'sex appeal. She had none.' There was nothing earthy about her. She was all effervescent laughter and teasing suggestiveness. Not for her the hurly-burly of passion. She believed in 'high ideals', in 'moral purity', in men who loved one and only one woman. If any man showing interest in her had a 'past' or was deflected from the path of constant adoration of Elizabeth Bowes-Lyon for even one moment, he fell off the face of her planet. According to the Duke of Windsor, 'She was pathologically jealous and had to be the centre of attention at all times.'

For all her supposed idealism, Elizabeth chose to fall in love with a man who had a past as well as a present and displayed no more than a glancing interest in her. Jamie Stuart was a neighbour of the Strathmores in Scotland. He liked her. He was nice to her. He even flirted with her and led her along. But he made no pretence at committing himself to her. It must have been galling and hurtful to this professional bewitcher to have her magic fail on the one man she wished to capture, but Elizabeth was nothing if not persistent.

At Lord and Lady Farquhar's ball on 20 May 1920, at 7 Grosvenor Square in London's Mayfair, she pulled out all the stops to bewitch Jamie Stuart. Instead, she hooked Bertie. Nor is this fanciful speculation, for he later told Lady Airlie that he had fallen in love with Elizabeth that very evening, 'although he did not realize it until later'.

Elizabeth now found herself in quite a pickle. Both David and Bertie were prone to falling in love with women whom they could put on pedestals and adore with slavish devotion. This was a pattern already established during their childhood, and it was one that neither prince would break during the course of his life. While such adoration was the very sort of love the dainty Lady Elizabeth required from her suitors, she did not want the drooling, shambolic Bertie salivating over her. Especially when doing so would ruin the hopes she had for something maturing with his equerry.

Unless one realizes how royal etiquette dictated that Prince Albert's equerry should put his master's feelings and desires before his own, it is impossible to appreciate the dilemma with which Bertie presented Elizabeth when he began showing an interest in her. In royal circles, service meant precisely that, and, no matter how illustrious the rank or how exalted the position of the servant, all servants remained servants and were expected to serve selflessly. Even had he wanted Elizabeth, Jamie Stuart would have had to step aside and let Bertie press his suit. Which is precisely what he did.

One does not need to possess a great deal of imagination to envisage the consternation and frustration that the young Elizabeth felt. Nevertheless, Bertie was second in line to the throne, and in aristocratic circles, where the Royal Family are the gods of the religion of monarchy, one could take pride from the attentions of even a stuttering, spluttering, drooling prince. Moreover, Elizabeth was no rebel. Her whole personality was geared towards pleasing. She was well known for her obedience and willingness to accommodate her parents at every turn. To this day, no one can find an instance when she did anything that might, even vaguely, have displeased or embarrassed them.

While Lord and Lady Strathmore were not in favour of the slavish self-abasement that went along with royal service, and the noble earl had even said that 'If there is one thing I have determined for my children, it is that they shall never have any post about the Court,' they were nevertheless both staunch royalists. Moreover, Lady Airlie, Queen Mary's lady-in-waiting, was one of Lady Strathmore's closest friends, and the Ogilvy and Bowes-Lyon children were in and out of each other's homes at Cortachy Castle and nearby Glamis Castle. Elizabeth had no doubt that both her mother and Lady Airlie wanted her to be nice to Bertie, so she was.

Bertie now set about turning his equerry's friendship with the Strathmore family to his own advantage. Jamie was asked to stay at St Paul's Walden Bury, their English country house, and Bertie, whose every request was a command, tagged along as well. Later in the summer, the Strathmores repaired north of the Border to Glamis and the Royal Family to Balmoral. Jamie was in attendance upon his prince, who made sure that they visited Glamis.

That June of 1920 Bertie had been made Duke of York, Earl of Inverness and Baron Killarney. Ever eager to please his hypercritical father, he wrote a touching letter of thanks, expressing the hope that he would live up to the honour. This he would strive to do throughout the succeeding sixteen years in which he remained a peer of the realm, but as June gave way to July, and the shooting season got nearer, he made plans to visit friends south of the Border after the Glorious 12th (of August, the official beginning of the shooting season). Jamie Stuart remained at Balmoral within easy reach of sweet Elizabeth, while his royal boss and Prince Henry headed for Newbury and the comforts of Sir Ernest Cassel's shooting estate in Berkshire.

Like his grandfather, Edward VII, Bertie was shooting mad. Nothing, then or in the future, would ever be allowed to interfere with this, his greatest pleasure. Not love of Lady Elizabeth Bowes-Lyon, left on her own in Scotland to pursue her interest with his equerry, nor ill health, and, indeed, the last activity he would undertake in his life would be to go shooting, the day before his death in 1952.

Doubtless, Elizabeth was relieved to be rid of her enamoured prince. She did not have long on her own with Jamie Stuart, however, for they were all back in London by the autumn. Once more the social whirl was in full swing, and once more Bertie pursued her with dogged devotion. He was now completely and unrestrainedly in love, to such an extent that his main topic of conversation was Elizabeth. 'He's always talking about her,' Queen Mary observed to her lady-in-waiting Lady Airlie.

That Christmas the bewitched Bertie asked his parents whether they would object to his proposing to Elizabeth. Queen Mary had already made the point to Lady Airlie that 'I don't know her very well,' and even though she thought that 'she seems a charming girl,' she told Bertie she would have to meet Elizabeth again before making up her mind.

King George V, on the other hand, seems to have had no reticence, save about the desirability of his son. 'You'll be a lucky fellow if she accepts you,' he said. This remark would later be construed as praise for his future daughter-in-law rather than a put-down of his son, but, as the Duke of Windsor complained, the King was notorious for making cutting comments to his sons, and, because he knew Elizabeth Bowes-Lyon even more slightly than Queen Mary did, he was therefore not yet in a position to sing her praises.

After gaining the tentative approval of his parents, Bertie did not rush off and see if Elizabeth might be interested in marrying him. On the contrary, he now let the matter drop. Historians have speculated upon the reasons for this, attributing it to a variety of motives, including caution, loss of nerve and enjoyment of his first worthwhile job.

Bertie was now President of the Boys' Welfare Society, an organization through which industry sought to improve the employment conditions of the workers. Scores of businesses were involved in an experiment that had, for the right wing, dangerous Bolshevist overtones. But Bertie loved his work. It was an outlet for his sympathies and his energies. This victim of an oppressive upbringing could empathize with the many forms of suffering and deprivation he encountered. As he clambered over construction sites, down mine-shafts and up into the driver's seat of a tramcar, his basic good sense and kindheartedness began to shine through in a way that no one since Lady Airlie had perceived, all those years ago when he was a little boy, seeking to hand her the Easter present he had made. Respect was a new experience for Bertie, but, as he asked sensible questions and gained sensible answers, this added to his rapidly burgeoning field of knowledge; he could see that the managers and overseers he spoke to respected him, not for the grandeur of his rank, but for his native intelligence and his forthright and caring approach.

It was not the rewards of his presidency of the organization, which soon became the Industrial Welfare Society, that deflected Bertie from his intention to propose to Elizabeth Bowes-Lyon. His detour came in an altogether more enticing form. During his researches for *Royal Feud*, a book about the Queen Mother and the Duchess of Windsor, Michael Thornton discovered that Bertie had met the beauteous musical-comedy star Phyllis Monkman. Through his friendship with various senior members of the Queen Mother's Household at Clarence House, he also learnt the full extent of the relationship that ensued, though he has never revealed it before. While Bertie had no intention of embarking upon a marital union with anyone as unsuitable as an entertainer, he was not about to forgo the satisfaction that came from an association with a woman of the world. In 1921, well-born maidens remained virgins until the time of their marriage, so there was no question of Bertie expecting Elizabeth to provide him with the delights that Phyllis Monkman could. The dainty, twinkling Elizabeth, was therefore put on the back-burner while he fried rather more worldly fish.

By late spring, however, the young Duke's thoughts had turned to something more permanent than passion. Once more the idea of marrying Elizabeth came to the forefront, and, even though her acceptance would mean that he would have to deny himself the pleasures of Phyllis Monkman, he got ready to make the sacrifice. Elizabeth, however, refused his proposal.

In her biography of the Queen Mother, Penelope Mortimer gives an indication of the reaction to this unexpected turn of events. Not only was Bertie pitied by the press but he also became the butt of his father's jokes and had to contend with his mother's outrage. Herself the product of a morganatic marriage who had managed to overcome the stigma by bagging the choice catch of all royals, Queen Mary had an exaggerated reverence for royalty. 'I can never forget my children's father is also their King,' she said by way of excusing her failure to intercede on their behalf when he abused them. But she did not spare herself either. She turned herself into a regal but emotionless automaton who was entirely subservient to her husband on the grounds that he was also *her* King. It should hardly be surprising, therefore, that she was outraged that some slip of a Scots girl, a mere Earl's daughter, could turn down the son of a King.

Although deeply depressed by Elizabeth's unexpected refusal, Bertie still had his other star, the musical-comedy star, to twinkle for him and brighten his nights. He also had the inevitable round of the social season: Royal Ascot, Cowes Week, shooting parties with Edwina Ashley and his cousin, the recently demoted prince of Battenberg who was now Lord Louis Mountbatten. Elizabeth was also a part of this whirl, but life was not turning out as she hoped. Lady Rachel Cavendish returned from Canada, where her father was Governor-General, and soon Jamie Stuart was as bewitched by her as Bertie was by Elizabeth. This was as devastating a blow for Elizabeth as it would be for any other human being in the same predicament, but there was nothing for her to do but accept it and continue with her life.

In August 1921 Elizabeth turned twenty-one. While half a century later this came to seem like no age at all, according to the custom of her day, Elizabeth had already started to get on in years. Girls aimed to be married during the year of their début, which meant that the successful ones were spoken for before the age of nineteen.

If this bothered Elizabeth, she gave no indication of it. Indeed, she took refuge within towering principles. Any man who married her had to be as pure as she was. He had to be religious, with impeccable behaviour, a blameless past and the promise of a shining future, in which his kindness, loyalty, upstanding virtues and high moral tone assured her a lifetime of adoration, protection, inviolability and sanctity. It is hardly surprising, therefore, that she was not interested in the Duke of York. Not only did he have the blemish of a past, but, added to his nervous failings, he also had the language of a sailor and an uncontrollable temper. Only that summer Louis Greig, his doctor-in-residence and tennis partner, had had to call him to order when he started ranting and raving on the tennis court, in full view of the other houseguests. To know the Duke of York might be to like him, but it was also to know all about his inability to control himself.

Despite Elizabeth's feelings – she told her close friend Helen Hardinge she found him 'almost repellent' – Bertie was still in love with her. Queen Mary therefore invited herself to stay at Cortachy Castle with her lady-in-waiting, Lady Strathmore's good friend Mabell Airlie. She planned to review the situation for herself. With Bertie in tow, she called upon Lady Strathmore at nearby Glamis Castle, but the venerable lady was ill in bed. Elizabeth had to act as hostess, and once more her skill at projecting herself was so remarkable that she actually won a victory she did not want. She so impressed Queen Mary with her considerable arsenal of social and personal skills that her future mother-in-law left convinced she would make an ideal wife for the socially inept Bertie. More to the point, though, Elizabeth's compulsion to please, even at the cost of her own objective, gave the shrewd Queen a valuable clue to the likely outcome if Elizabeth were handled skilfully. She therefore resolved to do what she could to forward the union.

Late in September, Bertie joined Elizabeth and her brothers Michael and David at Glamis for a shoot. By now Queen Mary was putting the considerable force of her character to work to realize her second son's desires. She recognized that Bertie would never stand a chance as long as his rival for Elizabeth's affections were around, so, as the year drew to a close, she formulated a plan. According to Michael Thornton, who got his information from one of the Queen Mother's oldest friends, at the beginning of 1922 'Queen Mary arranged for Jamie Stuart to be sent abroad.' Captain James Stuart, relieved of his duties as Equerry to His Royal Highness the Duke of York, was despatched to North America, to Canada, where Rachel Cavendish's father was Governor-General, and from there, to the oilfields of Oklahoma.

With Jamie Stuart safely out of sight, and, hopefully, if gradually, out of mind, Bertie was now reckoned to stand a chance. Certainly, the deck was being stacked against Elizabeth, as she herself knew only too well, for she soon learnt that Rachel Cavendish had put paid to any hopes she might have had for herself with Jamie, by capturing first his heart and then securing his commitment to marriage by way of a betrothal.

Between the romantic and marital phases of Jamie and Rachel's relationship, Queen Mary made her next move to entice Elizabeth into accepting Bertie's proposal. The idea was straightforward enough: draw her into their circle and let familiarity weave its seductive web. Queen Mary had a touching faith in the magnetic qualities of royalty, believing that most people would sooner or later be mesmerized into worshipping at the altar to which she herself paid obeisance. Bertie's only sister Princess Mary was due to marry Viscount Lascelles on 28 February, so Elizabeth was invited to be a bridesmaid.

So, too, was Rachel Cavendish, though the reason for that was different. To be a bridesmaid to a member of the Royal Family was an honour. Rachel was therefore being shown favour and glamorized, being made even more appealing to her suitor, the erstwhile equerry, who was now left in no doubt that the Royal Family looked upon his romance with Rachel favourably. Circuity and the bestowal of favours were the standard royal ways of delivering messages, and this would not have been lost on Jamie, who knew the language of the court. Nor can one have greater proof of the accuracy of that interpretation than subsequent events. Jamie married Rachel, they remained on excellent terms with the Royal Family, and the Hon. James Stuart became Viscount Stuart of Findhorn.

For all her charm, Elizabeth proved to be a harder nut to crack than even Queen Mary envisaged. Despite a second proposal during 1922, Bertie was still no nearer winning the hand of his Scottish lass. Historians have frequently attributed this to Elizabeth's reluctance to take on the heavy mantle of royalty, with its attendant responsibilities. To people who have known the former Lady Elizabeth Bowes-Lyon, however, the notion is preposterous.

To begin with, in 1922 there was no heavy mantle to bear. Royals made the occasional public appearance, but hardly on the scale that they did later. Their lives were private, protected and cosseted. They moved in a world of other royals and of aristocrats, who deferred to their every wish. Even the press was respectful. Their privacy was never violated, not even when the conduct of their personal lives was at variance with their public images. For instance, one of the King's sons (David) was involved with a married woman; another (George) was a cocaine addict and promiscuous homosexual at a time when both activities were against the law; his aunt, Princess Louise, Duchess of Argyll, had for many years been a notorious nymphomaniac who even had an affair with her younger sister Beatrice's husband, Prince 'Liko' of Battenberg; and his uncle, the Duke of Connaught, had had a mistress, Winston Churchill's aunt, Mrs Shane Leslie. Yet there was never any hint of scandal in print.

Nor did Elizabeth find the royal way of life unattractive. She liked the grandeur. She liked being entertained at Buckingham Palace, liked being praised with the extravagance that royal acolytes save for those they consider to be in royal favour, liked the cosiness and cossetedness of regal splendour. The transition from bearing the nickname of Princess to having the rank as a right was something that now appealed to her, but Elizabeth was still no nearer to finding the Duke of York palatable.

The Duke of Windsor provided Michael Thornton with the main reason for Elizabeth's continuing refusal. 'She conceived the idea of marrying me,' the Duke told the author. 'I liked her. She was great fun. I did not find her in the least appealing in that way. But there was no doubt about it. It was me she wanted to marry.'

This disclosure is in keeping with what is known of Elizabeth's character. From infancy, she had been reared to consider herself to be the best and to expect the best of everything. Not only was Bertie patently not the best in terms of masculine appeal, but in the royal scale he was second best. If she could not have the man she wanted, she would marry the best man available. There was no more eligible man in the world than Edward, Prince of Wales, not only because he was heir to the greatest position on earth but also because he was bright, witty, good-looking, stylish, charming and fun. 'She liked me. Of course she *liked* me,' the Duke of Windsor, recounted, 'but she was never in love with me any more than I was in love with her.'

The Duke of Windsor's interpretation of what was preventing the young Lady Elizabeth from marrying his younger brother certainly makes more sense than the implausible reasons historians have traditionally served up. However, fate, in the guise of the press, was standing by to give poor Bertie a helping hand. On Friday, 5 January 1923, while he was staying with the Drummonds at Pitsford Hall, and Elizabeth was with an old friend and admirer, George Gage, in Sussex, the *Daily News* announced that Elizabeth was going to marry David. This caused Bertie to fly into a fit of rage. It was bad enough for the whole world to know that she had refused him, not once but twice, but for everyone now to think that she was going to marry his more favoured brother was too much to bear.

Quite what Elizabeth thought of the report, no one can say. She confided her feelings to no one, though the diarist Chips Channon recorded her reaction as 'unhappy and *distraite*'. He also noted, 'She certainly had something on her mind,' and this, according to the Duke of Windsor's interpretation, was watching to see what his reaction would be.

This came immediately, for David was not prepared to have the press embarrass his brother on that account:

A few days ago the *Daily News* announced the forthcoming engagement of the Prince of Wales to an Italian Princess. Today the same journal states on what is claimed to be unquestionable authority that the formal announcement of His Royal Highness's engagement to a daughter of a Scottish peer will be made within the next two or three months. We [the Prince of Wales's Household] are officially authorized to say that this report is as devoid of foundation as was the previous.

Elizabeth appeared crestfallen, which is not surprising when you stop to think that she was bright and could not have missed the airy way in which her hoped-for husband flicked away the possibility of a marriage with her.

After three years of maddening sluggishness, developments now gathered momentum rapidly. The following week, Elizabeth went to tea with Lady Airlie. Members of the Queen Mother's Household told Michael Thornton that Mabell Airlie was the conduit through which Queen Mary expressed her desire of having Elizabeth as a daughter-in-law – and that that tea was the critical turning-point.

The subsequent course of events themselves reveals what happened. The Duke of York had told Viscount Davidson in 1922, prior to his second rebuff, 'The King's son cannot propose to the girl he loves, since custom requires that he must not place himself in the position of being refused, and to that ancient custom the King, his father, firmly adhered.' Lord Davidson advised him to disregard that stricture, which he did, but, when it did him no good, Bertie once more reverted to the royal custom of the intermediary.

Lady Airlie was the intermediary. She and Elizabeth discussed Queen Mary's wishes for the marriage. No one who took her position as seriously as

Queen Mary did would have overlooked the indignity that Elizabeth's continuing refusal of Bertie was causing the prince, especially when it was known in court circles that she had no objection to a marriage with David. The Royal Family really couldn't have a slip of a girl making them a laughing-stock in the press any longer, and it is entirely likely that Elizabeth would have recognized that this was her last chance. She must either marry Bertie or she must drop out of the royal picture altogether.

Viewed with the finality of an unstated ultimatum, marriage to Bertie did not seem such a terrible prospect. He was athletic, with a good physique and, when silent or in repose, quite nice looking. The raw material for an attractive man was there, if only he could be made to overcome his nervous habits. Moreover, he was second in line to the throne, and, while his wife would not enjoy the pre-eminence of being the Princess of Wales and later on, the Queen, she would rank above all other women except Queen Mary and the dowager, Queen Alexandra. People in royal circles were already predicting that David would never marry, for he was known to be enjoying a passionate association with beautiful socialite Freda Dudley Ward, and he exuded such an aura of unwillingness to settle down that the prospect of his becoming a bachelor King was only too real. If that were so, the Duchess of York would one day be the first lady of the land, and this is said to have had a powerful appeal to the adorable but narcissistic Elizabeth Bowes-Lyon.

On balance, therefore, becoming Duchess of York was not such a bad thing, and, before tea was over, Elizabeth told Mabell Airlie that she would accept Bertie's next proposal if he wished to tender it. This might seem like cold-blooded horse – or rather prince – trading to those of us who have been brought up in an era in which romantic love is prized above all else. Such sensibilities, however, were unknown in 1923 and certainly would have been lost on Queen Mary or the ladies in her circle. After all, Queen Mary herself had been engaged to King George V's eldest brother, the Duke of Clarence and Avondale, a notorious degenerate. No sooner did he die than Queen Victoria arranged for Princess May of Teck, as she then was, to switch her allegiance to his younger brother. This Princess May did as if it were the most natural thing in the world, which it was, of course, to someone whose objective was not to marry for the fulfilment of romantic fantasy but to marry as well as one could.

When Bertie heard Mabell Airlie's good news, he swung into action. That very weekend, he headed for St Paul's Walden Bury. According to Elizabeth herself, he proposed that Sunday at Welwyn, for the third and final time. This time she said yes.

So much for maidens in ivory towers possessing such high standards that they could not marry men with a past. Or for Hollywood-style romance, in which two innocents catch sight of each other across a room and, after a decent interval, plight their troth. Such notions might read well, but, in practice, that was not the way royal marriages were made.

CHAPTER FOUR

A Proper Release

*E*lizabeth took to public life with as much relish as Queen Leona took to running the Helmsley Palace Hotel. Already a star in her own world, Elizabeth merely broadened her horizons. The common people now had a chance to see her shine, the way her family, the aristocracy and the Royal Family did.

No sooner was the engagement announced, on 15 January 1923, than Elizabeth did something that was unprecedented in the annals of royal history. She obliged the newsmen gathered outside her parents' London house at 17 Bruton Street in Mayfair with a personal interview. Never before had an actual or prospective member of the Royal Family given a personal interview. While it was anodyne and would never be repeated – Buckingham Palace got on to the Strathmores as soon as the papers were off the presses, and Elizabeth was duly advised never to blab, ever again – it was nevertheless pivotal in establishing in the public mind the Elizabeth we have come to know and revere.

To begin with, Elizabeth's unprecedented co-operation gained her the affection of the press. They were therefore only too happy accurately to record how charming and delightful the undoubtedly charming and delightful bride-to-be was. This in itself was unusual, for, in that day and age, few people in public life were portrayed as human beings, with personal attributes like their less privileged fellows. Whether they were charming, or charitable, or saintly, these traits were as a rule never commented upon. What received attention were the effects of their actions. Their work, for better or for worse, was the focus of public attention, and the projection of Elizabeth as a personality, with human and desirable qualities, was as unusual as it was effective.

A star was born, and, as she was captured by the photographers smilingly choosing her wedding cake at McVitie & Price in Edinburgh, or smilingly opening a sale for the National Orthopaedic Hospital, or smilingly attending a reception at the Duchess of Portland's for the benefit of Nottingham's lace industry, or smilingly listening for hours while various convocations presented loyal addresses to her future father-in-law as a result of his son's engagement to her, suspicions about her sincerity and vanity arose. Surely anyone who smiled so constantly must be concealing a less pleasing aspect of herself? It was unnatural for anyone to be so perennially good-natured, and soon the word was that the Duke of York's future wife just might be hiding her darker side under the shining light of her bushel. But more of that later.

Buckingham Palace announced that the wedding would take place on Thursday, 26 April 1923. On the 24th, King George and Queen Mary hosted a reception to view the wedding presents. On the 25th, jostling for space with the newspaper photographs of such gifts as a full suite of ring, pendant, necklace and bracelet in diamonds and sapphires from Queen Mary and a pair of priceless antique vases from Japan's Prince Regent, was a photograph of Captain the Hon. James Stuart and Lady Rachel Cavendish, whose engagement was announced with exquisite, some might say cruel, timing.

To those in the know, however, the message was clear. Elizabeth was long over such aberrations as fancying herself in love with the youngest son of a mere Earl, for her heart had been ecstatically and unreservedly captured by the more desirable Duke of York. Fantasy was now meant to take over from reality and cloak the royal couple in a mantle of glamour called the mystique of royalty. The difficulty was, however, that Bertie was not a creature of glamour, and Elizabeth, for all her attributes, was not either.

The wedding took place on the appointed day at Westminster Abbey. Officiating were the Archbishop of Canterbury, Randall Davidson, and the Archbishop of York, Cosmo Gordon Lang. As if that were not enough, they were assisted by the Dean of Westminster, Bishop Herbert Edward Ryle, and, as a gesture towards the Scottishness of the bride, the Bishop of Brechin and Primus of the Scottish Episcopal Church, Walter John Forbes Robberds. The Abbey was thronged with the foreign royals who had not been toppled in the five years since the end of the Great War, as well as representatives of the great aristocratic families of the land. Dressed in the height of fashion, Elizabeth was attended by eight bridesmaids. Bertie was 'supported' by his brother the Prince of Wales, for royalty did not have a best man.

After the church service, which followed the pattern that has since become known throughout the world due to the televising of subsequent royal marriages, the bride and groom were driven back to Buckingham Palace in an open carriage. If it were possible, the overjoyed Bertie was even more radiant than Elizabeth, and, once inside the palace, the crowds outside in the Mall, then as later a feature of all royal weddings, demanded that the bridal couple appear on the balcony. At 1.15 p.m. they did, followed by other royal dignitaries. Elizabeth beamed beatifically in acknowledgement of the roars of delight from the crowd by rotating her right hand in a gesture of acknowledgement, which would thereafter become the Elizabeth wave, and by mouthing 'thank you' over and over again. King George, Queen Mary and the Duke of York stood by quietly and let the born charmer form her bond with the adoring masses.

Later that afternoon, the time came to step into the open landau that was to take Bertie and Elizabeth to Waterloo Station and thence to Polesden Lacey in Surrey. This magnificent mansion had been lent to them by one of the most notorious social climbers of that, or any other, age. It was the last word in luxury, with seven of the bedrooms possessing the unheard of refinement of *en suite* bathrooms. The consensus was that it possessed only one drawback. Its owner, Mrs Ronald Greville, was consistently loathed by as wide a spectrum of society as it was possible to achieve. Everyone from Sir Harold Nicholson, who called her 'a fat slug filled with venom', to Lady Leslie, who said, 'I would rather have an open sewer in my drawing-room than Maggie Greville,' reviled her.

There was only one exception to that general rule. Royalty adored her. That was not surprising, however, for she showered them with her considerable wealth, making them presents of expensive jewels and treating them to lavish hospitality in the age-old way that millionaires from Sir Ernest Cassell and Armand Hammer to Lynn Wyatt have done. Not even death stopped her generosity, for she included the York family, who became her pets, in her will. This was in 1942, when they had moved up the social ladder to its highest rung. Elizabeth was pleased to receive an invaluable necklace, which had originally been made for Marie Antoinette, and 'dear' Princess Margaret Rose £20,000 (a considerable sum in an age when the average wage was a few hundred pounds per annum).

From Polesden Lacey the Yorks headed north, for the chill of an Angus spring at Glamis. Elizabeth promptly came down with whooping cough, causing Bertie to observe in a letter to his father, 'So unromantic to come down with whooping cough on your honeymoon.' The mystery was where she picked it up, for she had been in contact with no one who had it. All her life, however, she would have the knack of getting slightly ill whenever she wanted to avoid something. For the Abdication Crisis, much later in 1936, she took to her bed with influenza, but what possible need could there have been for illness on her honeymoon?

In the circles surrounding Elizabeth, there has long been the suspicion that, so rare and precious a creature as she was, she felt a measure of distaste for the baser urges governing man's behaviour. Penelope Mortimer hinted at this in her biography when she said that Elizabeth's idea of courting was 'to hold hands in a boat'. This, allied to her feelings of repulsion towards the Duke of

York, made it likely that her whooping cough was a merciful respite while she adjusted to the more personal and, to her, less desirable aspects of married life.

So ethereal an approach to marriage requires some examination, if only because it would naturally have an effect upon both partners and the future conduct of their relationship. Throughout her life, Elizabeth has been a testament to the virtues of high principles and extensive moral precepts. There was never anything crude or basic about her, nor has she ever tolerated such traits in others. She sees anything short of highblown nobility as a failing and has never allowed the character for which she is justly famous to be sullied by the seamier side of humanity. This was as true of her before and during her marriage as it has been since her widowhood. With regard to her private life since the death of King George VI, she has maintained as chaste a reputation as it is possible to possess. Indeed, she could be said to be unique among women in public life, for she has never once been known to display any interest in any man. Most of the male figures who surround her are firmly established bachelors who have never been known to show any inclination for romantic attachments with ladies.

As we have seen, however, Bertie was a healthy and athletic young man. Although decent and dutiful, he had sufficient difficulty meeting the standards already set for him to function as a public figure without trying to raise them to an even more impossible degree of perfection. Moreover, he was a Windsor, and, as anyone who has ever had anything to do with any member of the British Royal Family knows, that means that he had normal appetites in rather larger measure than is the norm. His grandfather King Edward VII was a well-known rake, and, if respected columnist and author A. N. Wilson is to be believed, his father King George V also followed in the family tradition, though his preference was for professional ladies of the night. Certainly two of Bertie's three living brothers cut a swathe through the female population, and one, George Duke of Kent, did not even limit himself to that sex.

If Elizabeth's ethereality precluded much physical contact, it is inconceivable that Bertie would have done without satisfaction of the natural needs that all men expect from marriage. Whether the officially sanctioned version of the marriage, which is that Bertie was so desperately in love with Elizabeth that he would never have wanted to look at any other woman, is true or not, the alternative viewpoint also has to be considered in the interest of evenhandedness.

When he was researching *Royal Feud*, Michael Thornton discovered that there was a significant body of people surrounding Her Majesty who believed that Bertie continued his relationship with Phyllis Monkman after his marriage. This might seem incredible to those of us who have spent our whole lives with romantic fantasies about the perfection of King George and Queen Elizabeth's marriage. But to those at closer quarters, it was just a well-

known but well-kept secret. Michael Thornton, however, did not feel that he could in all conscience use such information in his book, for Clarence House had given him co-operation.

If the fact of Bertie's continuing relationship with Phyllis Monkman is true, the reasons are self-evident, though it is possible that Elizabeth never knew. 'She is a virulently jealous woman,' the Duke of Windsor told Michael Thornton, an assertion espoused by Penelope Mortimer and many others who have drifted into the Queen Mother's orbit.

Possibly, however, one should not look at the marriage from a late twentieth-century point of view, but from a Victorian and Edwardian one. At the turn of the century, it was acceptable for gentlemen to have arrangements that extended beyond the marriage bed. This was an age when there was nothing abnormal about women disliking intimacy.

Mrs Stanley Baldwin, whose husband was Bertie's first prime minister when he became king, has gone down in history for coining the expression, 'Lie back and think of England.' Such women were often grateful to be relieved of onerous responsibilities, as long as everything was kept carefully under wraps. It is entirely conceivable that someone as worldly, as sophistic-ated and as *fin de siècle* as Elizabeth shared a viewpoint typical of her own time, but, as such subjects were never discussed, even among close friends, we shall never know with any certainty. This seems so likely as to be a near certainty, for after Princess Margaret's birth Elizabeth withdrew her favours and turned a blind eye to the intimate friendship that Bertie then formed with Lady Maureen Stanley. Indeed, Elizabeth remained a close friend of the woman who was generally acknowledged within the royal circle to be Bertie's confidante. And Maureen, for her part, conducted herself with exemplary discretion, as befitted a daughter of the immensely rich Marquis of London-derry and his wife Edith, who was renowned as Britain's leading hostess and nicknamed Circe.

Before reaching the bridge of accommodation, however, Elizabeth and Bertie had to travel down the road of matrimony and at least reach the terminus of their honeymoon. This they did at Frogmore House, in Windsor Great Park, where Bertie had spent many of his early years. It was a vast and primitive museum, with none of the bathrooms, much less *en suite*, that Polesden Lacey boasted. But they were happy there. Elizabeth was not a Scot and Bertie a royal for nothing. They were both used to cavernous rooms, bad heating and walls that contained the chill of the ages. So while their first home, White Lodge, Richmond Park, was being made ready, they moved between Frogmore House and Windsor Castle, where Elizabeth captivated her father- and mother-in-law with her charm and eagerness to please.

White Lodge was Queen Mary's childhood home. But her parents Princess Mary Adelaide and the Duke of Teck never ever had any money, and while Queen Mary regarded her former home as good enough for anyone, Elizabeth had very definite ideas about the unsuitability of the small, lack-

lustre, suburban lodge. It was simply not good enough for a scion of Glamis.

Nevertheless, Britain's newest Duchess was nothing if not diplomatic. In June she and her adoring spouse moved to Richmond, whence she engineered to visit her parents at Bruton Street with such frequency that the uninitiated might have thought she and Bertie had taken up residence with the Strathmores. Bertie, however, did not complain. He had never known such joy. Not only were Lord and Lady Strathmore a genuine love match, but Lady Strathmore had a 'genius for family life', as Bertie himself acknowledged, and the family was a truly happy one.

For the first time in his life, Bertie had a life that was fun as well as relaxed and pleasant. The Strathmores played after-dinner games. They sang popular songs around the piano. They laughed loudly, conversed animatedly, exchanged a novel thing called ideas. At Windsor, Buckingham Palace, Sandringham and Balmoral, no such commodity as an idea was ever known to enter a conversation. No one ever laughed, or talked animatedly. After dinner, for an allotted length of time each guest paid his or her respects to the King and Queen, who maintained the dour expressions of majesty until it was time to retire to bed.

Queen Mary had been an entertaining and high-spirited young woman, but George was a dull, unimaginative bore whose only passions were sport and stamps. He had no sense of humour and did not see the need to be either entertaining or entertained. As life at court rigidly revolved around his tastes, his children grew up in a mausoleum from which all of them, with the exception of the vague and indolent Harry (Prince Henry, later Duke of Gloucester), wished to escape. David and George especially were of the opinion that there was no duller household in the land, and even the anxious-to-please Bertie and their father's favourite, Mary, agreed.

Where Bertie and Elizabeth were going to live became an issue early on. She point blank refused to stay at White Lodge. Bertie was beside himself. How could he insult his mother by informing her that his wife did not consider her childhood home good enough? Elizabeth did not care. 'They used to have terrific rows,' the Duke of Windsor told Michael Thornton. 'She has always had quite a temper and would go at him hell for leather.' This information would not have come as a surprise to the many people who were suspicious of her permanent public smile, and it is reassuring to discover that sweet Elizabeth possessed human failings beneath the benevolent façade after all.

Confronted with the dissatisfaction of an obstinate and strong-willed wife, Bertie moved Elizabeth to Curzon House on Curzon Street in Mayfair. She hoped to move into one of the Crown Estate mansions in Carlton House Terrace such as the late Prime Minister Gladstone had lived in, but when none became available, she settled for a Crown Estate property at No. 145 Piccadilly. Although not as chic an address, it was more in keeping with her taste than suburban White Lodge. It had twenty-five bedrooms, ballroom, drawing-room, dining-room, library, study and innumerable other minor

rooms. Elizabeth was now twenty-five and pregnant with her first child, but already she was gaining a justly deserved reputation for loving luxury and grandeur as well as for getting her own way. And Bertie? As long as Elizabeth was happy, so was he. And when she wasn't, he was miserable.

Pleased with her new home, Elizabeth settled back to give birth. On 20 April 1926 she went into labour. There was no question of having the baby anywhere but in a private house, in this instance, at her parents', as 145 Piccadilly was still being renovated. In those days, hospitals were for illness and giving birth was perceived as the ultimate, if most dangerous, form of health. Royal babies, however, could not come into the world without a wealth of witnesses. Ever since Mary of Modena was suspected of having substituted James the Pretender for a stillborn son, the Home Secretary and various other attendants had to be on hand. For the birth of Princess Elizabeth Alexandra Mary of York these included an obstetrician, Walter Jagger, and a surgeon, Sir Henry Simpson, because childbirth was a far riskier business than it is gratis modern medicine, and no one wanted the sweet Duchess of York taking her smiles to heaven before her time. It was just as well the doctors were in attendance, for it was a breech birth, and, after making a Caesarean incision, they pulled forth the future Queen of England at forty minutes past two o'clock on the morning of 21 April.

Bertie and Elizabeth were delighted with their baby. Both intensely family orientated, they settled back to enjoy the bliss of parenthood as the country became involved in a national crisis. On 2 May the famous General Strike of 1926 began. The country ground to a halt, and, to keep permanent paralysis from setting in, dukes took to driving buses while dustmen picketed the streets. While this undoubtedly perturbed Bertie's father at Buckingham Palace, a few hundred feet across Green Park the new leaseholders of 145 Piccadilly were too wrapped up in family life to be much concerned about anything but Little Elizabeth.

Nine months later, the exigencies of royal life demanded that Little Elizabeth be ripped away from the increasingly ample bosom of her mother. Elizabeth and Bertie were off to New Zealand and Australia, a major journey in those pre-aeroplane days. They were due to be away for six months, from 6 January to 27 June 1927, so Little Elizabeth was turned over to the control of her grandparents. One can only imagine the distress such loving parents as Bertie and Elizabeth felt, but they were dutiful, and neither would ever have dreamt of refusing to live up to his or her responsibilities to the crown.

Indeed, much preparation had gone into the tour of the Antipodes, not the least of which was Elizabeth's latest campaign to beat one of the nervous manifestations of Bertie's abused and deprived childhood. Ever since their marriage, she had been beavering away, trying to cure him of his twitches, his slobbers, his stammer and his rages. While she would never make much headway with the fits of temper to which he remained prone till his dying day, she did succeed elsewhere, though by 1926, Bertie had attempted several different cures for the worst of his ailments: his stammer, all of which had failed. Elizabeth, however, had heard of a medically unqualified faith-healer with a high success rate, and she wheeled Bertie to the Harley Street rooms of Lionel Logue.

The secret of Logue's success was to relieve the emotional disturbance underlying speech impediments by providing the patient with a spiritual antidote. He understood that no one stammers unless they are afraid of what they have to say and of the reception it is going to receive, so he gave his patients the tools to provide confidence in themselves and have faith in others. This he did partly by skilfully building a nurturing relationship with them, and partly by giving them the means, through such techniques as breathing exercises and breath control, to overcome the blockages that lead to recovery and through it to healthy independence.

Every day for nearly three months, Bertie and Elizabeth turned up at Logue's rooms, and, by the time they were ready to embark for down under, Bertie could speak, for the first time in his life since his childhood period of recuperation at Balmoral, with minimal hesitation. Even though fluency would always be beyond him, he was now an adequate communicator, and while he still lacked the glittering patina of his elder brother David, he had reached the point where his nervous ailments no longer made him a social embarrassment.

Elizabeth's mother had observed, prior to the marriage, that Bertie was the sort of man whose wife would make or break him. Her daughter was well on the way to making him. It was as if, having failed to bag the prince she desired, she was determined to make the prince she got into someone she genuinely wanted. Fortunately for her, and for the state of their marriage, he, like his brother David, was the sort of man who wanted a woman who would nurture him, and if it took being made over into her image of him to please her, then he was willing to pay the price. The key to the brothers' marriages was that they had married the mothers they yearned for. Maternal care, not sex, was the secret hold the indomitable sisters-in-law had in common over their husbands, and it would prove to be the most potent grip of all.

At this juncture, it is worth looking at the dynamics of Bertie's relationship with Elizabeth, for it had already achieved a recognizable form, which would remain unchanged for the remainder of their married life. There is no doubt that she had many engaging qualities, aside from charm, warmth and a sense of fun. She was loyal and responsible, strong and confident. Superficially, she was his opposite, for he came across as diffident and lacking in confidence.

Bertie shared one outstanding characteristic with his brother David, a need to be subservient to a woman. Both brothers married women who, for all their apparent differences, shared one basic similarity: Elizabeth and David's duchess, Wallis, the former Wallis Warfield Simpson, were superb homemakers. They were also dominant personalities. Beneath Wallis's sleek American chic and Elizabeth's frou-frou country-come-to-town costumes, the sisters-in-law ruled their roosts. Of course, they did it in the name of love, but the issue is not why they did it, but that they did.

To understand the brothers' exaggerated need for the warmth of a loving home life, and why they chose women whose personalities put theirs in the shade, it is necessary to remember that they not only had cold and distant relations with their parents during childhood. They also had the counterpoint with their grandparents. King Edward VII and Queen Alexandra were the ones who showed up the emotional desert of family life with George V and Mary by providing the children with an oasis of love, warmth and encouragement. Thereafter, all the children, but David and Bertie especially, remained not only emotionally hungry but also emotionally driven. They strove to reproduce the contented family life that they learnt about through their grandparents, not with the independence of fulfilled and emotionally balanced adults, but with the obsessiveness that men with parched throats display when they set about finding a permanent oasis to slake their thirst. As much as wives, David and Bertie needed mothers. Wallis and Elizabeth fulfilled both roles, in the process tying their husbands to their apron strings with knots that neither brother wished to loosen.

There is no doubt that Elizabeth established the structure of her married life and thereafter set its tone. In every sense of the word, hers was a matriarchal household. Bertie was happy to turn over all power to her, to fall in with her plans and allow her to dictate their way of life. Even parenting became her province, and, when their children were older, if they wanted to go somewhere or do something, he deferred all decisions to Elizabeth. 'Ask Mummy' was as close as he got to putting his foot down or saying yes.

Under the beaming light of Elizabeth's radiant personality, Bertie flourished as he had never flourished before. He still liked a drink, but he no longer drank to excess. He was still eclipsed by his charismatic elder brother David, now joined in the glamour stakes by his youngest and most handsome brother George. He and Elizabeth, though universally perceived as being dull, still undertook a not too onerous complement of official duties.

With each passing day, Bertie grew in stature and confidence while Elizabeth grew in size. She was no longer the dainty little flower she had been at the time of her wedding, but Bertie did not seem to mind, and she saw no reason to disallow the vast afternoon teas, with countless sandwiches and rich cakes and pastries, in the interests of retaining her figure. Then, on 21 August 1930, Princess Margaret Rose of York was born, at Glamis Castle in Scotland, the first member of the Royal Family to have been born north of the Border for centuries. Bertie and Elizabeth's happiness became complete.

CHAPTER FIVE

A Chance to Shine

*L*ife had settled into a most agreeable pattern. With the death of Queen Alexandra in 1925, Elizabeth was now the second lady in the land. She got a good press, though she was still suspected of vanity and insincerity. She had excellent relations with all the members of the Royal Family. King George was so fond of her that he even overlooked her habitual lack of punctuality with the comment, 'You are not late. The clocks must be fast.' Even David, with whom she later fell out, was an ardent admirer of her charm and wit, and she and Bertie were on cordial terms with him. As the Prince of Wales, he would be the next King, and there was no question of Elizabeth failing to please a power-that-was or would-be.

The early and mid-thirties were a period of fun for the younger members of the Royal Family. They were now all adults and, while only Bertie and Mary were married, David did have an established pattern to his life. Weekends were spent playing host to his friends at Fort Belvedere, a crown property near Windsor Castle. King George V had still not learnt that a bit of approval might get him what a plethora of disapproval would not. He remained David's most fastidious critic, lambasting him for such decadent behaviour as indulging in the new-fangled custom of weekends. The one subject on which he might, with some justice, have castigated his eldest son was the one he studiously avoided, so, as David reached his late thirties, and one mistress supplanted another, the King mentioned neither Freda Dudley Ward nor Lady Furness.

Both ladies were well-known figures in society. Both had been received at court by the King and Queen. But it was Thelma Furness who pointed up the way Elizabeth played the game of life. The American Viscountess, twin sister of Gloria Vanderbilt Sr, became such a fixture at Fort Belvedere that Bertie and Elizabeth grew to know her quite well.

By this time, they had left Frogmore House for the nearby Royal Lodge, also in Windsor Great Park, and dropping in on David during the weekend became a feature of their lives. Once, Virginia Water froze, and they all went skating on kitchen chairs. Elizabeth was such fun that Thelma opined, 'If ever I had to live in a bungalow in a small town, this is the woman I would most like to have as a next-door neighbour to gossip with while hanging out the washing in our back yards.' So, despite the avowed height of her moral stances, Elizabeth was not above the civilized acceptance of immoral arrangements, if they involved a greater power in the land than herself, and, as David was the next King as well as Bertie's brother, she had no difficulty accepting his mistress.

Not even David's next mistress caused Elizabeth a moral dilemma. Wallis Simpson was married and living with her husband, but, then, so too was Viscountess Furness for the early part of their affair. Although she did not drop over to Fort Belvedere as often as Bertie, who got to know Wallis well, Elizabeth definitely knew her. The problem was not with the moral acceptability of the Prince of Wales's arrangement, but with the intensity of his feeling for her and of Wallis's attitude towards Elizabeth.

David was crazy about Wallis in a way he had never been crazy about Thelma Furness or Freda Dudley Ward. To him, she was what Elizabeth was to Bertie. Elizabeth resented the fact that another woman had been able to trigger a love that she had wanted for herself but had not achieved. Wallis, moreover, did not behave towards Elizabeth as if she were her social inferior.

By this time, Elizabeth had become used to the obeisance everyone paid her. She had a reverent and jealous regard for the overweening importance of her own position. As we have already seen, beneath the pleasing though strong-willed façade lurked a temper, which her brother-in-law David described as 'vicious'. It was this that Wallis triggered off when she treated Elizabeth as just another woman and not a figure of reverence, and matters were not helped when Elizabeth once dropped in at the Fort just as Wallis was mimicking her to friends.

Elizabeth felt that Wallis was not acknowledging her or extending her her due. Thelma had certainly never forgotten her place, yet here was Mrs Ernest Simpson treating the second lady in the land as if she were her equal. All this antipathy Elizabeth was able to glean from relatively few encounters, but she was accurate. Wallis did not consider herself inferior to anyone, so, rather than subject herself to the ignominy of being treated as an equal by a woman whose superior she considered herself to be, Elizabeth kept herself scarce.

If the jealous Elizabeth withdrew behind the rank that she had acquired with marriage, others born to it did not. In November 1934 Prince George married Princess Marina of Greece. The Duke and Duchess of Kent, as they now were, were frequent guests at Fort Belvedere, as were Prince Harry, who married the Duke of Buccleuch's daughter Lady Alice Montagu Douglas

Scott in November 1935. So, too, were the former prince of the house of Battenberg and his wife, Lord and Lady Louis Mountbatten. According to Princess Alice, Duchess of Gloucester, David and Wallis were 'very loving together', and Wallis was a 'wonderful hostess', though the family, naturally enough, 'were unhappy with the liaison'. They wanted David to settle down with a nice girl whom he could marry, but, in the meantime, they had no objections to enjoying happy times with him and his paramour.

If such accommodations appear to be hypocritical, those on the receiving end of the stick did not think so. As long as David was going to be King, they either kept in with him or lost out on the favour he would one day be in a position to bestow. Once he was not King, of course, they were in a better position to give vent to the full force of their feelings without danger of losing any of the privileges by which they lived. They, in fact, were then in a position to do something for him, for they were above him in rank, and, as the members of the Royal Family resident in Britain and within the fold, their acceptance of him and his wife was crucial to the maintenance of his dignity. It is hardly surprising that he was shocked and embittered to discover that people who had spent week after week, year after year, enjoying his hospitality, should then claim that they could not accept as his wife a woman whom they had accepted as his mistress. And, to him and to Wallis, the crowning insult was the courtly tone of principle.

On Monday, 20 January 1936, everything changed, not only for David and Wallis but also for Bertie and Elizabeth. King George V had been seriously ill for some days. Predictably, as soon as trouble arose, Elizabeth took to her bed, so Bertie had to do without the support of his wife when Lord Dawson of Penn, the doctor, administered a fatal injection to bring his sovereign's life to a close, in time for the news to make the morning edition of the papers. The King had been perilously close to death some years before and had managed to rally. This time, however, all chance of recovery was taken out of the hands of God, nature or the resilience of the King's body. As if that were not unbelievable enough, this was done with the full support of Queen Mary, who stood vigil in the room with the Princess Royal while the Archbishop of Canterbury read psalms. Needless to say, George V did not collude with his wife and doctor in the commission of an act that the law classified as murder. As far as the Archbishop was concerned, there was no crisis of conscience, for the breaking of one of the most important Commandments was committed not by mere mortals, but by a Queen and a Peer of the Realm.

Whether the royal brothers were not alerted because they might have objected, or whether this were a mere oversight, no one now knows, as they are now all dead, but history records that they remained downstairs, not knowing their father's death was imminent until after the event. This came at five minutes before midnight. David was now King Edward VIII.

The new reign began well enough. David showed a touching sensitivity, which could not have come from either parent. He even organized his brothers to stand vigil over the coffin of their father, which so affected Queen Mary that she had a painting done to commemorate the occasion. Nevertheless, David was not popular with the powers-that-be at court. Making what would prove to be a fatal mistake, he reappointed the senior members of his father's staff to positions of influence on his own. Lord Wigram, the Private Secretary, was of retirement age and asked to be relieved of his duties after the funeral, so that left the post of private secretary as well as those of deputy and assistant to be filled. The new King invited his old private secretary to renew his old job in this new post, but Godfrey Thomas refused on the grounds that he was not sufficiently qualified. He agreed to remain as assistant, however, so David asked Major Alexander Hardinge, later the 2nd Baron Hardinge of Penshurst, his father's deputy, the husband of Elizabeth's good friend Helen Hardinge and brother of one of her bridesmaids Diamond Hardinge, to fill the main slot. This the Major agreed to do, and Captain Alan Lascelles, the late King's Assistant Private Secretary, became the deputy.

From the very outset, Hardinge and Lascelles resisted David's every attempt at updating the institution of the monarchy. In 1934 Chips Channon had written, 'It is high time that such dreary narrow-minded fogies were sacked, as, indeed, they will be, in the next reign.' The breadth of their minds had not increased, but they now had even more power than they had had before. The post of private secretary was an important one. In her acclaimed biography of Queen Victoria, Lady Longford describes how Sir Henry Ponsonby 'peremptorily refused' to carry out his sovereign's orders when he did not agree with them. Private secretaries still displayed an astonishing independence, for they considered themselves to be the guardians of the crown. The King was merely the transient occupant of a throne and should remain subservient to its interests. They saw their job not as functionaries who obeyed their boss, the sovereign, but as advisers and watch-dogs whose duty it was to steer a potential troublemaker away from trouble. They, not their charge, knew what was best for the crown, and woe betide anyone who forgot that.

Although Queen Victoria had had a mind of her own, King Edward VII and King George V did pretty much as they were told. As far as Hardinge and Lascelles were concerned, Edward VIII was much too opinionated and independent for his own, their own and the crown's good. He wanted to alter traditions and practices, which they and their predecessors had spent years formulating. To the dispassionate observer, such changes might have been all to the good, but not to the men whose power and influence were threatened by their implementation. They therefore took it upon themselves to thwart the King, to withhold the red boxes that held Cabinet papers and to slur his name by alleging that he was unsound, had dangerous political opinions and might betray the secrets of his realm. They actively disliked Mrs

Simpson, with her American forthrightness and, worse, her egalitarian approach to life. Like Elizabeth, they were antagonized because she failed to defer to them. To her, they were not the King's bosses but his servants, and she was encouraging their recalcitrant charge to become too big for his boots. They therefore waited for the first opportunity that presented itself to get rid of her and to bring the new King to heel.

With the uncanny innocence of someone who has never had to fight for any advantages in life, Edward VIII presented Hardinge and Lascelles with their opportunity before the year was out. He wanted to marry Mrs Simpson. With that in mind, he encouraged her to divorce Ernest Simpson, which she did in October 1936. The upcoming divorce was the pretext for which Hardinge had been waiting. He went to see the Prime Minister, Stanley Baldwin, whose wife lay back and thought of England. He asked Baldwin to intervene and ask the King to stop the divorce, thereby instigating what became the Abdication Crisis.

From that moment until the King's Abdication on 10 December, Hardinge played a crucial role. According to royal biographer Lady Donaldson, 'Baldwin never seems to have been quite certain what he should do.' Hardinge had no such doubts. Nor did his wife Helen, who was Elizabeth's good friend. They were both of the opinion that Edward VIII was not fit to be King. So, too, was Alan Lascelles, Hardinge's deputy. Vociferously and in the full knowledge of how to tilt the balance in their favour, the two private secretaries undermined the King's position, not only in Britain but in the Dominions as well. They had always fancied themselves kingmakers; now they showed that they could also be kingbreakers.

By the end of the plotting and scheming, Edward VIII was off his throne and George VI on it in his place. Hardinge and Lascelles had got what they wanted: a malleable King. Elizabeth had also got what she wanted: riddance of the competition, even though, true to form, she once more took to her bed until the denouement was achieved.

The Abdication Crisis revealed a fundamental issue at the heart of the crown. Whether Wallis Simpson was fit to be Queen should never have been the issue. The real issue was whether a tiny cabal of powerful courtiers should have been allowed to undermine the position of the rightful King to the extent that he felt the only way of having a fulfilling life was to abdicate.

Since then, the British Establishment has assailed Edward VIII's reputation with almost as much vigour as they have defamed Wallis. It is virtually impossible to extract a rational judgement out of anyone remotely connected to it. However, if you go farther afield, there are people, with no axe to grind, who can tell you what sort of man and woman the Duke and Duchess of Windsor were.

One such is John Pringle, the scion of one of Jamaica's grandest white families and the founder of the internationally famous Round Hill Hotel in Montego Bay. In his time, he has been Jamaica's Director of Tourism as well as the head of other governmental organizations. He is a film producer, an international socialite and an astute businessman whose acumen has increased his family's wealth considerably. At the end of the Second World War, he was also the Duke of Windsor's aide-de-camp in Nassau. Over the years, he has never had anything but good to say about both the Duke and the Duchess. Contrary to the misinformation put out to the public by the British Establishment, he never witnessed the Duke or Duchess skiving off on their duties; he never saw them befriending criminals, rakes or other disreputables; nor did they conduct themselves with anything but dignity and decorum.

The Windsors might have been pariahs in London, but in Paris and New York they were superstars in the social firmament. This was clear in the late 1960s in New York. When I was at school there, I had the pleasure of crossing paths with them, and observed that they were never less than dignified. Many of the events they attended were fund-raisers for charities, and it strikes me as arrogant hypocrisy for the British Establishment to pillory them for mindless socializing when they were only doing abroad what the other members of the Royal Family were doing at home, namely supporting worthy causes.

Elizabeth has often been blamed for leading the campaign against the Windsors. The Duke and Duchess themselves blamed her. According to Michael Thornton, 'They believed that she was the prime mover behind the scenes.' An overview, however, reveals that she was but one of the prime movers. She was like-minded with Hardinge, his wife Helen and Lascelles, who set about establishing their authority with breath-taking speed and indecent callousness. It must be remembered that Bertie and Elizabeth had never ever shown any inclination to break new ground, rock the boat or do anything but please, and now that they were King George VI and Queen Elizabeth, they happily fell into the established line. Hardinge and Lascelles, needless to say, were delighted to have the sort of sovereign and consort they wanted, and they were equally vociferous about proclaiming their approval for the obedient Bertie and the obliging Elizabeth.

To those who covet power, its possession is pointless without exercising it. This Hardinge and Lascelles knew, and almost the first advice they gave the King was to disassociate himself from everyone who had supported his brother. The first head to roll was Lord Brownlow, Edward VIII's lord-in-waiting who had accompanied Wallis to the South of France when she fled the country just before news of the Abdication Crisis broke. Brownlow's only failing was to serve his master well, but that was enough for him to be discharged in as humiliating a manner as Hardinge and Lascelles could devise. He was not even informed that he was discharged. On the day he was due to report to the Palace for duty, he was told that there was no need to, as the King was only receiving the Archbishop of Canterbury at 145 Piccadilly, where he and Elizabeth were still residing. The following morning he picked up *The Times* to see that he had been replaced by the Marquis of Dufferin and Ava. Upon ringing the Palace for an explanation, he was coldly informed that the resignation that he had never tendered had been accepted. 'Am I to be turned away like a dishonest servant, with no notice, no warning, no thanks, when all I did was obey my master, the late King?'

'Yes,' came the reply from Lord Cromer, the late King's trusted servant.

Chips Channon heard that there was to be a blacklist at the Palace, and that all friends of the late King's were to be included. This must have been true, for the next head to roll was David and Wallis's good friend Emerald Cunard. Queen Mary herself witnessed the execution, which she recounted to the Prince Regent of Jugoslavia: 'In my presence, Bertie told George (Duke of Kent) he wished him and Marina never to see Lady Cunard again and George said he would not do so.'

Nor was Queen Mary above a bit of blacklisting herself. She also told Paul of Jugoslavia, who was married to the Duchess of Kent's sister Princess Olga of Greece, 'I am hoping that George and Marina will no longer see certain people who alas were friends of Mrs S and Lady Cunard's and David's.'

Elizabeth shrewdly did not commit pen to paper. Nevertheless, she quickly gained a reputation within society for the vengefulness of her pursuit of the Windsors, as they became upon their marriage in June 1937. Nor did she and the private secretaries fail to devise a wedding present for the man who had not wanted to marry her, calculating that it would ruin his happy day. Walter Monckton, who had acted as King Edward VIII's intermediary during the Abdication Crisis, arrived for the wedding with a letter from the new King bearing the news that he was pleased 'to declare that the Duke of Windsor shall, notwithstanding his Act of Abdication . . . be entitled to hold and enjoy for himself only the title, style or attribute of Royal Highness, so however that his wife and descendants, if any, shall not hold the said title or attribute.' Rather pathetically, the malleable King, knowing only too well what an underhanded swipe this was, continued by saying he hoped David would not regard the painful course he had had to take as an 'insult'.

David's reaction, however, was virtually identical to the King's. 'He received the news,' Walter Monckton said, 'almost in the same words his brother had used when he sent me off. "This is a nice wedding present."'

Using the same phrase to describe an act of treachery was where the brothers' similarity ended. Bertie was not the victim, but the instrument without whose ultimate consent such weapons could not have been used. David, on the other hand, was the victim, and victim he remained, as Bertie stood by impassively and allowed the cabal to break one agreement he had made with David after another.

For instance, David owned Sandringham House and Balmoral Castle.

These he leased to George VI in an intricate but legally binding formula, which would have ensured the abdicated King a comfortable income for life had it been adhered to. It was not, however, and he never received the agreed amount. He tried, with that and other breaches of accepted procedure, such as his wife assuming his rank, to get the court to honour the actual or implied terms of his Abdication, first by exercising patience and understanding, then by agitating for the restoration of his rights. For that he was roundly condemned, and, short of taking his own brother to a court of law, there was nothing he could do but accept the perfidy to which he was subjected for the remainder of his life.

There is no doubt that King George VI allowed much that is questionable to be done in his name. There has never been any suggestion, however, that Bertie was a malicious or vengeful person, and that, encouraged to pursue his inclination, there would ever have been a vendetta against his elder brother. The Duchess of Windsor herself said, by way of explaining how she and the Duke came to be posted to such a backwater as the Bahamas for the duration of the war, 'We owe this to a woman's jealousy.' She did not specify who the woman was on the grounds that the identity of the culprit was so obvious as to need no affirmation.

A famous Scottish Duchess, who was a friend of the Windsors and has known Queen Elizabeth the Queen Mother for much of her life, says, 'It was common knowledge at the time that the Duke and Duchess were hounded with the open connivance of Queen Elizabeth. She worked with the Hardinges and, to a lesser extent, Alan 'Tommy' Lascelles. But she wasn't motivated by sour grapes alone. She was convinced the British public preferred the Duke to King George VI and used to sit around devising ways of eroding his popularity so that the King would have a chance to shine in his own right.'

After their accession, Bertie and Elizabeth were not as popular as they subsequently became. People were stunned by the Abdication, and while the press tried to shape public opinion by roundly condemning the previous King, memories were not so short that the diffident George VI and the dumpy Queen Elizabeth had yet overtaken the glamorous and charismatic Edward VIII in the desirability stakes. David still had his supporters, as Elizabeth knew only too well.

When life returned to normal, the only point of glamour left in the Royal Family was the stylish and beautiful Duchess of Kent, formerly Princess Marina of Greece. Grey had replaced colour, Bertie and Elizabeth were low-key but obliging, and, if the nation was supremely unimpressed by their King and Queen, at least Hardinge and Lascelles were happy.

Then Elizabeth showed her mettle and did something that shocked the court to such an extent that, thereafter, her husband's advisers walked in fear of her. She made Bertie dismiss Alexander Hardinge, not because he had been treacherous to his previous master and might therefore perform in character with Bertie, nor because he was an incompetent who was out of touch with the realities by which the sovereign should rule, but because word had got back to her that he had mooted the idea, at the height of the Abdication Crisis, of replacing Bertie and the dim-witted Prince Harry on the throne with the more attractive Duke of Kent.

The turn round in the British public's perception of Bertie and Elizabeth came in the summer of 1939, when the sovereign and his consort made an official visit to Canada and the United States. She was a triumph, even if Bertie was, in the words of one observer, a 'letdown after his brother'. Elizabeth pulled out all the stops, wearing exotic hats and furs in the day and *Gone with the Wind* dresses at night. She socked the provincial Canadians between the eye with her interpretation of glamour. She glittered and sparkled and charmed, not only with her clothes but also with her smiles and her radiant appreciation for everything and everyone. Beside her lack-lustre husband, who was providing such an ideal counterfoil for her brilliance that they might well have been dreamt up by a Hollywood film studio, she shone all the brighter.

Lord Tweedsmuir, the Governor-General of Canada, claimed, 'The Queen has a perfect genius for the right kind of publicity.' Not until her grandson married Lady Diana Spencer would royal watchers be treated to another such spectacle.

What the British had perceived as the vain posturings of a plump narcissist, the Canadians took to their hearts. So, too, did the Americans, when Bertie and Elizabeth descended upon the White House to stay with President and Mrs Franklin Delano Roosevelt. The two men got along well, bound as they were by a deep appreciation of what it was like to be handicapped, Bertie with his nervous afflictions and Roosevelt with polio-induced paralysis. Eleanor Roosevelt, however, was heartily fed up with the demands of the royal couple and their courtiers. There was one fuss after another, from demanding dining chairs that were identical to the unique pair the presidential couple normally used, to insisting that messengers – and chairs for them to sit upon – be posted outside the passage that connected the King and the Queen's bedrooms. This last requirement was one too many for Mrs Roosevelt, who condemned it as seeming 'foolish to me, since the rooms were just across the hall from each other'. Had she lived in England and been privy to the gossip, that Bertie had not been granted Elizabeth's favours since the birth of Princess Margaret, the need for messengers might have become more apparent.

Uninitiated though she was about such necessities, Mrs Roosevelt nevertheless witnessed Elizabeth's ascendancy from mere queen to international darling. The American press were as taken with her as the Canadian had been, and by the time she and Bertie arrived back in Britain aboard the

Empress of Britain, everyone back home looked upon their King and Queen with new eyes. At Southampton and in London the crowds went wild and, later, the masses in the Mall would not depart until the newly acknowledged international superstars appeared on the balcony and waved. Finally, the great British public and the press woke up to the fact that they had a veritable galaxy of their own. Elizabeth the Great and the Good had finally been born, sixteen long years after she had first appeared in their midst. Thereafter, she and her public would guard their perception of her with jealous regard, for so precious a commodity as national adoration was not something to disregard, not now that the public had got around to viewing Elizabeth as she, the King and her many other admirers viewed her.

Adulation, Bertie discovered, suited him almost as much as Elizabeth. Shortly after his return home, he went to the Guildhall to make a speech about the ideals of the Commonwealth. He spoke well, indeed fluently, conveying not only the conviction that shaped his thoughts but also the steel that Lady Airlie had discovered lurking beneath his good and decent character – all those years before when he was a little boy, and she grew to know him after he thrust his Easter present in her hand.

Elizabeth now had everything she had ever wanted. She possessed an attractive and acclaimed prince, his love, the love of her children, as well as the love of her family, peers and nation. She had, it was true, never made it as the wife of the Prince of Wales, but she now sat upon the throne of England as his brother's consort. She was the first lady in the land. She had achieved mythical status within her lifetime.

This was the high point of her life, and she relished it. Always one to enjoy herself, she gave full rein to her life-as-a-party tastes, surrounding herself with congenial and amusing friends and relations such as Lord and Lady Fermoy, her favourite brother David Bowes-Lyon, the other members of the Royal Family, even the Hardinges, with whom she remained on sociable terms. Like most of her Strathmore relations, Elizabeth had discovered that the pleasures of drink were conducive to the maintenance of a feeling of well-being in a way that a hefty tea consumed in the mid-afternoon was not. This was ironic, for she had spent the early days of her married life trying to keep Bertie's drinking under control. He, however, was now too busy to overindulge to the point of drunkenness, though he still drank more than was good for him. He was up early every morning for a full day of engagements. Whether they were public or private did not matter. Bertie was an active man and had always been. He was also conscientious and allowed his private secretaries to bury him under a mountain of work.

For her part, Elizabeth was not a *fin de siècle* lady for nothing. She was a product of a generation who did not believe that well-born women had to do anything but get married, produce the regulation heir and spare, then dedicate themselves to whatever pursuits took their fancy.

The Surveyor of the King's Pictures, Kenneth (later Lord) Clark was 'shocked to see how little' she did with her day: 'She never rose before eleven.' She undertook the occasional official duty, sometimes with the King, sometimes without, and retired to bed late at night, after a riotous time singing and playing charades with her friends. Often, other members of the Royal Family were present, for Elizabeth remained on excellent terms with most of them, especially Queen Mary. She did, however, have cool relations with her sister-in-law Marina. Word had got back to her that the Greek Princess, daughter of a Russian Grand Duchess and great-granddaughter of a Tsar, had referred to her and Prince Harry's wife as 'Those common little Scots girls whom my husband's brothers married.' There was no question of freezing Marina out, though she undoubtedly would have consigned her to social Siberia along with the Windsors if she could.

David and Wallis, as the whole world knows, were still banished. The year before, when the Duke and Duchess of Gloucester were visiting France, they had been asked to make a detour to Paris to see Harry's brother and his wife. According to Princess Alice, Duchess of Gloucester, the reason for doing this was to test the water for a reaction in England. In the event, there was virtually none. One or two old ladies wrote letters to the Palace, but there was nothing to be concerned about. The cabal, however, used the existence of those letters as a reason for perpetuating the banishment, leaving some in royal circles to question whether sending the Gloucesters had been a genuine attempt to seek the repatriation of the Windsors, or just a clever ruse to protect the cabal's reputations in the eyes of posterity.

Undoubtedly, a more compassionate person than Elizabeth might have decided that this was the time to slacken her hold on the bars preventing the Duke and Duchess of Windsor from returning home. She had had only one valid concern in wishing David to remain away from Britain, and that was the well-founded fear that he might be more popular than Bertie. This no longer applied, however, so the perpetuation of the banishment had to be for more personal reasons. 'Jealousy,' the Duke and Duchess of Windsor both said to Michael Thornton, and if it was not that, it could only have been a staggering lack of compassion. But then, Elizabeth was a hardy Scot. Whatever her virtues, compassion had never been among them. She was well known for her toughness, for possessing an exacting and critical disposition beneath the smiles and the gestures of softness. Hers were hard virtues, not soft ones, and they left room only for success, not for failure. Even her much vaunted moralism was of the brand that did not allow for compassion or for the acceptance of anything like human failing or failure. It was geared towards being on life's winning team, and it had worked, for her and for Bertie.

CHAPTER SIX

The King is Dead, Long Live the Queen

*T*he war years solidified Bertie and Elizabeth's image in the public mind and increased his workload, but insofar as their married life was concerned, little changed. With a bit of help from Lady Maureen Stanley, they remained a happy, self-contained family unit. He still adored Elizabeth, and she was still happy to be adored by him, even though she had gone through a phase of flirting so outrageously with Kenneth Clark, who was clearly besotted with her, that King George VI had had to bawl them both out. This, however, was very much an Elizabethan sort of flirtation, all show and no go, and though Bertie remained jealous of the 'competition', he soon realized it was no threat to the sanctity of his union with Elizabeth.

With the passage of the years, Elizabeth had grown to love Bertie in a way that she had not at the time of their marriage. But theirs was not quite the placid union the public has been led to believe. They no longer squabbled over where they were going to live, but she had habits that drove him to distraction, and his eruptions were frequent and loud.

The biggest bone of contention, Kenneth Clark aside, was her perpetual inability to be on time. He was a stickler for punctuality, to such an extent that he was known to wait on a train that was early, before disembarking at the scheduled time of arrival. Elizabeth, on the other hand, had never been known to be on time for anything, and to this day, she is invariably late. Five minutes late in arriving was early for her, ten to fifteen minutes usual and twenty nothing out of the ordinary. Royal schedules are precision planned, however, and the result was that she threw the works completely out.

But that was only the beginning of the story. Elizabeth moved in slow motion, taking her time, to walk, talk, wave, beam beatifically and soak up the pleasure of being where she was. This was as divergent from the quick, precise Bertie as it was possible to be, but the more he tried to rush her, the slower she became.

According to Michael Thornton, 'Her household was full of stories about the King losing his temper with her. Before they were due to go anywhere together, he would pace up and down, waiting, waiting. "Where is that fucking woman?" he once shouted, for he had the strong, earthy language of a sailor, and when he lost his temper, he used it.' Once they were at their appointed venue, getting Elizabeth to adhere to the schedule was like trying to get hold of a wet and slithering child. The King did not use foul language then, but he was known to try to speed her up with curt prompting.

For all the conflict their differing concepts of time caused, Bertie never lost his touching reverence for Elizabeth. Whenever they were together he always hung back and let her take centre stage. Even when the war had brought him the deep respect of the whole world, he still remained the same old Bertie, in awe of and grateful to Elizabeth for having him.

Like his father and grandfather before him, Bertie was a heavy smoker. So, too, was David. Smoking, in the form of chronic bronchitis and pulmonary problems, killed King Edward VII and King George V. In July 1948 it started to kill King George VI, too, as it would later kill the Duke of Windsor. Bertie, in residence at the Palace of Holyroodhouse in Edinburgh, was out walking towards Arthur's Seat with Group Captain Peter Townsend, his equerry and later Princess Margaret's lover. All of a sudden he exclaimed, 'What's the matter with my legs? They won't work properly.'

For someone as athletic as Bertie, the sudden failure of his well-developed legs was a worry, but, try though he did to take a sensible and unsensational view, the problem worsened. Within a matter of weeks he was in constant pain, and by the time the court returned to London in October, his left leg was permanently numb. Elizabeth called in the King's medical team, and Buerger's Disease was diagnosed.

Buerger's Disease is a condition caused by heavy smoking. The arteries narrow and the blood, which is normally circulated throughout the body, ceases to reach such extremities as the legs. One of the dangers of the condition is gangrene, and Bertie's doctors feared that his leg would have to be amputated. To avert that, they prescribed a period of bed rest and exercises. Like most active men, Bertie did not take kindly to a period of enforced rest, but rest he did, and with a minimum of fuss too. His eldest daughter, Princess Elizabeth, Duchess of Edinburgh, known within the family as Lilibet, was due to have her first baby, and indeed Prince Charles was born while King George VI was recuperating. It did little good. By March 1949 Professor Learmouth was forced to advise performing a lumbar sympathectomy.

After this, Bertie's health did improve slightly, though it was still evident just from looking at him that he was a very sick man. Chips Channon records that the King wore heavy make-up to conceal his pallor, and Michael Thornton recalls seeing him when he was a little boy and wondering why on earth the King's face was concealed beneath a thick mask of cosmetics.

By spring 1951 Bertie's condition had deteriorated once more. He had a hacking cough, which simply refused to go away. Summer was spent, as always, at Balmoral. While out shooting, on Princess Margaret's twenty-first birthday, Bertie caught a chill, and by 1 September his condition was sufficiently alarming for Elizabeth to send for the doctors to come up from London. They advised that he return to London for an X-ray, which he did by overnight train on 7 September. Matters now moved quickly. On 16 September, Elizabeth learnt that Bertie had cancer. On the 23rd his diseased lung was removed. So, too, were some of the nerves in his larynx, to which the cancer had spread. The very real threat of never speaking again in a normal voice now existed, after all the time spent learning to speak unhindered by stammering. When he had recovered enough to talk, the King did in fact do so in a raspy, whispery voice, but he was alive and seemingly cured, and on 9 December, his recovery was celebrated with a National Day of Thanksgiving.

Elizabeth's way of coping with Bertie's illness was reflective of the sort of woman she was. She was admirably supportive, vigilant for her husband's well-being and involved in the course of his treatment. The more virulent aspects of her personality were carefully hived off so that they could be directed at those for whom she felt no love. Bertie could not be blamed for having smoked himself into death's doorway. Bertie was her husband, and Bertie could not therefore be held responsible for anything so tawdry as dying from the side-effects of smoking. No, the fault had to lie elsewhere. It had to lie with someone who was not as fine and noble and moral and upstanding as she or anyone whom she loved. She did not have to thrash around long to find a scapegoat. As soon as the initial phase of Bertie's illness was diagnosed, Elizabeth had alighted upon the culprit. In fact, two culprits. The Duke and Duchess of Windsor were once more in the dock.

According to Elizabeth's theory, Bertie would never have developed Buerger's Disease if David had remained on the throne and had taken all the strain of kingship during the war years. The fact that he had avoided doing so was entirely due to Wallis Windsor's existence. They were therefore respons-ible for Bertie's illness.

Having achieved what she regarded as a correct attribution of the blame, Elizabeth next set about ensuring that the world would not be misled as to what was truly responsible for her husband's fading health. The name Buerger's Disease did not actually sit well, not when it could be arterio-sclerosis under another name: a name that did not brand its sufferer as both the perpetrator and the victim of his habits. Yes. Arteriosclerosis, with its vague and indeterminate sources of origin, made a more pleasing impact. Elizabeth called it arteriosclerosis, and the doctors, ever eager to oblige a grand patient, did not press the unwanted name of Buerger's Disease upon the charming and appreciative Queen. So arteriosclerosis it became.

By the time Bertie had to have his lung resectioned, David and Wallis already knew that they were being blamed for his illness. They were stunned at being made scapegoats yet again for something that was palpably not their fault. Bertie's health had never been good, not even when he was a little boy, and, while it was possible that the anxieties to which he was subjected during the war did have a physical effect as well, the largest part of the blame for his state of health had to rest with his smoking habit. David and Wallis had hoped that the passage of time would lessen the hostility that the British Establishment pointed in their direction, but here again was Elizabeth finding another way of keeping the hated David and the detested Wallis away from her hallowed and sanctified domain.

With her enemies at bay and Bertie on the mend, Elizabeth brought in the new year of 1952 at Sandringham, in keeping with Royal Family tradition. She and Bertie did return south at the end of January, to see Lilibet off at London Airport. She was replacing her parents on an official visit to Australia and New Zealand, and in those pre-jetplane days, all journeys, even those that covered less than half the globe, as Lilibet's would cover, were noteworthy.

When Lilibet disappeared through the open door of the aeroplane, she did not know it, but it was the last time she would ever see her father alive. Physical suffering, allied as it was to a childhood and early adulthood of emotional anguish, had etched deep lines into the face of a relatively young man, for the King was still less than fifty-seven. With his high cheekbones, gaunt visage and straightforward expression, King George VI was a magnifi-cent, if haunting-looking man. He was still an avid sportsman, however, so as soon as he bid Lilibet farewell, he and Elizabeth returned to Sandringham.

On 5 February Bertie, whose great love had always been shooting, joined the Sandringham estate workers, local gentry and tenant farmers for the Keepers' Day Shoot. This was a mopping-up exercise, to pick up all the game that had survived to the end of the season. It was a good day, and Bertie enjoyed himself thoroughly. When Elizabeth and Margaret returned from a day out with the artist Edward Seago, they had a 'truly gay' dinner (in the old-fashioned sense). It was the last they were to have. The following morning Bertie's valet discovered him dead in bed. Elizabeth was informed by the equerry, Sir Harold Campbell, as she drank her tea in the privacy of her own bedroom.

To say that Elizabeth was grief-stricken would be to put her condition mildly. An intensely emotional woman, Elizabeth had grown to love Bertie with all the devotion and passion that a high-minded woman brings to a sanctified union. Bertie the lame duck had become first the prince of her heart then the king of her dreams. Even before his metamorphosis from shambling wreck to heroic royal, his was a character so fine, a heart so unsullied by malice, that any woman would sooner or later have succumbed to the considerable charms Mabell Airlie had once discerned lying beneath the painful surface. By the time of his death, he was universally revered for qualities that are every bit as admirable in a humble man as in a king. The whole world felt it had lost a dearly loved friend, but Elizabeth knew she had lost the one and only adorer she would ever have.

For three years Elizabeth foundered. Death had deprived her not only of her husband but also of her King. No more was she a reigning Queen Consort. No more did the world revolve around her. Her daughter was now Queen. She was merely a dowager, though she took care, as Penelope Mortimer points out in her biography, to ensure that she got the style and dignity of Queen into her so far unique title not once but twice: Queen Elizabeth the Queen Mother.

Sir Winston Churchill, her daughter's prime minister, is credited with resurrecting Elizabeth's sense of purpose and interest in life. He pointed out that she still had many admirers. She could still lead a useful public life. She might have stepped down a peg or two, but she was still wanted by a great many people. Armed with that reassurance, she did gradually emerge from the shadows of depression. A star was reborn. The legend of Queen Elizabeth had been preserved: that of Queen Elizabeth the Queen Mother was nascent.

If the effects of the war were debatable where King George VI's health was concerned, they were not on the lives of his daughters. Lilibet and Margaret Rose were thirteen and nine when the Second World War broke out, so many of their most important early years were spent subject to the restrictions of a war-time family, which had to guard against the ever present danger of being kidnapped by the enemy.

In the rearing of the two Princesses, as in so many other things, Elizabeth had her own way. Little Elizabeth, whose name had been shortened to Lilibet by Margaret Rose when she was learning to speak, was more her father's daughter than her mother's. She was soft and kind, introverted and reserved, conscientious and obliging, but passionate and dedicated. These latter qualities would show, before the war was out, in a most unexpected way, but in the meantime she was kept younger than her years because of the deprivation entailed by being reared in Windsor Castle with only her younger sister as a companion.

Lilibet, moreover, did not shine the way Margaret Rose did. Margaret was prettier, cleverer, funnier and more endearing. Even Queen Mary acknowledged that Margaret could be badly behaved, but she was so adept at wrapping everyone around her little finger that she got away with it. No one would have won prizes for guessing whence she had inherited such charm. She did diverge from her mother's considerable talent for getting her own way, however, by behaving in a less acceptable manner than the socially impeccable Elizabeth.

Victory in Europe Day in 1945 was jubilant for everyone on that continent. The British Royal Family were as exultant as anyone else, and, while the tens of thousands of celebrants in the Mall were milling around shouting for the King and Queen to appear on the balcony and give them a wave, Elizabeth and Margaret were given the very first taste of freedom they had had in their lives. They were allowed to slip out of the Palace and join the throng. Shouting for your King and Queen and walking about the streets surrounding Buckingham Palace might not seem like very much to the average person, but to a nineteen and a fifteen year old, both of whom had never rubbed shoulders with ordinary people before, the mere act of blending into the scenery was unimaginably thrilling. Neither sister ever forgot it.

If Margaret Rose were still a child, which is how fifteen year olds were perceived in those days, Lilibet was now a young woman. Moreover, she was the one who had inherited her father's passionate and dogged nature, and, true to her Windsor heritage, she had allowed her heart to be irredeemably captured. Prince Philip of Greece was the object of her desire, and while her parents were not happy, for differing reasons, about the prospect of a match, she was adamant that this was the man for her. Queen Mary told Lady Airlie, 'They have been in love for the last eighteen months. In fact longer, I think. I believe she fell in love with him the first time he went down to Windsor, but the King and Queen feel that she is too young to be engaged yet. They want her to see more of the world before committing herself, and to meet other men. After all, she's only nineteen, and one is very impressionable at that age.'

There is no doubt that those were the sentiments motivating King George VI, but there has long been the suspicion among friends of both Queen Elizabeth II and Queen Elizabeth the Queen Mother, that the mother's concerns for the daughter were based on more personal and instinctive grounds. Prince Philip of Greece was very much a man of his time. Overtly masculine, he was not a docile character, but strong, assertive, and forceful. A born and trained leader, he commanded every environment in which he was placed. There was no question but that he would be the man of any house that became his. Moreover, he had intelligence and education, and these maximized the natural characteristics of a personality already endowed with more than its share of masculine thrust.

While Lilibet was thrilled to the depths of her being by Philip's masculine presence, Elizabeth had a natural antipathy towards it. She had none of the crackling passion of the House of Windsor, nor did she consider her lack a failing. The men she surrounded herself with were either weak personalities, such as her husband had been, and still was with her, or they were confirmed bachelors whose distaste for matrimony confirmed the innate direction of their desires.

Elizabeth's natural antipathy towards the more robust aspects of masculinity would have far-reaching effects later in the lives of mother, daughter and son-in-law, but for the moment she retreated behind Bertie's reasons for concern.

Philip was actually a far more interesting person than anyone else around Lilibet. Her choice of him says much for her taste. Nor was he interesting in isolation. He came from a long line of fascinating personalities. Compared with his antecedents, the Windsors looked like stodge.

Philip was the fifth and youngest child of Prince and Princess Andrew of Greece. He was born on 10 January 1921, at a Regency-style villa named Mon Repos, which for half a century had been the residence of British Commissioners on the island of Corfu. He had four elder sisters, but he was the only son, and his prospects of one day sitting upon the Greek throne were not remote. 'If the child will be a boy, he will be sixth in succession to the Greek throne,' his mother observed shortly before his birth. 'As things are today, with Alex [King Alexander of Greece, a nephew] dead [of blood poisoning from a monkey's bite], Tino [King Constantine, a brother-in-law] threatened by Venizelos [the prime minister, who soon got rid of the monarch], and George [another brother-in-law] and Andrew [her husband] unacceptable, my son, if God wills, could become one day the King if monarchy prevails.'

Princess Andrew was right to question whether the monarchic system of government would continue. The prime minister was notoriously republican and Greek politics were notoriously turbulent. Of the three Kings of the Schleswig-Holstein-Sonderburg-Glucksburg dynasty, one had been assassinated, one deposed in favour of his son, and the third had died horrifically, opening the way for his father's reinstatement. But King Constantine sat on a shaky throne and would lose it the year after Philip's birth.

The Greek monarchy was not old. Prince Philip's grandfather, King George I, was the second King of the Hellenes. The first was Prince Otto of Bavaria, who sat upon the throne for thirty years after the Greeks gained their independence from the Ottoman Empire. In 1862, however, he was forced to abdicate, and in 1863 the vacant throne was offered to Prince William of Denmark, after Queen Victoria's second son, Prince Alfred, Duke of Edinburgh turned it down.

Enthroned as George I, Willy, as the King was known within his family circle, married the Grand Duchess Olga Constantinovna of Russia and went on to produce eight heirs to the throne. Of these, seven survived to adulthood, and all had lives of such overwhelming interest that there must have been times when they yearned for the solace of boredom. Philip's father and mother were not the only influences on the young Philip's life. All the Greek aunts and uncles helped to shape Philip into the man Elizabeth loved, and he himself frequently said that his father's family have too often been downplayed at the expense of his mother's. According to him, this is unfair as well as inaccurate, for his early life was spent almost exclusively with his Greek relations.

King George and Queen Olga had a happy marriage, and their children led relatively informal existences for royalty. They were poor by royal standards, and their son Christopher recalled that the Old Palace in Athens had 'only one bathroom in the whole place, and no one had ever been known to take a bath in it, for the simple reason that the taps would scarcely ever run and, on the rare occasions when they could be coaxed into doing so, emitted a thin trickle of water in which the corpses of defunct roaches and other strange animals floated dismally.'

The eldest child was the Crown Prince, Constantine, born in 1868. George followed in 1869, Alexandra in 1870, Nicholas in 1872, Marie in 1876, Andrew in 1882 and Christopher in 1888. A daughter, Olga, born in 1880, died at the age of three months.

Constantine made the fatal mistake of marrying the German Kaiser Wilhelm II's sister Princess Sophie Dorothea in 1889. This eventually cost him the throne after his father's assassination in 1914, for Queen Sophie was popularly believed to be influencing her husband to take neutral Greece into the Great War on the side of the Central Powers, headed by her brother, while the Allies were trying to sway Greece in their favour. In fact, Sophie hated her brother Wilhelm, but the relationship proved a valuable tool for Aristide Briand, the French Prime Minister and Foreign Minister, when, on 25 September 1916, some French sailors were killed in Athens. He proposed to the other Allied governments the deposition of the King and the recognition of his political adversary, the pro-Allied Eleutherios Venizelos, as Prime Minister.

This scheme took some months to bear fruit, but on 12 June 1917, Constantine was forced to leave Greece and to surrender the throne to his young and malleable second son, Alexander. After Alexander's death in 1920, he was restored, but two years later he was forced to abdicate in favour of another son. This time it was the Crown Prince, who ascended the throne as King George II. In the way of Greek politics, this event was quickly followed by yet another return to power of the Prime Minister Venizelos, who celebrated by sending the entire royal family into exile.

While Constantine was bobbing back and forth between exile in Switzerland and his throne in Athens, his parents' second son was leading what he himself described as 'a life of bourgeois privacy'. His father's namesake, Prince George of Greece and Denmark, had been badly battered in May 1891, when his reputation was dealt a deadly blow. He had accompanied his cousin Nicky, the Tsarevich and later last Tsar of Russia, on a cruise, which took in Ceylon, Java, Siam, China and Japan among other places. In Otsu, one of the policemen guarding the royal cousins drew his sword and delivered two fierce blows to Nicky's head. He was spared from serious injury or death only because his bowler hat protected him and because George intervened, but the incident caused an international uproar. As is the way with royal courts, the Tsarevich's entourage tried to deflect any hint of blameworthiness, which might devolve upon the future Emperor as a result of policies that had instilled such hostility in the Japanese, and blamed George for provoking the attack. This sullied his honour in an age when a man's reputation was his most prized possession, and George never recovered from the blow.

There was more to the blonde and gentle giant than just an air of scandal, however. Prince George's wife was one of the most remarkable women of her time. Born Princess Marie Bonaparte, she was descended from Napoleon's youngest brother Lucien on her father's side, and on her mother's, from Francois Blanc, who owned 97 per cent of the Casino in Monte Carlo, the Société des Bains de Mer, the Cercle des Etrangers, as well as being Monaco's principal real-estate developer. More than merely being one of the richest women in the world, Marie was a brilliant intellectual who became first a pupil then later a disciple of Dr Sigmund Freud. She and his daughter Anna became the only two lay practitioners of psychoanalysis whom he acknowledged. It was thanks to her generosity that the Institute of Psychoanalysis was founded, and by the time of her death in 1962, she was regarded as one of that discipline's pillars.

But there was even more of interest to Princess George of Greece and Denmark than her intellectual accomplishments or her wealth. Frigid throughout much of her life but desperate for a cure, she had her clitoris surgically removed closer to her vagina on three separate occasions. She had many lovers but only two great loves. One was Aristide Briand, the very Prime Minister and Foreign Secretary at the time of her brother-in-law Constantine's difficulties with the Allies. Female sexuality became her speciality as a psychoanalyst, and when she and her husband came to London for the wedding of their niece Marina to the Duke of Kent, she did something that went unnoticed then, but which in latter years would have caused a media stir. She gave a lecture on female sexuality to the British Psycho-Analytical Society.

Princess George despised family life, especially her husband's. 'It's too much for me,' she said, discounting them as 'All royal bourgeois, these Danes, bourgeois virtues and defects, united, honest, good, simple, kind, desperately treading the common path.' She refused on principle to send her two children, Prince Peter and Princess Eugenie of Greece, to private schools, though she paid for the education of her exiled brother-in-law Andrew's children at private schools, reasoning that they deserved the education they would have received had the dynasty continued to reign in Greece. It was this Bonaparte princess, therefore, who paid for Prince Philip's education, not the Mountbattens, as has so erroneously been claimed over the years, and verification of this can be obtained from an inspection of Marie's papers.

All Prince Philip's other aunts and uncles also married interestingly. Aunt Alexandra became the Grand Duchess Paul of Russia and Aunt Marie the Grand Duchess George. Both Grand Dukes were executed during the revolution, along with the Tsar's brother Grand Duke Michael and other members of the Imperial Family. This was a double blow to Uncle Nicholas and his wife Helen, whose daughter Marina became Duchess of Kent, for Helen was also a Russian Grand Duchess. The baby of the family, however, married less grandly but more adventurously and ultimately more profitably. Christopher's first wife was an American heiress called Nancy Leeds née Stewart, and after her death the immensely rich widower married Princess Françoise of Orléans. This raised eyebrows in France, for the Greek Royal Family now had sisters-in-law who represented the two opposing ruling houses of France: the Bonapartists and the Orléanists.

Of all the brothers, the most unfortunate was Prince Philip's father. Prince Andrew was the most Hellenic of his brothers and sisters. So caught up was he with the idea of being Greek that he obstinately refused to speak any other language, in a family where German, French and Danish were the more usual tongues. As far as Andrew was concerned, he was as Greek as any fisherman from Pireaus, and while he did not deny that he was the grandson of a Danish King of German extraction, the blood of his forebears played no part in the assimilation of his identity. It was therefore all the more devastating for him when the exigencies of Greek politics denied him a host of rights denied to no other Greek male.

The first right to go was that of serving in the army. In 1909, Venizelos, who kept on bobbing up like a cork in water, forced through the Military League the edict that Andrew and his brothers had to resign their commissions. This was especially disruptive for Prince Andrew, who was a dedicated officer with plans for a lifelong career in the army.

Had the Military League not rescinded their order in 1912, when they needed the princes to lead the Greek armies into war against the Ottoman

Empire, Prince Andrew's life might have taken a less tragic and traumatic turn. However, the order was revoked, and Andrew rejoined his beloved army. For the next decade Andrew was a serving officer amid the turbulent ebb and flow of Greek politics. The First World War ended, and the Ottoman Empire disappeared, leaving only the rump state of Greece's traditional enemy, Turkey. The Allies then besieged the relict of their former enemy, and Prime Minister Venizelos, scenting the opportunity for realizing his dream of restoring Greece to its ancient glory, made plans to attack Turkey. The ineptitude of the Greek government was so great, and their intransigence at refusing to listen to any advice so absolute, that Prince Andrew decided in September 1921 he had no other choice open to him but to distance himself from the débâcle that was bound to occur. He therefore secured his release from his military duties and headed for Mon Repos, where the infant Philip was living with his mother and elder sisters. Within a year, his forebodings materialized. The Allies did not come to the aid of Greece, and Turkey thrashed Greece roundly.

In October 1922, one month after Andrew's brother had been forced to abdicate, and shortly before his nephew King George II was driven off the throne, Andrew was summoned. In contravention of the agreement reached a year before with the government, he was required to go to Athens to testify against three former prime ministers, two former ministers of state and the former Commander-in-Chief of the Army, General Papulas, who had been charged with high treason. The government needed scapegoats for their failings, and scapegoats aplenty they were intent on dishing up to the agitated populace, whom they had whipped up into a frenzy of confidence with unrealistic assurances of certain victory. To show that no one, no matter how eminent, was beyond their reach, they arrested Prince Andrew as soon has he reached the capital city he had loved since boyhood. The charge was high treason. Any hope the Royal Family had for an equitable outcome to what was nothing but a show trial was dashed when the first batch of 'traitors' was tried on 13 November. Found guilty, they were summarily executed.

Prince Andrew's trial was scheduled for 2 December. According to his younger brother, Prince Christopher, 'No one was allowed to go near Andrew except his valet. Guards kept strictest watch and confiscated all letters and parcels. Finally, I hit on the expedient of writing a letter on cigarette paper, rolling it tightly and putting it with cigarettes into his valet's case. Andrew answered with a short note full of courage, but I knew that he had no hope of regaining his freedom. Andrew had just had a conversation with a former school-fellow, Pangalos, now Minister for War and instigator of his trial, that left him small grounds for optimism. "How many children have you?" Pangalos had asked suddenly, and when my brother told him, he shook his head: "Poor things, what a pity, they will soon be orphans."'

In desperation, Prince Christopher went to their nephew, King George II, and asked him to intervene, but he was a puppet in the hands of the

Venizelos government and was powerless to do anything but hang on to his throne for a short while more.

Princess Andrew, however, was not prepared to accept without a struggle the fate that awaited her husband. Leaving the baby Philip and his sisters on Corfu, she went to Athens to orchestrate the campaign to save her unfortunate spouse. She wrote letters left, right and centre: to King Alfonso XIII of Spain, who was married to her cousin Victoria Eugenia of Battenberg; to the Pope; to the President of France; and to her brothers George and Louis.

Fortunately for Princess Andrew, royalty was intricately interconnected. Louis took the problem to their cousin King George V, who was also the first cousin of Prince Andrew (the prince's father and the King's mother having been brother and sister). The King paved the way for Louis to see the prime minister. Andrew Bonar Law then turned the matter over to the Foreign Secretary, under whose jurisdiction it fell. Lord Curzon, outraged at such a patent miscarriage of justice, swung into action, despatching the former Naval Attaché in Athens, Commander Gerald Talbot, to Greece. So necessary was stealth that Talbot entered the country with doctored papers and a false beard.

King George V, meanwhile, decided that he was not going to permit any other relation of his to be sacrificed due to his inactivity, as had happened when he refused David Lloyd George's offer of asylum to the deposed Tsar and Tsarina of Russia and their children. The blood of those cousins on his hands was quite enough for the King, and, calling upon his powers as Commander-in-Chief of the Armed Forces, he instructed the Admiralty to order a cruiser to Athens to back Talbot up. On the evening of 29 November, the day before the rumoured starting date of Andrew's trial, the *Calypso* cruised into the Bay of Athens under the command of Captain H. A. Buchanan-Wollaston.

As the ship steamed into the harbour, Talbot was in conference with Minister of War Pangalos, whom he had known from his posting in Athens. The pro-republican minister was adamant that he could not oblige the commander by acceding to his pleas for compassion. Prince Andrew of Greece was going to be executed, just as the other 'royal traitors' had been. Nor could Pangalos be budged from his stance until an assistant entered the room with the news that a British cruiser was in the harbour with its guns aimed towards the shore. Doing a complete volte-face, the Minister of War, immediately saw the sense of clemency. Talbot duly returned to the British Embassy, from which he sent to London a telegram stating that he had 'obtained this evening promise from Minister of War and also from Colonel Plastiras, the two leaders of government, that Prince Andrew will not be executed but allowed to leave the country in charge of Talbot.'

If nothing instilled compassion so much as the guns of a warship, there was no power on earth that could spare Prince Andrew from the ignominy that awaited him at his trial. Found guilty, before the first word was uttered, of disobeying orders and abandoning his post, he was stripped of his rank and title, deprived of the Greek citizenship that he had always held so dear, sentenced to imprisonment and banished. 'But consideration being given to extenuating circumstances of lack of experience in commanding a large unit,' the verdict continued, 'he has been degraded and condemned to perpetual banishment.'

Pangalos himself escorted Prince Andrew from prison under cover of darkness to the *Calypso*, where Princess Andrew was already on board. They set sail immediately stopping off the following day in Corfu to pick up the five children, and headed for the port of Brindisi, which they reached the day after. Disembarking, they headed for London via a circuitous and leisurely route. They stopped off in Rome to thank the Pope for his support. They visited relations along the way, then ended up at Kensington Palace, where Princess Andrew's mother resided. The whole family remained undyingly grateful to King George V for saving Prince Andrew's life, and the King himself was proud of the part he had played. It mitigated, if only somewhat, his failure in saving the lives of his Russian cousins.

The courageous Princess Andrew was a woman of commendable spirit and quiet indomitability. According to Marie Bonaparte, 'She smiled a lot but seldom spoke, because she was deaf.' Highly intelligent but deaf since the age of four, she used what little hearing she had while she was a child to teach herself to lip-read in several languages. Born Princess Alice of Battenberg, she was the daughter of Queen Victoria's granddaughter Princess Victoria of Hesse. Her aunt was the last Tsarina of Russia, Alexandra Feodorovna being the sister of her mother. Her father was Prince Louis of Battenberg, son of Prince Alexander of Hesse and his morganatic wife, the former Julie von Haukc.

Suffering, strife and scandal were the stuff on which the beautiful Alice was weaned. Her husband's disgrace was not her first experience of misfortune. She had had to endure the public humiliation of her father only eight years previously, and, as this would colour the way Prince Philip perceived the world, it is worth recounting.

Prince Philip's grandfather Prince Louis of Battenberg was judged by his peers to be the most brilliant naval mind of his generation, but even this, and the other sacrifices he made for Britain, did not spare him from the fate that ultimately awaited him. At the age of twelve, he had given up his German citizenship to come to England to join 'the greatest navy in the world' as a cadet. By the outbreak of the First World War he was First Sea Lord and generally acknowledged to be the one man capable of sparing the British navy from defeat by the German.

Prince Louis's German birth, however, stuck in the craw of the gutterpress, especially a bombastic tabloid called *The Globe*. As soon as war with Germany was declared, it mounted a campaign of vilification, calling into question his loyalty to his adopted country and blaming him for the sinking of ships such as the *Audacious*, a dreadnought, which struck a German mine off Lough Swilly. Honour bound to do the correct thing, Prince Louis felt he must offer his resignation, which he did, on 28 October 1914. There is no doubt that the government should not have allowed itself to be brow-beaten by a small and vicious segment of the press, which was more intent on whipping up a frenzy in which to sell newspapers than on practising ethical journalism. But the prime minister, H. H. Asquith, and the minister under whose portfolio the navy fell, Winston Churchill, accepted the resignation rather than take a potentially unpopular course and oppose press and public opinion.

Although Prince Louis's good friend and cousin, King George V, showed solidarity and trust by naming him a privy counsellor, and the eulogies soon flooded in, a brilliant career had been destroyed not only at its peak but also when it could have most profited the nation. Moreover, Prince Louis experienced real financial hardship as a result of the loss of his position. He had no real money of his own, and, without the salary and perks of a serving officer, he had no option but to borrow a house on the Isle of Wight, where he and his family lived in genteel but straitened circumstances.

As so often happens in life, once the very people who could and should have defended Prince Louis and preserved his career had had the opportunity to consider the disgracefulness of their omission, a feeling of shame about the way he had been treated became the pervasive emotion. This fortunately was acted upon, and in 1921 the First Lord of the Admiralty, Lord Lee of Fareham, recommended to King George V that he promote Prince Louis to the rank of Admiral of the Fleet on the Retired List by an Order-in-Council. This was done on 4 August 1921. Vindicated, even if his career would never rise Lazarus-like from the dead, Prince Louis was finally at peace. Within days he was dead.

The whole Battenberg family, which had been renamed Mountbatten in 1917, was bitter about the way Prince Louis had been hounded from office. This overriding sense of injustice became the spur that drove his son, Lord Louis Mountbatten, to excel in the navy and to cover himself in honours. It left Alice shaken to her core, but she had strength born of being handicapped, and she used this experience to enhance further her already spiritual approach to life.

Nor did Alice allow the trauma of nearly losing her husband to the executioner to shake her profoundly spiritual philosophy. Captain Buchanan-Wollaston, who escorted them out of Greece recounted, 'They were rather amusing about being exiled, for they so frequently are.'

The happy times continued when the family reached London. The newly exiled couple felt the need for a break, however, so they left the children behind in London with Alice's mother, now the Dowager Marchioness of Milford Haven, having previously been known by the royal titles of Princess Victoria of Hesse and Princess Louis of Battenberg. Andrew and Alice crossed the Atlantic and went to stay with Prince Christopher and his heiress wife Nancy, who had by then less than a year to live.

When the time came to return home, Andrew and Alice had to ask themselves where home should be. The whole royal family was still exiled, but even if they had not been, Andrew was so bitter about his mistreatment at the hands of the politicians that he would never have elected to live in Greece again.

Paris was the home of Andrew's brother George and his wife Marie Bonaparte, and it was there that the dispossessed family found refuge. First, they were put up in a suite of rooms in the magnificent townhouse that Marie had built for George on the Rue Adolphe Ivan, on the edge of the Bois de Boulogne. But, this arrangement was not suitable for a large family with young children, so they moved to Marie's mini-estate outside Paris, at St Cloud. Situated in the extensive grounds of this lavish mansion was a lodge, which Marie turned over to Andrew and Alice for their exclusive use. It was there, surrounded by his four sisters, his Nanny Roose and the other trusted retainers who came from Greece to continue serving their master and mistress for little more than board and lodging, that Prince Philip of Greece spent his boyhood.

CHAPTER SEVEN

A Passionate Alliance

P rince Philip's childhood was enchanted. Despite the relative penury of his parents, he grew up with most of the advantages of royalty, but without many of its attendant disadvantages. Being exiles, the Greek royal family did not have to worry about official duties, did not have to curtail their activities with an eye to the possible effects upon public opinion, nor be subject to any of the many restraints governing reigning royals.

As both Prince George and Prince Christopher were married to exceedingly wealthy women, the Greek royal family all managed to live comfortably, even if the poorer members did not have money to throw around. Moreover, many of their closest relations still sat upon thrones, so they were able to enjoy the luxury of visiting cousins who lived in splendid state. As a result, Prince Philip's earliest memories revolve around magical times at Cotroceni and Sinaia with the boy king, Michael of Romania and Princess Alexandra of Greece, later Queen of Yugoslavia.

Michael and Alexandra were his exact contemporaries as well as his cousins, being the children of the former Princess Helen of Greece and the late King Alexander of the Hellenes, who had died of the monkey's bite. When Philip was not off on some exciting family holiday in Romania with them, his family stayed on the Baltic at the Greek royal family's home at Panka. There were also frequent visits to Alice's family home at Hesse-Darmstadt, where her uncle the Grand Duke lived in regal splendour, as if he had not been deposed and the monarchies of Germany abolished. His lifestyle was every bit as elegant as that enjoyed by their Danish relations, whom they also visited and who had the good fortune to occupy a throne, although they, too, were relatively poor in royal terms.

The Danish connection had another valuable offshoot. All the members of the Greek royal family were members of the Danish royal family. As such, they were entitled to style themselves Princes and Princesses of Greece and Denmark and, more importantly, to hold Danish passports. They therefore did not have to travel on stateless documents and be subjected to the ensuing hassle.

The cosmopolitan nature of Prince Philip's formative years was nowhere more obvious than in his schooling. In 1927, he was enrolled at the MacJannet Country Day and Boarding School at St Cloud, called the Elms because its three buildings, one of which had been Jules Verne's house, were situated in a pleasant garden shaded by huge elm trees. This was a progressive kindergarten run along American lines by an American who had formerly taught at the National Cathedral School in Washington and was catering to American children. The result was that Philip was soon speaking English with a broad American accent, even though he had learnt the language from his mother, who spoke it to her children. He was also fluent in German and French, the native tongues of many of his relations.

Philip's teacher in grade III, Catherine Pegg Levitsky, remembered him as a bright and helpful young man with exquisite manners. 'He would sit on my right hand at the dining table, not as an honoured guest but because he was particularly agile and a careful carrier of hot dishes. He would never wait for the maid to carry in the different courses, for, as he explained to me, his mother had taught him that a gentleman does not allow a woman to wait on him.'

Kindness and compassion were also virtues that Philip manifested at an early age, and that have motivated much of the work he has undertaken throughout his life. Due to his mother's deafness, Philip was raised with an appreciation of how necessary those qualities are. His cousin Alexandra recalled the occasion of a trip to the beach, when they were all children on holiday at Berck. Toys had been brought for all the able-bodied children but not for an invalid cousin who was bedridden with a tubercular leg. Without being prompted by anyone, Philip took his toys and gave them to the forgotten child.

At kindergarten the young Philip displayed early signs of the sportsmanship, for which he became renowned in adulthood. Catherine Pegg Levitsky described him as a 'rugged, boisterous boy' who was 'full of energy'. Already a good swimmer from his family holidays on the Baltic and in Romania, he developed a passion for baseball, boxing and the other competitive sports such as football to which he was exposed. Like King George VI, he was a born athlete who enjoyed nothing more than physical activity, and, like his future father-in-law, he liked to win.

Hélène Cordet, a childhood friend of Prince Philip, gave me an insight into the family life of the young Philip. 'Prince Philip and I have known each other all our lives,' the former Hélène Foufounis says. 'I remember their lives in Paris very well. He was much younger than his sisters, by about eight years. He was very much loved by the whole family. Because the age gap was so big, he was very close to his mother. She was a wonderful woman. Very, very nice and kind and very good with him. He was also close to his father. Prince Andrew was very nice too. He was dashing and elegant. They really were a very nice family.'

Beneath the surface, however, tensions were brewing for Prince and Princess Andrew. Exile and the trauma to which Prince Andrew had been subjected were leading to increasingly divergent lifestyles. Andrew's interests were daily becoming more sybaritic while Alice's were fast heading towards ascetic spirituality.

Andrew needed to wash away the sour taste of injustice, to make his mark in some positive way. Without scope for any other activity, he turned in the one direction where he knew success would be assured. Women became his refuge as well as his interest. 'The grown-ups talked, but he was no more naughty than anyone else,' Hélène Cordet said defensively when I broached the subject with her. That was both true and fair, for the custom among Continental noblemen and royals was for them to have outside interests, which the indelicate termed mistresses.

As we have seen, this was as much an accepted practice within Andrew's family as within society as a whole. Indeed, a lady or two on the side was hardly anything to rant about, not when the Danish and Greek royal families were a study in marital infidelity and odd sexual liaisons. There was Prince George of Greece, who was besotted by his decade-older uncle, Prince Waldemar of Denmark. There was the pleasure-loving Andrew, who whiled his hours away in other women's beds when he was not throwing away what little money he had on the gaming tables. He had always had an eye for the ladies, and Alice, in keeping with the ladies of her time, had turned a blind eye throughout their marriage. Exile, however, made wilful blindness that much harder a policy to maintain, especially when it was allied to a gambling problem. She had lost all the props that protected her in Greece. Gone were the structure and activity of official duties, behind which an errant husband could shield himself from his pliant wife. With nothing to do on a daily basis, everything one did was painfully visible.

Prince and Princess Andrew were now confronting the logistical difficulties that unfaithful bourgeois couples all over the world face. Had she been more dependent or less spiritually motivated, Alice might have continued to fail to see what was staring her in the face, but she had reached the point in her own life when she wanted to dedicate herself to the greater good of humanity. Without fuss or acrimony, therefore, she and Prince Andrew laid the ground for separation.

The first item on the agenda was arranging marriages for their four daughters. Separation and divorce were volatile subjects among their contemporaries, and while Prince and Princess Andrew did not plan legally to end their marriage, they had no intention of allowing its practical termination to affect their daughters' future. They would therefore have to be married before Andrew and Alice could proceed to separate. Between 1929 and 1930, they secured good matches for all four daughters, whose engagements were announced one by one.

The marriages took place between 1930 and 1931. The youngest, Sophie, was a mere sixteen when she stood before the altar with her cousin, Prince Christopher of Hesse. The penultimate daughter Cecile also married into the Hesse family, securing her first cousin the Hereditary Grand Duke George Donatus for herself. The candles had barely been snuffed out by their tapers before the eldest daughter, Margarita, found herself exchanging vows with yet another cousin, Prince Gottfried von Hohenlohe-Langenburg, whose grandfather had been Queen Victoria's second son, Prince Alfred, Duke of Edinburgh. Finally, Theodora's future was secured as the Margravine of Baden with the Margrave Berthold, whose father Prince Max of Baden had also been the father of the Weimar Republic and the last Chancellor of Imperial Germany.

Prince and Princess Andrew were not so distracted by the various engagements and marriages that they forgot about Prince Philip's future. He had reached the age when boys are sent to prep school. Prince Andrew himself was 'so English', according to Captain Buchanan-Wollaston, though he had no English blood flowing through his veins, and Alice considered herself English despite the preponderance of German blood in her family tree. It was therefore only natural that they would choose a British education for their only son, and they chose Cheam School, one of the oldest preparatory schools in the country.

Cheam was founded in 1447 in London, but moved to the Surrey village, after which the school took its name in 1665, to avoid the Great Plague. Near to Richmond, which Elizabeth had regarded as too suburban for her tastes when she was offered Queen Mary's childhood home, the school had already moved within the village once, to its present thirteen-acre site, and would move again the year after Prince Philip's departure, to the more rural terrain of Headley, near Newbury, Berkshire. Cheam was Alice's choice. Her father had sent her brother Prince George of Battenberg there as a result of being impressed by the conduct of two midshipmen, who had been schoolmates at that school. George, by now the 2nd Marquis of Milford Haven, sent his own son David, Earl of Medina, there. And in 1930 Alice arranged for her son Philip to attend.

This was Philip's first foray into the world at large. By all accounts, it was as great a success as his earlier schooling had been. A born extrovert, he revelled in being with boys his own age. He was as successful off the playing fields as on and within weeks had a coterie of friends. High-spirited and fun-loving, young Prince Philip of Greece got up to his share of mischief, to such an extent that, when he and Princess Elizabeth attended the tercentenary celebrations in 1947, he introduced his headmaster to the present Queen with the rider, 'My late headmaster who used to cane me.'

Aside from discipline, Cheam instilled independence and hardiness into its pupils. Philip had to sleep on an antiquated iron bed, which he had to make up each morning. The dormitories were not heated, nor were the boys allowed to leave them in a mess, and after he, David and the ninety other boys had eaten breakfast, they went to classes, which were of a high academic standard. Philip, however, was no bookworm. He found studying boring, but, being intelligent, managed to achieve acceptable, though by no means outstanding, marks. He excelled only in French, which was hardly surprising, considering he was fluent in it, and in sports, coming first in a diving competition and the high jump and captaining the soccer team in his final year.

For three years Philip led the life of a typical son of English gentlefolk. His exeats were usually spent at Lynden Manor with cousin David and his Uncle George and Aunt Nada. For longer holidays, he either returned to the Continent to see his mother and occasionally his father, or he stayed with a host of relations, both Continental and British. Although his family had fractured, he was still close to his parents, by his own reckoning, though his good friend Michael Parker would later opine that the lack of his father's presence left a void in Philip. Whatever the truth of these differing opinions, Philip and Prince Andrew maintained a vital correspondence, and even if he saw less and less of his father with the passage of the years, he never felt that he was being purposely deprived of his attention or affection. On the contrary, he adored his father and did everything in his power to excel in the ways in which he knew the prince would approve.

In 1933, Philip's first English sojourn came to an end. The time had come for him to return to the bosom of his Greek family. His sister Theodora had married the headmaster of Salem, a school run along English lines in the family's schloss in Germany. Founded by Berthold of Baden's father, Prince Max, who had also been the first Republican Chancellor of Germany, Salem had started out as an experiment geared towards changing the Prussian élite from militarists into humanist leaders. Prince Max believed that Waterloo had indeed been won on the playing fields of Eton and, with that in mind, hoped that the school he founded would provide Germany with similarly successful leaders.

The school started after the Great War with only four students, one of whom was Prince Max's own son, Berthold. As it grew, the former statesman turned its care over to his former private secretary. Kurt Hahn not only became its headmaster but went on to develop a reputation as an accomplished educationalist. Salem was well on the way to fulfilling Prince Max's hopes when Hitler came to power in January 1933. On 5 April, Germany's

Nazi chancellor ordered the boycott of all Jewish establishments. Hahn, being a Jew, was arrested and imprisoned. He was released only after Berthold of Baden orchestrated a campaign for his release, which included an appeal from the British prime minister, Ramsay MacDonald, to the German president, Field Marshal von Hindenberg, resulting in the ancient war hero ordering Hahn's release. He promptly fled to Britain, where he opened another school modelled on Salem: Gordonstoun.

The original plan had been to have Philip return to the bosom of his immediate family. Schooltime would be spent with his sister and brother-in-law. Being on the Continent, he would be more accessible for visits to his parents, especially to his mother. As with many other well-laid plans, this one came a cropper. Germany was in the grip of Nazism, and the young Philip had no more tolerance for ridiculous practices than the older Philip would later have. He regarded the many ways in which the Nazis exhibited their power, such as the salute to the Führer, the goose-stepping, the parades, the heel-clicking and the *heil*, as ludicrous nonsense, and he showed his contempt with savage mimicry.

On one notable occasion, he goose-stepped through the market square at Uberlingen, stopping to give the Nazi salute and commenting acidly that in his opinion the soldiers wished to use the lavatory, for the motion of the outstretched hand was the same that he, and all other students of boarding school, used to ask permission to be excused so that they could relieve themselves. Funny as this might now seem to those of us who did not live under the Hitler yoke, this was no laughing matter in 1933 Germany. The principle of Aryan supremacy was the cherished platform on which the Nazis were building their political credo, and they did not take kindly to anyone mocking it. This premise, however, was yet more proof to the intelligent Philip that Nazism was ridiculous, and he did not shy away from saying so to anyone who would listen.

Nor did Philip lack opportunity to get his point across. His brother-in-law Prince Christopher of Hesse, husband of Sophie, was an early Nazi, and only his death in action in 1944 spared him the disgrace of being hauled before a War Crimes Tribunal and being tried for his crimes against humanity. This would certainly have scuppered Philip's chances of marrying Princess Elizabeth, for there was no way a British King could have allowed his daughter to marry the brother-in-law of a war criminal.

But Sophie was as fortunate as her brother where matrimony was concerned. At the end of the war she made another good marriage, to yet another cousin, Prince George of Hanover. Their good fortune did not extend to her in-laws, however. Christopher of Hesse's brother Philip was also a Nazi. He ended up in prison and at the end of the war was tried and found guilty of war crimes by the Allies. His wife, Princess Mafalda of Italy, had an even more distasteful end. Thrown into Buchenwald Concentration Camp when her father King Victor Emmanuel took Italy into the war on the

Allied side in 1943 under General Badoglio, she was killed there in 1944.

In 1933, however, the horrors of war and defeat were still very much in the future. Nazi Germany was reawakening as a great and mighty power, and Philip's family realized the danger in which he was placing all of them. 'We thought it better for him and for us if he went back to England,' his sister Theodora said with classical understatement. He was duly despatched back to Uncle George and Aunt Nada. And to the Salem experiment.

Kurt Hahn, in exile in Britain, bought Gordonstoun House and its 300-acre estate in 1934 with the intention of reproducing Salem in a new environment. Situated in the Highlands of Scotland near Lossiemouth, birthplace of the British prime minister who had interceded to save Hahn's life, Gordonstoun school had only thirty students, including Prince Philip, when it started. The boys had to do everything, from taking turns emptying the garbage and converting stable blocks into dormitories to building a dining-room. After the stifling paranoia of Nazi Germany, Philip gloried in the fresh air of Highland naturalism. He was as co-operative at Gordonstoun as he had been unco-operative at Salem under the Nazis.

According to Kurt Hahn, 'When Philip came to Gordonstoun his most marked trait was his undefeatable spirit. He felt the emotions of both joy and sadness deeply, and the way he looked and the way he moved indicated what he felt. That even applied to the minor disappointments inevitable in a schoolboy's life. His laughter was heard everywhere. He had inherited from his Danish family the capacity to derive great fun from small incidents. In his schoolwork he showed a lively intelligence.'

For four years Philip flourished. He enjoyed being challenged, not only at school but also out of it. The world in which his family lived had become even more exotic and cosmopolitan with the restoration of the Greek monarchy in 1935. His first cousin once more reigned as King George II. Crown Prince Paul had married another cousin, Princess Frederika of Brunswick, and she recalled how, 'When he was about fifteen, he used to spend part of his holidays with us.'

He could now add the warmth and the glamour of Greece to the lengthy list of places where he vacationed. But Greece was not all airy palaces and sun-swept beaches. Alice had moved back to Athens, where she set up a charity catering to the needs of the poor. She lived very simply, almost poorly, preferring to spend her money and her energy on doing good for the needy rather than in maintaining a royal way of life. When he was in Greece, Philip naturally saw a lot of his mother.

Back in England, Philip was not deprived of colourful relations. Both his maternal uncles had married women who cut a scandalous swathe through society. Aunt Nada was the former Countess Nadeja Torby, a famous lesbian and aesthete who spent much of her married life travelling the world and seducing men's wives. She was even reputed to have had an affair with her own sister-in-law Edwina Mountbatten, though there is no proof that this actually took place, and judging from Edwina's rampant interest in the opposite sex, a relationship of that nature would have been very much out of character.

Nada's sexual proclivities were not the only aspect of her life to keep the *cognoscenti* entertained. In a day and age when anyone of mixed blood was classified as belonging to the darkest race coursing through their veins, Nada could have been categorized as a Negress. That is certainly how Tsar Nicholas II viewed Nada's mother, Countess Torby, who was descended from an Ethiopian slave named Hannibal as well as the great Russian writer Alexander Pushkin. It was also the reason why he forbade Nada's father, the Grand Duke Michael, from marrying the crinkly haired Countess. Love, however, won out, and the Grand Duke made the Countess his morganatic wife, moved to England, produced two daughters who married well and lived happily thereafter.

Philip's other aunt, Edwina Mountbatten, was equally exotic, the marriage equally adventurous in terms of race and lifestyle. Born Edwina Ashley, Lord Louis Mountbatten's wife was Jewish by origin, the grand-daughter of Sir Ernest Cassel, the German-born Jewish financier who was King Edward VII's good friend. One of the greatest heiresses of her day, Edwina was also renowned for her promiscuity. Moreover, she did not limit herself, as most profligate women of her caste did, to men within her social orbit.

At a time when classes and colours did not mix, Edwina liked her lovers in all sizes, shapes and colours. She had too many lovers to list, but only three great loves. The first was Paul Robeson, the black American singer who immortalized 'Ole Man River'. That ended badly in May 1932 when the *Sunday People* ran a story linking 'one of the leading hostesses in the country, a woman highly connected and immensely wealthy' to 'a coloured man'. Although neither Edwina nor the man was named, her reputation was such that even the general public was able to identify her. It was well known that she had had a torrid affair with another 'coloured' entertainer, the famous night-club singer/pianist Hutch (Leslie Hutchinson), and he was popularly but erroneously believed to be the man referred to. Buckingham Palace was in a fury with Edwina for bringing scandal into the Royal Family's periphery, and she was made to know in no uncertain terms that she had to sue to restore her reputation. This she did, winning the action, which began in June 1932. The upshot, however, was that she was warned to be more discreet. She therefore dropped Paul Robeson unceremoniously, inflicting a deep wound from which he never recovered.

Edwina's two other lovers were 'Bunny' Philips, whom she wished to divorce Mountbatten to marry, but who discarded her to marry her sister-in-law Nada's heiress niece Georgina Werhner, daughter of Nada's sister Lady

Zia Torby and Sir Harold Werhner. The treasures of Luton Hoo were infinitely preferable to those of Broadlands, but Edwina bounced back, ending her days as the inamorata of the Indian Prime Minister, Jawaharlal Nehru.

Although the Mountbatten men were not as sexual as their wives, the teenaged Prince Philip of Greece's uncles nevertheless set him an example of the way *civilized* men conducted their lives. They slept with whom they pleased, but did so quietly. Both brothers behaved so discreetly that there was conjecture as to whether they actually did more than dine with ladies. In the case of Lord Louis, he was even suspected of being homosexual, though this has been discounted by everyone who knew him well, including his private secretary of some three decades. What John Barratt did confirm, however, was that Lord Louis did have a lifelong romance with Madame Henri Letellier. Although there was no doubt that the *soignée* Yola Letellier and the handsome 'Dickie' Mountbatten were the closest of friends, companionship, not sex, was the most important aspect of their relationship, which lasted until death parted them in 1979.

Rather more turgidly motivated was the other man in Prince Philip's life. Prince Andrew of Greece was indeed 'naughty', as the grown-ups whom Hélène Cordet overheard described him. Although still embittered by his treatment at the hands of the Greek government in 1922, still fearful of what might happen if he returned to live in his homeland, he had found a measure of peace and harmony in the South of France, at the gaming tables and in the ample bosom of his simple mistress.

Meanwhile, Philip's school-days were drawing to a close. He had excelled at Gordonstoun, to such an extent that he was made guardian, or head boy, during his last year, and at the end of the summer term, 1938, he packed his belongings and headed south.

Already it was apparent that the handsome and dynamic young prince was cut out for great things, and, if destiny did not allow him to walk on the path of greatness, his talents would be wasted. Kurt Hahn assessed the character of his departing student by writing, 'Prince Philip is universally trusted, liked and respected. He had the greatest sense of service of all the boys in the school. Prince Philip's leadership qualities are most noticeable, though marred at times by impatience and intolerance. He will need the exacting demands of a great service to do justice to himself. His best is outstanding; his second best not good enough.'

The summer he left Gordonstoun was also the last one Philip would see his Uncle George, who died suddenly of cancer in autumn 1938. By then, Philip was enrolled at Cheltenham, where Mr Mercer coached him for the entrance examinations to the Royal Naval College at Dartmouth. Philip had decided that he wanted a career like his Uncle Louis, fast rising to the top in the British navy, and his grandfather, the disgraced Prince Louis of Battenberg. His prospects of ascending the Greek throne had retreated with the passage of the years and the arrival of progeny to his cousins. He would therefore have to tread the path of other penniless princes. He would have to work, at least until he could follow the example of his Uncles George and Christopher, and marry well.

On 4 May 1939, Philip entered Dartmouth. This was an ominous though exciting time to be entering the navy, as storm clouds were already gathering over Europe. The eighteen-year-old prince determined to excel. Although his entrance examination results had been a modest sixteenth out of the thirty-four cadets admitted, by the end of the first term he had been awarded the King's Dirk as the best cadet of the term. He had resolved to live up to the splendid example set by his uncle, Lord Louis Mountbatten, who was placed first out of the whole Naval College in his final examinations. But Dartmouth would prove to be more than just the setting that allowed the handsome Prince Philip of Greece to excel. It was also the place where he won the heart of the most eligible heiress in the world: Princess Elizabeth.

Passion was the driving force behind Prince Philip and Princess Elizabeth's relationship. The emotion, however, did not come from him, but from her. Lilibet was her father's daughter, as fervent and obstinate as she was dutiful and obliging, and there is no doubt that the subsequent marriage would never have taken place had she not become as obsessed with the tall, well-built, blue-eyed, Nordic god as her father did with her mother.

Elizabeth's obsession arose as a result of an accidental encounter between Philip and herself. Her parents had just returned from the triumphal visit to Canada and the United States that made the British public aware how their King and Queen were now perceived as international superstars. Accompanied by Lilibet and Margaret Rose, King George VI and Queen Elizabeth began their summer holidays by embarking upon a cruise on the royal yacht, the *Victoria and Albert*. Also on board was Bertie's naval aide-de-camp and cousin, Captain Lord Louis Mountbatten. On the afternoon of Saturday, 22 July 1939, the yacht put into the River Dart, and the King and his cousin, with the Queen and the two Princesses, disembarked to begin a trip down memory lane. Both men had been cadets at the Royal Naval College at Dartmouth, and they were eagerly anticipating their two-day stay. What neither could have envisaged was that the budding Lilibet would be struck by sexual lightning.

Lilibet already knew her cousin Philip. Reports that claim they first met at Dartmouth do not take into account how they had certainly met on numerous occasions beforehand, such as at the wedding of Philip's first cousin Marina of Greece to Lilibet's uncle, George, Duke of Kent, and at smaller family gatherings. They were, after all, cousins, and the British Royal Family was well known at that time for drawing its friends from within its family circle. All his life, therefore, Prince Philip had been a constant though not frequent visitor to Buckingham Palace and Windsor Castle, and his grandmother, with whom he sometimes stayed, lived in Kensington Palace along with other members of the Royal Family. But six-year-old Lilibet seeing eleven-year-old Philip was not the same thing as thirteen-year-old Lilibet being thunderstruck by the thrusting energy of the masculine, eighteen-year-old Philip.

It was only natural that the elders would delegate the older cousin to take care of the younger girls. According to Philip's cousin, Queen Alexandra of Yugoslavia, 'My Aunt Elizabeth [the present Queen Mother] and Uncle Dickie [Lord Louis Mountbatten] put their heads together' and hauled Philip out of his previous duties to entertain Lilibet and Margaret. 'Philip rather resented it, a youngster of eighteen called to help entertain a girl of thirteen and a child of nine,' Alexandra recounted.

It was a claim substantiated by Marion Crawford, the girls' nanny, who stated that he was 'rather offhand in his manner. He said, "How do you do" to Lilibet, and for a while they knelt side by side playing with the trains. He soon got bored with that. We had ginger crackers and lemonade, in which he joined, and then he said, "Let's go to the tennis courts and have some fun jumping the nets." She never took her eyes off him the whole time. At the tennis courts I thought he showed off a great deal, but the little girls were much impressed. Lilibet said, "How good he is Crawfie! How high he can jump." He was quite polite with her, but did not pay her any special attention. He spent a lot of time teasing plump little Margaret.'

Philip might not have been struck by Lilibet, but she was riveted by him. And like the true Windsor she was, she could not be deflected from her goal once she had caught sight of it. Though neither of them yet had any idea what the ultimate outcome would be, she already knew enough to want to see as much of Prince Philip of Greece and Denmark as she could. And, as King George and Queen Elizabeth were indulgent parents, Philip was relieved of his other duties and delegated to amuse his two cousins.

Six weeks later, the Second World War broke out. Lilibet and Margaret were moved to the safety of Windsor Castle, where they would remain, almost prisoners, for the following five and a half years. There was the constant fear that Hitler might send spies to kidnap the two princesses and take them back to Germany, so their activities, always restricted, were even more curtailed than they had been prior to the declaration of war. Cut off as they were from even the limited contact they had had with friends of their own age, Lilibet and Margaret were almost entirely dependent upon the adult members of their household for companionship. Occasionally, however, cousins of their own age came to visit for lunch, tea or dinner, or to stay for a few days. Lilibet's great favourite became Philip, whom she engineered to have asked with such frequency that the secret of her love for him was soon out of the bag.

Marriage is not treated in royal and aristocratic circles with quite the romanticism that it receives from the general public. Everyone understands that marital unions are for more than love. Philip needed a wife who could provide him with the means to live up to his birthright, while Lilibet's eventual need was for a husband who would be a suitable consort for a reigning monarch. These considerations might seem cold to someone who is not used to taking a dispassionate view of matrimony, but to the families of Prince Philip of Greece and Princess Elizabeth of the United Kingdom of Great Britain and Northern Ireland, they were of the utmost importance, and they were addressed as soon as Lilibet's interest was noted. The fact that she was a mere fourteen did not make the subject inappropriate or premature. In royal and aristocratic circles, good potential matches are sometimes nurtured from the cradle. Philip's own sister Sophie had only been sixteen at the time of her first marriage, so Lilibet's age did not rule out consideration, even if it did preclude quick action.

By 1941, the subject of a marriage between Philip and Lilibet had gained sufficient acceptance within the family circle for Chips Channon to record that he had attended 'an enjoyable Greek cocktail party. Philip of Greece was there. He is extremely handsome, and I recalled my afternoon's conversation with Princess Nicholas [his Aunt Helen, mother of Princess Marina, Duchess of Kent]. He is to be our Prince Consort, and that is why he is serving in the Navy.'

Although Princess Nicholas sounded definite, the match had not been formally arranged. It was more of an understanding than a betrothal and, as such, was by no means irrevocable. From Philip's point of view, it was desirable. He would marry the most eligible girl in the world, one who would bring him riches beyond his wildest dreams, as well as a secure and prestigious position upon the world stage. Lilibet, moreover, was 'very sweet', as her putative fiancé described her on several different occasions. In terms of the sort of marriage he had been reared to make, this was the quintessential good match.

From Lilibet's point of view, the prospective marriage was also fortunate. Not only was Philip endowed with good looks, intelligence, rugged physicality and palpable masculinity, but he was also a real prince. In regal terms, he was better bred than she was, for Lilibet was only half royal, while Philip was wholly so. This might not seem like much of a recommendation to the average person, but to Lilibet, who has been known over the years to remind her mother, 'You weren't born royal, I was,' Philip's complete royalness was a major consideration.

Everyone in the family was pleased that Lilibet and Philip's future had been so suitably settled, except Elizabeth. She was careful to couch her disapproval behind saccharine smiles and benevolent displays of maternal concern, but her profound lack of enthusiasm could have become a major problem had she encountered anyone less persistent and determined than her elder daughter. 'Lilibet is too young to think of marriage,' she would say whenever the subject came up, then rush to invite young noblemen to Windsor Castle so that Lilibet could be distracted away from the charms of the athletic Philip.

Lilibet, however, knew her mother only too well. She knew that Queen Elizabeth was not one to wage war by direct confrontation. Her method was subtler, to smile sweetly, then introduce the cannon when her opponent's defences were down. In this case, the technique manifested itself with the abovementioned lack of enthusiasm, with put-downs about Philip's uncle Louis Mountbatten, whom Elizabeth did not like, followed by men she considered more desirable. Her choices, however, were more in keeping with her effete taste in men than in her daughter's rugged Windsor interests. Lilibet also knew that the only reason her mother wanted her to marry a British nobleman rather than a foreign prince was because Elizabeth herself was a British noblewoman. Her lack of royal blood was one of the few Achilles heels this indomitable woman possessed. She knew only too well that other royals scorned her for being what Princess Marina called 'a common little Scot', and her attempts at deroyalizing the Royal Family even further were sometimes interpreted as a self-centred attempt to hold her own against her more illustrious connections.

Throughout the war years, Lilibet was too young for Elizabeth's disapproval to be a real issue. This would only happen when the young couple wanted to become officially engaged. In the meantime, they courted in pristine tradition. Philip was often away on tours of duty, firstly on the *Valiant*, then in 1942 on the *Wallace* and after 1944 as the First Lieutenant on the *Whelp*. He had a photograph of his teenaged cousin in a silver frame beside his bed, and they corresponded frequently. When they did see each other, they went for long walks holding hands in Windsor Great Park. They were never alone for long, and there was no question of any impropriety taking place.

By the end of the war, Lilibet was nineteen. She was now old enough to be married. Elizabeth, however, had other ideas. Queen Mary told Lady Airlie that Lilibet and Philip were 'in love', but that King George VI and Queen Elizabeth thought she was too young to settle down. They wanted her to meet other men first. As has been seen, the King left all aspects of his daughters' lives up to their mother, so it is possible, with reasonable confidence, to exclude Bertie from the formulation of obtuse delaying tactics, which were the province of his strong-willed wife.

For the next two years, Lilibet doggedly held her ground while her mother sweetly tried to undermine it. There were no scenes, no fights to mar the smooth surface of family unity. Without even openly acknowledging the tussle of wills, Elizabeth and Lilibet maintained their positions with determination. Elizabeth was still hoping that one of the antiseptic chinless wonders whom she was trotting beneath her daughter's nose would entice her away from the rugged charms of the strong-jawed Greek prince. Lilibet, on the other hand, could not be swayed, and she even went to the length of asking Philip to stay for a whole month at Balmoral during the family's summer holiday in 1946.

Lilibet was fast approaching the indisputable age of legal majority. She was due to be twenty-one in April 1947. From that point onwards, her mother would not be able to retreat behind Lilibet's youthfulness. She therefore took matters into her own hands and informed her parents that she and Philip wished to become engaged.

Faced with a *fait accompli*, Elizabeth tried one last delaying tactic. The King, Queen, Lilibet and Margaret were due to undertake a tour of South Africa in February 1947. So Elizabeth suggested to her malleable husband that he get Lilibet to wait until after they had returned before making a final decision. Her latest attempt to wear Lilibet's defences down, however, was as successful as her earlier efforts had been.

While Lilibet was away, the issue of Philip's nationality was addressed. He applied for naturalization, which was granted on 18 March 1947. This move, in fact, was unnecessary, for Philip was already a British subject, by virtue of an Act of Parliament passed in 1705, which stated that all descendants of the Electress Sophie of Hanover were British subjects as well as Princes and Princesses with the style and dignity of Royal Highness. This was later substantiated when his brother-in-law, Prince George of Hanover, sued the British government for acknowledgement of his right to British citizenship.

In 1947, however, the last thing anyone connected to the Royal Family wanted was a reminder of their German origins. Wounds caused by the war were still too fresh. This had an unexpected effect for Philip, who renounced his rights to the Greek throne. It affected his name. Having been born a Prince of Greece and Denmark, he was a member of the House of Schleswig-Holstein-Sondenburg-Glucksburg. However, the family did not have a surname. On the other hand, all British subjects had to have a surname. The College of Heralds suggested that Philip adopt as his surname the Anglicized version of the Danish royal family's original German dukedom of Oldenburg and become Philip Oldcastle. They further suggested that he be made Prince of Oldcastle, as it would not do for the heiress to the throne to marry a commoner. Cheuter Ede, the Socialist Home Secretary, advocated using the name his mother's family had adopted, on the grounds that Mountbatten 'is certainly grander and more glittering than Oldcastle'. This idea appealed to Philip's vain uncle, the recently ennobled Earl Mountbatten of Burma, and while Philip refused the offer of an interim British title, he accepted the recommendation King George VI approved of and became Lieutenant Philip Mountbatten, RN.

Shortly after Lilibet's return from South Africa, she took matters into her own hands. She and Philip were going to be married. Elizabeth gave way as graciously as she had opposed the match, and on 19 July 1947, the engagement was announced. The only lasting effect of Elizabeth's opposition was that she and her future son-in-law would never enjoy a warm relationship. A straightforward man, he could never quite bring himself to either like or trust the woman whose smiles had meant the opposite of warmth.

CHAPTER EIGHT

Happy Days

On the eve of his wedding, Lieutenant Philip Mountbatten was created a Knight of the Garter by his future father-in-law. The following morning, it was announced that he had been, in the words of King George VI 'created a Royal Highness and the titles of his peerage will be: Baron Greenwich, Earl of Merioneth and Duke of Edinburgh.' He had not been re-created a prince and would have to wait until 1957 before he regained the rank to which he had been born. Ignoring such an obvious fact, Bertie continued, 'It is a great deal to give a man all at once, but I know Philip understands his new responsibilities on his marriage to Lilibet.' Philip did not go on record with his thoughts about honours that gave him no more than he had surrendered, but he has since made it plain that his status did not result from his marriage to Elizabeth of England or through the Mountbatten family, but as a result of having been born into a Royal House of greater age than his wife's. For those reasons, he has always been particular to keep his father's family to the forefront.

Philip and Lilibet were married on 20 November 1947 in Westminster Abbey, in a ceremony that brought the only light and colour that post-war Britain, in the grip of an austerity programme, would see until well into the next decade. There was nationwide rationing, and only the government's decision to make the day special allowed the citizenry the pleasure of experiencing a full-blown royal wedding.

Not since the funeral of King Edward VII in 1910 had there been so many foreign royals parading themselves in exotic costume in London. All the best suites in the capital's leading hotels were taken over to accommodate them, and the list included the King and Queen of Denmark, the King and Queen of Yugoslavia, the Kings of Iraq, Norway and Romania, the Queen of the Hellenes, the Queen Mother of Romania, the Belgian Prince Regent, Princess Juliana the Regent of the Netherlands and her consort Prince Bernhardt, the Grand Ducal family of Luxembourg, the deposed royal family of Spain including their English Queen Victoria Eugenia (born a Battenberg and, as such, a double cousin of the groom as well as a single cousin of the bride) and Queen Salote of Tonga.

Also in prominent attendance was Philip's mother. Alice was now a widow, Prince Andrew having died and been buried in 1942 in the South of France, where the Monegasque Royal Family were able to give him a suitably regal funeral. Since then, Alice had been trying to found a new religious order amid staunch opposition from the Greek Orthodox Church. Her habitual mode of dress was a nun-like costume with flowing headgear, but she put these aside and turned up at the Abbey in a smart lace gown and matching hat.

After the marriage ceremony, there was the traditional wedding break-fast at Buckingham Palace, following which the young couple set off on their eagerly awaited honeymoon. The first week was spent at Broadlands, the Hampshire home of Philip's Uncle Dickie and Aunt Edwina. After a stopover in London to announce their gratitude to the millions of well-wishers, Philip and Lilibet headed northwards, to Birkhall, a house near to Balmoral Castle on the Balmoral Estate, where they continued their honeymoon in freezing conditions.

This was an idyllic time for Lilibet. Snow or no snow, she had finally got the man she wanted. And what a man he was. He could warm her cockles the way no fire could. Philip was no sanctimonious prayer-book pusher. He brought a wealth of personal experience to his marriage. 'He was', in the words of one cousin, 'his father's son.'

Philip had had countless girlfriends, none of whom could ever complain that his idea of romance was similar to his mother-in-law's fanciful concept of chastely holding hands in a row-boat. One of his closest friends was Baron, the fashionable photographer, through whose studio a limitless trail of beauties paraded. Prior to his marriage, Philip was often there, meeting new girls with whom he would embark upon delicious but short-lived flirtations. At the time, as he was also courting the heiress to the throne, discretion was not only desirable but crucial. Tact, however, did not preclude satisfaction, and Philip was already well known for the Schleswig-Holstein-Sonderburg-Glucksburg appeal, which coursed through his amorous veins.

While Philip was on honeymoon introducing Lilibet to the delights of matrimony, London was ablaze with the rumour that he was the father of two young children. Had this story been denied forthwith, repetition might not have lent it credibility. However, all the parties ignored it in the mistaken belief that it would eventually go away. By the time the lady around whose identity it flourished started denying it, it had been around for so many years that many people were convinced it was true. They refused to believe Hélène Foufounis Cordet, the striking Greek entertainer, when she explained that she and Philip had known each other all their lives, and that they were like brother and sister, not lovers. She told me that 'The stories were nothing but lies, all lies,' and indeed her son finally felt forced to go to the extraordinary length of making a public announcement to the effect that Prince Philip was not his father.

It would be several more years before Lilibet's peace of mind was perturbed by the stories about Hélène Foufounis Cordet, and the legion of other women with whom Prince Philip is purported to have been involved. In the meantime, she was able to finish off her honeymoon and begin her married life in a state of blissful satisfaction.

Philip was the young Duchess of Edinburgh's introduction to life as well as to the pleasures of marriage. Until she began her life with him, Lilibet was cosseted and protected and kept well apart from ordinary as well as aristocratic life. First, there had been the war to curtail her activities, and, when it ended, there was her parents' insistence that she meet the world from the security of royal palaces. Lilibet had never been allowed even the protected liberty of an aristocratic young lady. She had never gone to stay with friends for weekends, nor been to restaurants and night-clubs. Her parents and grandmother Queen Mary did not approve of royalty mingling with anyone outside the family. The fact that her uncles David and George had led normal social lives while they were bachelors rated not as a precedent to be followed but as a warning to be heeded.

Nor was Lilibet's socializing the only aspect of her life that was severely restricted until marriage. Her education up to this point had been sorely inadequate. Even Queen Mary, who had been well educated, had felt compelled to question what Lilibet was being taught while she was still young enough to be in the schoolroom. The heiress to the throne was unable to fulfil the simplest standards of mathematical deduction for children her age, and her grasp of such basic subjects as biology and general science was also woefully lacking. Elizabeth, however, brushed aside her mother-in-law's intervention as successfully as she had imposed her will elsewhere. Lilibet was her daughter, and she intended to see that she was educated in a way and with an emphasis that she, Elizabeth, wanted. It did not matter if neither of her daughters understood the first thing about trigonometry as long as they had good manners, knew how to play the piano, behaved well and remained subservient to their parents' will. According to Elizabeth's reasoning, that was all the education any girl needed. Whether she became a queen or not was quite beside the point, as she herself had proven. After all, that was all the education she had had, yet here she was, the most popular queen in Christendom. What was good enough for her was good enough for Lilibet.

Deprived of exposure to life as well as to knowledge, Lilibet was not the most outgoing of young brides. She was not exactly lacking in confidence in herself so much as aware of the gaps in her knowledge, for she was a classical example of the product of a parent who has a narrow but confident, almost arrogant, outlook. All her life she had been raised in the belief that royalty was special, so there was no question of her considering herself inferior. But she was far more down-to-earth than her mother, and, now that she was married to someone as intelligent, sophisticated and experienced as Philip, she was quick to spot the deficiencies in her upbringing and soak up the nourishment she had lacked to date.

The first years of Lilibet's marriage were happy. She led a far more normal life than she had hitherto done, and this period became the halcyon days not only of her marriage but also of her youth.

Like all newly-weds, Lilibet and Philip needed a home of their own. The King came to their rescue, giving them not one but two homes. In town they had the use of Clarence House, a grace and favour palace owned by the crown opposite St James's Palace on the Mall. Her father also gave her Sunninghill Park, another grace and favour house, this time near Ascot in Windsor Great Park, as a weekend retreat. Before work could begin on the renovations needed to restore the damage caused by an enemy bomb as well as its wartime use by the army, however, Sunninghill Park was gutted by fire. Arson was popularly suspected, but neither Buckingham Palace nor the police would confirm this, despite a secret report indicating that as the cause. Nevertheless, Lilibet and Philip needed a country house to which they could escape on weekends, so the King paid the rental on Windlesham Moor near Windsor in Surrey for them.

Although Lilibet's marriage was happy in the personal sense, its public start was a harbinger of how controversy would dog her throughout her married life. The first row was over money. Philip came to the marriage with two suits (one his uniform, the other a worn lounge suit), savings of £6 10s 0d in the bank, a naval lieutenant's salary of some £11 per week and a wife's supplementary allowance of £4 7s 6d. Clearly the young couple had to rely upon the Civil List to bankroll a regal way of life. King George VI therefore sent a message to parliament 'relying on the liberality and affection of my faithful Commons' with the request that the Labour government vote suitable allowances for Princess Elizabeth and Prince Philip.

To Bertie's fury, the Leader of the House, Herbert Morrison, turned over the responsibility to a select committee, which voted, by thirteen to five, to increase Lilibet's annuity to a mere £50,000 and to allocate Philip the measley sum of £10,000. When the King stopped to think that Prince Albert had been awarded an allowance of £30,000 upon his marriage to Queen Victoria, when the purchasing power of the pound was five times higher than it was in 1947, his rage increased to a glorious pitch.

Moreover, the government could muster only £50,000 for the refurbishment of Clarence House, which, though sumptuous when used by King William IV as the Duke of Clarence in the early days of the last century, had never been lived in since the Duke of Connaught had vacated it prior to the First World War to live in Bagshot. Even though the government was in the grips of an austerity programme, the sums awarded were so small that they were insulting, and there was a tremendous fuss made all the worse for being public. After complaining to his Prime Minister, Clement Attlee, an impotent Bertie turned over £100,000, which he had saved out of the Civil List during the war, to his daughter and son-in-law, so that they could start life in reasonable style.

While Clarence House was being refurbished, Lilibet and Philip lived in a suite of rooms at Buckingham Palace. From the outset, Philip's adjustment to what Queen Wilhelmina of the Netherlands called 'the gilded cage' was uneasy. The courtiers did not like him. He was too straightforward, too sure of himself. But what antagonized them from the outset was his innate dislike of empty and meaningless rigmarole. Just as he had laughed at the pretentiousness of Nazi protocol, so, too, he now brought his incisive wit to bear on the treasured practices of the Buckingham Palace courtiers. They were no more amused than his father-in-law had been when Philip had viewed with levity being forced into a too short, hand-me-down kilt in Scotland and had curtsied to the King. Bertie made sure that Philip understood that he could never consider the practices of the monarchy as humorous, not even if he thought them meaningless and irrelevant.

Significantly, Lilibet's approach to monarchical tradition had still not set into a mature pattern. There is no doubt that her father's influence upon her was profound. Lilibet always was a stickler for protocol and tradition and remains so to this day. Fortunately for her, however, she was sufficiently open to her husband's influence to assimilate his sense of humour about many of the traditions that she and her father held so dear. The result has been a unique combination of her father's reverence for the traditions of the monarchy and Philip's appreciation of the ridiculous, which was best displayed in public at the time of the Prince of Wales's investiture at Caernarfon Castle. Both she and her heir nearly burst out laughing in the middle of the solemn ceremony when Charles's too large crown threatened to lodge itself Goon-like on the bridge of his nose.

If Philip brought levity and interest and freedom into Lilibet's life, she brought stability into his. For the first time since he was sent to Cheam School at the age of nine, Philip had the security of knowing where his next meal was coming from and with whom he would be eating it. The intervening years might have been interesting and stimulating, but they had also lacked any discernible pattern. Shuffled back and forth between his various relations, he had never known from one month to the next where his place of residence would be. This had instilled an appreciation of novelty and excitement, which has remained with Philip to this day, but beneath the restlessness, he yearned for the stability that a settled home life would bring. This he now had, along with the financial security that had also eluded him hitherto.

The true purpose of Philip and Lilibet's marriage, however, was not the expansion of her mind or the fulfilment of their beings but the production of an heir to the throne and a spare to ensure the succession if something went wrong. Of the four Kings this century, two had been second sons, George V's elder brother having been the dissolute Duke of Clarence and Avondale who has often been erroneously suspected of having been Jack the Ripper. And George VI's elder brother, of course, was the abdicated Duke of Windsor.

With their responsibilities to the crown uppermost in their minds, Lilibet and Philip set about living up to this most pleasurable aspect of their duty. So successful were they that she gave birth to His Royal Highness Prince Charles of Edinburgh almost a year to the day after her wedding. Waiting only a year before becoming pregnant again, she produced Princess Anne nearly twenty-one months to the day after Charles. The succession was assured.

Throughout this period, there was a dark cloud hovering over the newly-weds' appreciation of their halcyon days. Bertie's health, never good, had become worrisome. The trouble had started while Lilibet was pregnant with Charles, when George VI's leg grew numb on that walk with Group Captain Peter Townsend. The operation coincided with Prince Charles's birth, and though his health improved somewhat between then and Princess Anne's birth, it was nevertheless sufficiently delicate for everyone in the family to remain concerned.

Inexperience is often youth's best bulwark against despair, and so this axiom proved in the case of Lilibet and Philip. Though they knew her father's health was precarious, neither one expected him to die. They therefore laid down the bricks in the courtyard of their married lives as if they would be there to use it for many years to come.

Clarence House, into which they moved shortly after Prince Charles's birth at Buckingham Palace, had been reappointed to a suitably luxurious standard, much of it at the personal behest of Philip. He was the man of the house, the partner who, by his own admission, 'naturally filled the principal position'. The Duke and Duchess of Edinburgh might have been any young aristocratic couple, fulfilling the traditional roles of the protective male and the retiring female, but for two factors. They were royal and as a result they both had to work.

Between the births of the two children, however, King George VI's health was stable enough for both the Duke and Duchess of Edinburgh to pursue their own lives. Philip was innately ambitious and wished to excel in his chosen career. He therefore derived profound satisfaction out of being instructed in April 1948 to take a naval course at Greenwich as well as being appointed as the youngest member to the Admiralty's Operations Division shortly after his marriage. These were indications that the powers-that-be at the Admiralty viewed him as material for the highest naval rank.

Between 1948 and 1949, however, Philip's royal rank kept on interfering with the furtherance of his naval career. Although King George VI seemed to have recovered from the operation to cure his vascular problems, the general consensus among his senior staff at court, among his doctors and the ever vigilant Queen Elizabeth was that the King's health was too delicate to be taxed. Medical stabilization of his condition and full recovery were two different things, and, with that in mind, Lilibet was roped in to assume many of her father's responsibilities. These affairs of state were not duties that Philip could share, and the King shrewdly advised his son-in-law be given his own sphere of influence so that he would not feel like a gooseberry. Philip's interests were taken into account, and he was appointed President of the National Playing Fields Association in 1949.

Having been reared by his uncle Berthold of Baden and Kurt Hahn in the best traditions of absolute commitment, Philip threw himself into his new appointment with a dedication that struck some of the more dispassionate courtiers at Buckingham Palace as irritatingly excessive. For all their sneering, he was infinitely more effective and successful than they could ever have been. Hard work did not frighten him the way it did them, and he spent hour after hour, day after day, week after week, mounting appeals, getting in touch with the leaders of industry, and, in his own words, 'squeezing all the rich people I know for all the juice I can get out of them'.

Frank Sinatra helped him raise £16,000 by coming to London to sing at the Royal Albert Hall, and Philip himself co-starred in a film with Bob Hope about the poor children of London whose playgrounds were the streets. This raised another £84,000, though fund-raising was not the young Duke's only success. His sense of commitment motivated others within the charity to previously unthought of feats of accomplishment, and, as the organization opened more and more playing fields and provided recreation for more and more underprivileged youths, the work grew proportionately until Philip was travelling several thousand miles per annum. 'I will go anywhere to open a new playing field,' he said, and while his detractors at the Palace derided such sentiments, those whom he benefited admired him all the more for this latest manifestation of excellence.

By the middle of 1949, Bertie's health had improved to such a degree that the pressure was off Lilibet and Philip. He was appointed first lieutenant of *Chequers*, which was the leader of the flotilla based in Malta, arriving there on 17 October.

Both Philip and Lilibet jumped at this opportunity to have the life of an ordinary married couple. Philip's Uncle Dickie Mountbatten was posted there. He and Edwina lived in sybaritic style in the Villa Guardamangia, and it was here that the young couple made their home. Life was busy for Philip. He continued to be an active president of the National Playing Fields Association, confining the many letters he had to write on its behalf to the few free moments he had when he was not on naval duty or otherwise engaged on shore, for he and Lilibet had a full social life.

For Lilibet, the sojourn in Malta proved to be 'one of the happiest periods of my life'. She went out dining, to dances, to the beach. She sailed, swam and even embarked upon the astonishing (for her) adventure of going into a hairdressing salon instead of having the hairdresser come to her. This was yet another first in a life that was gathering many other primary moments.

Philip was also gathering firsts. The one that gave him the greatest feeling of achievement was in September 1950, when he was appointed Commander of the frigate *Magpie*. Much to his disappointment, this would prove to be his first as well as his last command, for the King's health took another turn for the worse, and in July 1951 he was recalled to Britain 'on indefinite leave'. 'The past eleven months have been the happiest of my sailor life,' he confessed to the crew as he bid them farewell.

The crew of his ship was not the only thing Philip was bidding farewell to, however. Although he did not yet know it, he was also saying goodbye to his naval career. He and Lilibet were ordered to replace the ailing King and his sprightly Queen and embark upon a tour of Canada and the United States in the autumn. Just before they were due to depart, they learnt that Bertie had cancer. There was talk of abandoning the tour, but Bertie would not hear of it. However, they missed their departure date of 25 September on board the liner *Empress of Britain*. This created another and totally unnecessary drama, for the government and the courtiers would not allow the heiress to the throne to fly across the Atlantic. Philip, however, dug his heels in and demanded that they fly instead of altering their schedule and disappointing a large number of people by deleting the first part of it. The King and Lilibet supported him and, faced with the implacable opposition of the three royals, officialdom backed down. It was Philip's first victory against a group of people who were shaping up as his enemies, but it would also be his last one for many a year to come.

Philip and Lilibet's American and Canadian tour would have established them as global media stars, had they not been ones already. As it was, their international pre-eminence was merely ratified. They were young and good-looking, unassuming but regal. Dignity was the word that first sprang to mind when meeting them. Despite the obvious warmth of her personality, Lilibet was punctiliously royal in a way that no other female member of the Royal Family had been since Queen Mary. Her natural shyness enhanced the aura of reserve that royal protocol inevitably brings in its wake, and while Philip did his best to bring her out and to break the ice of formal occasions with witticisms, he, too, was careful never to step over that invisible line that separates royals from mere mortals.

So powerful was this element of unattainability that it eclipsed all else. Although Lilibet was very pretty in person (she never photographed well), had an excellent figure and dressed well, she never became a fashion plate. That role was reserved for her younger and more lightweight sister. Yet she and the Duke of Edinburgh were undeniably the most glamorous couple in the world. The public could never see enough of them, or of their two babies. Knowing that it was their responsibility to turn in impeccable performances in the execution of their public duties, and both being personalities who were almost dutiful to a fault, Philip and Lilibet never put a foot wrong. The result was that the public soon began raising their pedestals even further. As they did so, they also clamoured for more and more information about the private lives of the enchanting Duke and Duchess. The royal soap opera was about to begin.

In 1952 Lilibet and Philip substituted for her parents on yet another tour. This time the intended destinations were Africa, India and Australia. They only reached as far as Kenya. They were viewing wild animals from Treetops, an observation post beside a watering hole, when her father died. Cut off from all modern means of communication as they were, in the middle of the African bush, they did not learn the news until the following afternoon when they had returned for lunch to Sagana Lodge, a wedding present from the people of Kenya, where they were staying. Nowadays, of course, it would be impossible for one monarch to die and another to succeed without the whole world knowing it in a matter of minutes, but four decades ago happenstance played a large part in communication.

So it did with the way Lilibet came to receive the information that she was Queen. Her private secretary, Major the Hon. Martin Charteris, was *en route* to lunch when a reporter from the *East African Standard* told him that there had been a Reuter's message about the King's death. Although he could not obtain official confirmation (the governor and his staff were *en route* to Mombasa to meet the royals, so a pile of ciphers lay unscrambled and unanswered at Government House), he telephoned Sagana Lodge and told Prince Philip's private secretary and closest friend, Lieutenant Commander Michael Parker. Parker managed to catch Philip's eye and signalled him through the bay window of the sitting-room that looked out onto Mount Kenya to come outside. 'He's not the sort of person to show his emotions,' Parker says. 'But you can tell from a man's face. How he sets his features. I'll never forget it. He looked as if half the world had dropped on him.'

It is indicative of the nature of the relationship between Philip and Lilibet that he insisted that the news be withheld from her until it was confirmed. Only when he could no longer avoid inflicting pain upon the woman he had undertaken to protect, did Philip himself tell her. Her reaction was as different from his as night is from day.

'I remember seeing her moments after she became Queen,' a courtier says. 'Moments, not hours. And she seemed almost to reach out for it. There were no tears. She was just there, back braced, her colour a little heightened. Just waiting for her destiny. It was quite different for Philip. He sat slumped behind a copy of *The Times*. He didn't want it at all. It was going to change his whole life. Take away the emotional stability he'd finally found.'

Lilibet's ascension did more than rob Philip of the emotional stability he had not had for so much of his life. It robbed him of his career and his position as the head of his family. He was now the First Gentleman of the Realm, but he was also now a subject of his wife, The Queen. 'I wanted none of it,' Philip himself says. 'I never sought any of it. Not the position or the appointments I received. They were invitations. It was not my ambition to be President of the Mint Advisory Committee or President of the Worldwide Fund for Nature. I'd much rather have stayed in the navy, frankly.'

CHAPTER NINE

The Death of Romance

'*T*he marriage of The Queen and The Duke of Edinburgh ended, in the romantic sense, shortly after she ascended the throne,' Michael Thornton remembers Sir Martin Gilliat, Queen Elizabeth the Queen Mother's private secretary, telling him this in the days prior to *Royal Feud*, when the Clarence House set regarded him as a friend.

What destroyed the marriage was the manoeuvrings of a few well-placed courtiers and members of the government, who were jockeying for positions of influence over the new monarch. Politics is a dirty business, whether it is conducted from a palace of a queen or the office of a president, and by the time Lilibet and Philip realized just how dirty a business it could be, the romantic side of their marriage had been well and truly killed off.

The end, however, was not sudden, though the beginning of the end was. Lilibet and Philip had chased across the African skies to return to London at the earliest possible moment so that Queen Elizabeth II could start her reign with all the panoply officialdom could muster. The first official ceremony of any reign is the Accession Council, part of which had to be delayed until Lilibet's return from Africa. Just before ten o'clock on the morning of 8 February, she left Clarence House on the arm of her husband. Crossing the road, they walked over the cobbled courtyard of St James's Palace towards the front entrance, from which the Levee Room and the Throne Room are accessible. Most of the Privy Council were assembled in the former room, the latter being the holy of holies into which only a few select courtiers and members of the government could gain admittance.

When Lilibet and Philip reached the entrance, however, the unbelievable happened. The officials handling the accession ceremony informed their twenty-five-year-old queen that protocol forbade her husband from accompanying her. Under the rules of precedence, his rank was not sufficient to warrant such an honour. The highest ranking adult male in the kingdom was her uncle, Harry, the Duke of Gloucester, and he would have to take her in. The way was firmly barred to Philip, who had to gain admittance to his wife's palace through a back door. He was accompanied by Michael Parker, his private secretary.

Nor did matters improve once he was inside. Philip was firmly excluded from the Throne Room, the main scene of action. He had to remain, with the other privy councillors not important enough to gain admittance, in the Council Chamber. Both Philip and Lilibet were humiliated and perplexed by what they regarded as callous, inconsiderate conduct, but neither one did anything about it at the time. They were both too new in their positions, both feeling their way, both too unsure of the lie of the land to know what to do. So they bided their time and did nothing for the moment. But their passivity, his especially, was only momentary.

It soon became apparent that the senior members of the Royal Household were not going to be the only contentious arm of officialdom with whom Philip and Lilibet had to deal. Within weeks of Elizabeth II's accession, the prime minister became a problem. An avowed lover of history and a sentimental monarchist, Sir Winston Churchill had the romantic notion that he and Lilibet would duplicate the Eliza Dolittle relationship that Lord Melbourne and Queen Victoria had had. Queen Victoria, however, had been eighteen and unmarried, not twenty-five and married, when she succeeded to the throne. The difference in age and the existence of a husband made a significant shift in the degree of dependence the Queen would need to devolve upon her prime minister. It is now impossible to say whether Churchill took these factors into account and purposely decided to overlook Philip, or whether he allowed his fancies to colour the facts. But what is well known is that he believed himself to be the man destiny had chosen to shape the young monarch so that she would become a great queen who would preside over a second Elizabethan Age of golden glory.

It could, of course, be purely accidental that officialdom was doing its level best to marginalize Philip at the very moment that Churchill was trying to fashion the sovereign into the image he wished. Churchill's pronouncements, however, leave room for doubt. He was renowned for his dislike of Lord Mountbatten, whom he blamed for 'dismembering the Empire' and 'giving away India', and there is every indication that he lost sight of where the uncle ended and the nephew began.

Unluckily for Philip, he had adopted the name Mountbatten, and this put him firmly in Churchill's firing line as the old man pursued his campaign of 'keeping Dickie in his place'. Lord Mountbatten, Churchill learnt, was going around London saying that the House of Mountbatten now reigned. This was indeed the legal position, for Lilibet had traded the surname of Windsor for Mountbatten upon marriage, in keeping with the accepted custom that a woman relinquishes her maiden name and adopts her husband's last name. However, Lilibet was also a constitutional monarch, bound to act upon the instructions of her prime minister. So when Churchill discovered how Lord Mountbatten was boasting about the reigning dynasty sharing its name with his, the prime minister informed his queen that the dynasty must continue using the name Windsor, as laid down formally in King George V's declaration of 1917. The *London Gazette* therefore announced on 9 April 1952:

> The Queen today declared in Council Her Will and Pleasure that She and Her Children shall be styled and known as the House and Family of Windsor, and that Her descendants, other than female descendants who marry, and their descendants, shall bear the name of Windsor.

Philip was incensed. Not only had he not had any desire to assume the name forced upon his mother's family at the time of their demotion from princes in 1917, but he had done so only to facilitate his father-in-law's advisers. The name Mountbatten itself meant nothing to him. What mattered were his rights as a father and as a man. He was being singled out, Wallis Windsor style, for discriminatory treatment. 'I'm just a bloody amoeba, that's all,' he was quoted as saying, but privately he said, 'All they wanted was my sperm. I'm nothing but a fucking sperm factory to them.' His anger was fed by the knowledge that the politicians had not acted alone. Queen Mary and Queen Elizabeth the Queen Mother had both been active behind the scenes, encouraging Churchill. And while he could understand and forgive the reasons for the old queen wishing to perpetuate the will of her husband, he was not so accommodating where the Queen Mother was concerned.

If the issue of the dynasty's name caused pressures that would colour Philip and Lilibet's married life, it was just one of many problems that overwhelmed them at the time. The young couple wished to remain at their home. Churchill, however, was insisting that they move out of Clarence House and into Buckingham Palace, on the grounds that the sovereign must be seen to reign from the seat of royal power. This, at least, was one move that was not popular with the recently widowed Queen Elizabeth the Queen Mother. Like Queen Alexandra before her, she wished to remain ensconced in the bosom of monarchy for as long as possible. Always happy to fulfil the wishes of others, Lilibet had no objections to her mother taking whatever length of time she required to move. She also floated the idea to Churchill that she use Clarence House as a family home and Buckingham Palace as her office and official residence for entertainment purposes. He was adamant, however, that she had to leave the home she and Philip loved.

Although officialdom seemed to be winning all the battles, there was one issue on which Lilibet refused to relent. Precedence had been used as the excuse for forbidding Philip to accompany her into her own Accession Council, and precedence was now being used to keep him out of just about every affair of state that any female consort would have partaken of. On 30

September 1952, she therefore declared in the *London Gazette*:

> The Queen has been graciously pleased by warrant bearing date the 18th instant to declare and ordain that His Royal Highness Philip, Duke of Edinburgh . . . shall henceforth upon all occasions . . . except where otherwise provided by Act of Parliament have, hold and enjoy Place, Pre-eminence and Precedence next to Her Majesty.

Making her next move, Lilibet got parliament to increase Philip's Civil List allotment from £10,000 to £40,000. She also showed where her heart lay by appointing him Chairman of the Coronation Committee and a member of the Court of Claims, which dealt with people who claimed to have a historic right to partake in the coronation. These were shrewd moves, for the establishment was gripped with what Chips Channon called 'Coronation Thrombosis', and by giving Philip positions of influence Lilibet was declaring to one and all that she stood by her man.

Loyal though Lilibet was to Philip, neither she nor her consort was a match for the wily courtiers who now enveloped her in the busiest year of her life. 'They bombarded her with work,' Philip recounted to a relation, showing how they managed to drive an unsuspected but effective wedge between him and his wife. From early in the morning till late at night, the late King's private secretary, Sir Alan Lascelles (who had helped to ease King Edward VIII off the throne and was now Lilibet's private secretary), backed up by Sir Piers Legh, the Master of the Household, and Sir Ulick Alexander, the Keeper of the Privy Purse, ran her off her feet. Starting as he intended to continue, as soon as Lilibet returned to Britain from Africa, Sir Alan presented her with the Red Boxes, which contain the government papers of the day, and informed her that she had to get through them then and there. He knew that Lilibet was like her late father, punctilious to a fault, and, when she did not resist – and assert who was boss – he buried her in work, thereby becoming the man who really called the shots.

Ostensibly, Sir Alan, Sir Piers and Sir Ulick were teaching Lilibet the ropes, but they were also isolating her from her husband and the influence they, the prime minister and the Queen Mother feared Philip had over her. Up to that point, Philip had been Lilibet's protector, not as a Svengali, but as a loving and traditional husband. They were a close and loving couple, and it was this normal marital bond that the Palace clique now set about loosening. They were almost paranoid about Lord Mountbatten becoming the power behind the throne, which was a genuine irony, for, as Philip himself has often said, 'I was never as close to my uncle Dickie as everyone thought. Lilibet, in fact, was closer to him.' By the time all of the in-fighting had subsided, however, Lilibet was even closer to Uncle Dickie than she might ever have been had events been allowed to unfurl naturally.

To the chagrin of Elizabeth and the Palace clique, Lilibet had also developed a genuine closeness with Philip's mother Alice, which went way beyond the formally correct relationship she had with her own mother. True, she spoke to Queen Elizabeth the Queen Mother most days. True, she was careful to be a dutiful daughter. But when she wanted to let her hair down, to relax and be unguarded, Lilibet turned to her saintly mother-in-law, who was now a nun and utterly beyond the manoeuvrings and machinations that she had seen her smiling mother perpetrate upon her many stunned victims.

Fighting for the soul of the sovereign, and the influence that went along with whomever gained her ear, the Palace clique now created an atmosphere of such overwhelming exclusion that Lilibet and Philip had to fight for him to enjoy literally any of the many rights that a female consort of a monarch as a matter of course possessed. For instance, Elizabeth had always sat beside King George VI at State Openings of Parliament. Yet Philip was relegated to a chair some way beneath Lilibet's throne, and it was only later that she was able to insist that he be placed beside her. On and on and on the obstacles went, some so outstandingly petty that there were times when Philip and Lilibet could hardly believe that they had to expend so much energy on combating trivia. Yet they had no choice, unless they wanted molehills to develop into mountains. For instance, the courtiers decreed that Philip could not ride in the same carriage as his wife. This was another battle that Lilibet won, but she was having to be careful, as she knew only too well that she could not afford to alienate her senior advisers. It was therefore a case of trying to facilitate two warring factions.

Lilibet's tact and diplomacy with Philip's denegrators, however, had an adverse effect upon her husband. He knew that Sir Alan Lascelles had been Queen Elizabeth the Queen Mother's man from the days of the Abdication Crisis. He also knew that his mother-in-law had never approved of him and was no more fond of him than she had ever been. He sensed her hand behind many of these difficulties, so whenever Lilibet adopted a softly, softly approach with his detractors, Philip felt she was not standing up enough for him and for herself.

From Lilibet's point of view, however, fighting too vigorously brought consequences that were as painful for her as tact and diplomacy caused her husband. Unless she kept in with the Palace clique, she was in danger of antagonizing people whom she needed to run the monarchy.

Another regrettable effect of the turmoil and overwork in the early days of Lilibet's accession was that she was alienated from her children. She tried to see them for at least half an hour each morning and an hour each evening, but that basic schedule had to accommodate day trips as well as trips abroad. Between the tours she had had to undertake for her father and mother, and the worldwide Coronation Tour, which was now scheduled to celebrate her ascension to the throne, she saw so little of the children that there were times when they treated her more like a visiting godmother than a dearly beloved mother. This distressed her, and she tried to do what she could to partake of activities such as bathtime, but the sad fact was that she was so caught up in the demands of majesty that she simply did not have time for a family life.

The strain on Lilibet, on Philip and on their marriage was tremendous. By the time the coronation took place in June 1953, Lilibet was already cut off from her husband and her children. This, however, was not a fact she appreciated at the time, and as she continued to be tossed to and fro with the demands of the monarchy, she did not even have the time to notice that her family was disintegrating under her very nose.

For Philip, this period was even more difficult in emotional terms than it was for Lilibet. He was no longer master in his own house, and while Lilibet tried to mask that fact by allowing him to remain the principal partner within their family, he saw only too clearly the realities of his predicament and the way he was perceived by those surrounding them.

To someone as traditionally masculine and assertive as Philip, this was tantamount to being robbed of his manhood. Moreover, he is innately and intensely dignified, and he bitterly resented the indignities to which he was subjected. Without even realizing it, he began repeating the pattern of resentment and anger that had been the fate of his father and grandfather. In the process, he had lost his 'emotional centre' and became a volatile man given to extremes. Since then, he has been someone who can charm the birds off the trees one moment, give vent to the most bilious invective anyone has ever heard before you have finished blinking, then switch back to being charming as if nothing untoward has taken place. He now lacks the ability to relate to people on an even keel and can no longer call upon any of the virtues of emotional moderation.

With Lilibet otherwise engaged with the demands of her role, Philip who was far more emotionally dependent upon her than anyone but his closest relations realized, found himself with time lying heavily on his hands. This he tried to fill with useful endeavours, but he discovered that the Palace clique did not wish to give him sufficient responsibility to utilize his time effectively. Having learnt the hard way during the long days of his eventful childhood that human beings must be resourceful and realistic, Philip, who had always had a fun-loving disposition, channelled his energies into pleasure. This was not an ideal solution, for the serious-minded student of Kurt Hahn did want to make his contribution to the world in which he lived. But, deprived as he was of a platform from which to perform professionally, he had no choice.

His cousin Alexandra had married King Peter of Yugoslavia, and Peter noted, 'It was as if a volcano had been stoppered up. You could feel it all underneath.' The King wondered 'how long he can last . . . bottled up like that.' The answer was: an irascible but pleasureable lifetime.

Like his father before him, Philip approached the business of pleasure as thoroughly as if he were running half the navy. He had always been intensely athletic, so he utilized some of the time he had to hone his sailing and polo playing to world-class standards. Rather more contentiously, he also sought to excel in the arena in which the disenchanted Prince Andrew of Greece had excelled as well. Feminine appreciation therefore became a yardstick by which he could measure the success he would have preferred to gain professionally. Returning to his bachelor haunts with his best friend during his single days, Philip and Baron the fashionable photographer soon cut a swathe through feminine London. They were also founder members of the Thursday Club, an all-male affair, which met for lunches at Wheeler's Restaurant in Old Compton Street, Soho. According to Michael Thornton, 'One starchy courtier told me they indulged in quite lewd talk.' When pressed for more details, the courtier explained that the talk revolved around graphic accounts of the antics the men had got up to with the beautiful bits of fluff with whom they were dallying.

Back at Buckingham Palace, the very advisers who had forced Philip into a life of leisurely satisfaction were horrified. But they knew that lascivious lunches were only the tip of the iceberg. Philip and Baron were lunching and dining in the company of the beautiful models and entertainers who provided conversational fodder for the Thursday Club, and within a matter of months all of smart London was ablaze with talk of assignations at Baron's studio, and of the use of his flat as a 'safe house'.

In the pre-Accession days, it had been almost a relief when gossip had centred on two well-known and respectable young ladies. The first was Pat Kirkwood, and the second was Hélène Cordet. Pat Kirkwood was an extremely sexy and striking blue-eyed brunette who was the highest paid musical star throughout the 1940s and 1950s. Billed as Britain's answer to Betty Grable because of her magnificent legs, when she met Philip in 1948 she was starring at the London Hippodrome in the Starlight Roof revue, which introduced a twelve-year-old soprano named Julie Andrews to the West End stage. They were introduced in her dressing-room by Baron, who also presented Philip's naval equerry, Captain 'Basher' Watkin, after which the four of them went to Les Ambassadeurs, a private club in Mayfair.

Philip offered Pat Kirkwood beer, to which she disdainfully snorted, 'Beer?! I'd like some champagne, please.' After having a late supper, they adjourned to the Milroy night-club upstairs, where Philip spent the remainder of the evening dancing exclusively with the beautiful 27-year-old star. Rumours of this episode spread like wildfire throughout London and reached the ears of the King, who was furious because Lilibet was pregnant with Prince Charles at the time. 'I was told at Clarence House that the King sent for Philip and gave him a colossal dressing down, to his great resentment,' Michael Thornton says.

There were two reasons why Philip was resentful. The first reason was that nothing had happened of which either he or Pat Kirkwood should feel guilty. And the second was that he was not a little boy and felt he should not be treated as if he were one.

Miss Kirkwood insists she and Philip only ever met again at Royal Variety Performances. Despite this, there were persistent rumours about a continuing friendship. 'There was even talk of a white Rolls-Royce that Philip is supposed to have given Miss Kirkwood, which she dismisses as "fantasy",' Michael Thornton says.

For years Pat Kirkwood has used the law to ensure that no one perpetuates rumours of a romance between the Queen's consort and herself. When Tim Herald was preparing his authorized biography, *The Duke*, in 1991, Hodder and Stoughton, his publishers, received a letter from Daynes Hill & Perks, Miss Kirkwood's solicitors, warning them that she would sue for libel if there were any suggestion of a romantic relationship. Prince Philip's private secretary, Brian McGrath, telephoned Miss Kirkwood at her home in West Bruton on the North Yorkshire Dales and made the extraordinary suggestion that she should write out what she wished to appear in the book concerning herself and Prince Philip. He told her that the Duke of Edinburgh, who was checking the proofs of Mr Herald's authorized work, would ensure that her account appeared exactly as she wrote it.

Rather less litigious has been the other lady whose name was bandied about by the rumourmongers as the first flush of romance paled slightly in the Queen and Prince Philip's marriage during Lilibet's pregnancy with the first child. Hélène Cordet had been Philip's oldest friend to whom he was not related. There had been talk in the Greek community when they were both children that they might marry when they grew up. The Foufounis family were eminent Greek royalists, comfortably off rather than rich, and the prospect of a union between Hélène and Philip must have had great appeal for them. It might also have proven attractive to the Greek royal family had not Lilibet conceived this great passion for Philip, but once there appeared the prospect of a union between the Greek and British royal houses, all alternatives paled into insignificance. Moreover, Hélène and Philip seemed keener to remain friends than to become lovers, and she married her first husband in 1938.

'I've known Prince Philip more or less all my life,' Hélène Cordet told me. 'My family lived in Marseilles and his in Paris when we were children. This was before I went to school in Switzerland and lived in Egypt. I've been married twice. The second time in 1945. I have two children, a boy who is forty-nine, and a girl who will be forty-eight in February 1993.' Gossips attributed paternity of the children to Philip, which so annoyed them that the prince's putative son felt compelled in adulthood to make that announcement that his father was the man named on his birth certificate and not the Duke of Edinburgh.

By the time Lilibet ascended the throne, Hélène Cordet was the toast of

London. 'My parents did not approve when I went into show business. They thought my choice of career *infra dig*. I started as a singer then I presented a TV show called *Café Continental*, which was a great success and became the No. 1 show. This was in 1951.' The gossips could not believe that Philip and Hélène were anything as innocent as mere friends, or that he was just happy to let his hair down among old and sympathetic figures from his past.

Word of Hélène's friendship with Prince Philip had spread throughout London. It did her career no harm, and when Philip and Lilibet's marriage came under courtier-imposed strain, Philip knew he could always be assured of a welcome from his childhood friend. By this time, Hélène and her second husband had opened up a restaurant at 6 Hamilton Place on the site of the Inn on the Park. 'It was a success but made no money, what with food going off and pilferage and all the other wastage that restaurants suffer from,' Hélène Cordet said.

Meanwhile, Philip and Lilibet's marital problems continued to gather pace while Lilibet slaved away at being queen, and Philip played at being his father's son. Baron's studio in Park Lane remained the place where Philip met many a young and attractive girl with whom he could enjoy a short flirtation followed by a discreet goodbye. The object of the exercise was not to create a scandal or to embarrass Lilibet, to whom Philip remained devoted, but to have a good time and prove himself in areas over which the Palace clique had no control.

As so often happens in life, the *coup de grâce* was not issued by an enemy, but by a loved one. Princess Margaret had always been her sister's closest friend. It was therefore only natural that it was to Lilibet that Margaret turned when she fell in love with Group Captain Peter Townsend. Margaret had long since had a crush on the tall, handsome airman who was her father's equerry. After George VI's death, Townsend was appointed Comptroller of Queen Elizabeth the Queen Mother's Household and moved into Clarence House with Margaret and her mother when she and Lilibet finally swapped residences. The handsome airman had recently been divorced from his wife because of her adultery with the artist Sir Philip de Lazlo's son, and John Dean, the Duke of Edinburgh's valet, summarized the view of many in the palace, his employer included, when he said, 'Our view was that it would be regrettable if a man in Mr Townsend's position allowed Princess Margaret's interest to grow into anything stronger than the friendly feeling which would naturally exist between them, meeting as often as they were bound to do.'

Margaret, however, was headstrong, the pampered darling of her father, who could never deny her anything, and of her mother, who went along with the King's regimen of indulgence. Elizabeth, moreover, had never indicated that she disapproved of a man whom she herself treated in the mildly flirtatious way that Southern debutantes reserved for their faithful swains. But what was acceptable for a widowed queen in pursuit of preserving her feminine vanity was not acceptable for her single daughter to act upon in earnest, though it would take a couple more years and a lot of heartache for that fact to penetrate through the layers of artificial consideration and superficial concern that permeated the hothouse atmosphere of the sophisticated yet moralistic dowager queen's household.

In April 1953, with just a few weeks to go before the coronation, Margaret informed her mother and her sister that she wished to marry Peter Townsend. Their reactions said a lot about the sort of people they were.

Both Elizabeth and Lilibet liked Peter Townsend. Indeed, Elizabeth was dependent upon him for the smooth running of her household. She also treasured the cosy and good-natured way he fitted into 'my knitting brigade', as Elizabeth calls the scintillatingly gay and majestically precious environment in which she exists. Overtly, she evinced neither approval nor disapproval, either of the affair or of the prospect of a marriage. She had long since preferred the art of distancing herself from anything unpleasant, and her attitude was: If it is possible, so be it. The paradox between this position and the high moral stand that she had taken with David and Wallis did not bother her, and Margaret was, naturally enough, relieved not to have the opposition of her formidable mother.

Lilibet also responded in keeping with the deeper aspects of her character. Not judgemental or controlling by inclination, she was wholeheartedly in favour of her sister having this chance of happiness if it were possible. However, Margaret was only twenty-three, and under the Royal Marriages Act of 1772, Lilibet had to give her sister permission until she was twenty-five.

Bound as Lilibet was by the constitutional demands of her position, she had to consult the prime minister and act upon his advice. No one wanted the new reign to begin with a major scandal, and Sir Winston Churchill, mindful of the 1936 Abdication Crisis, in which he had ironically enough, taken Edward VIII and Mrs Simpson's side, advised the Queen to withhold her consent until Margaret was old enough to marry without it. He also suggested moving Townsend from Clarence House to a post abroad, but, this being out of his brief, the Queen left Margaret's lover right where he was, at home with her and her mother. At this juncture, the Queen, the Queen Mother and the prime minister all gave Princess Margaret the impression that there would be no objection to the marriage when the two-year wait had elapsed.

Coronations are solemn and majestic occasions, carefully rehearsed so that every contingency is taken care of. Queen Elizabeth II's was no exception, but human beings cannot rehearse out every bit of spontaneity, especially when a couple is in love, and, as the ceremony ended and Margaret and Townsend were waiting to depart, she artlessly dusted a speck off his immaculate uniform. Such an intimate deed would have spoken volumes wherever it had taken place, but in such an awesome setting it made a noise that reverberated worldwide when the photographs were published. Within days, the affair knocked the coronation off the front pages, and everyone wanted to know: Would Margaret marry her divorced Group Captain?

While the question preoccupied the government as well as the readers of newspapers all over the world, Margaret and her mother prepared to embark upon a tour of Rhodesia. Townsend had been scheduled to accompany them, but Churchill intervened now that the romance had become a political issue. Once more he advised the Queen that the Group Captain must be sent abroad, as air attaché to an embassy of his choice, and that he and Margaret must not meet for at least a year. When they did so, it would have to be in conditions of the utmost secrecy.

Unadvisedly perhaps, but with the noble intention of protecting his wife wherever he could, Philip stepped into the mêlée. He advised Lilibet to stand aside and stop supporting her sister. He did not want her being embroiled in a political controversy so soon after her coronation, nor did he want her making needless enemies when they had quite enough problems of their own without fighting Margaret's battles for her. Never one to mince his words or cover his tracks, Philip made his position so clear that Princess Margaret quickly got word of the position he was taking. She was furious. She needed her sister's support for what was possibly the most important event of her life. Yet here was Philip 'buggering things up', as Margaret later told a friend.

Moreover, Margaret's friends did not consider Philip's motives to be based purely upon the desire to spare Lilibet from unpleasantness, distress and difficulty. He had never got along with his parents-in-law as well as Peter Townsend did. Over the years, he had had many an occasion to see how the late King favoured his beloved and tactful equerry over his more rambunctious son-in-law, and how the Queen Mother much preferred the equable companionship of her adored comptroller to the grit of the robust Philip. Peter Townsend was the ideal courtier, all smooth corners compared to Philip's sharp edges, and several of Margaret's circle believe to this day that the competitive Philip was secretly delighted when the wonder-boy Townsend found himself in a predicament that might reflect adversely upon him and his monarchical protectors, the late King and the Queen Mother.

Whatever Philip's motives, Margaret set off for Rhodesia reluctantly, albeit cheered by the promise that she would be able to see her lover one last time when she returned home. As the tour drew to an end, however, she was devastated to learn that Peter Townsend was departing for Brussels before she got back. The politicians and court had let her down. So badly did she take this news, which she called 'a betrayal', that she was unable to function and had to be put to bed, where she stayed, in a state of awful hysteria, which could be overheard by everyone else in the residence for two days.

By the time Margaret returned to England, she and Philip were barely speaking. She no longer liked or trusted her brother-in-law, but she still clung to the hope that she would be allowed to marry the man of her dreams when she reached twenty-five. This she did in August 1955.

Townsend returned to England, and the furore surrounding the impending marriage blew up again. Most of the tabloids were firmly in favour of a marriage, but in the intervening two years some of the protagonists had had a chance to see how the land would lie, and they marshalled their troops accordingly. Chief among these was Queen Elizabeth the Queen Mother, who had come out against the marriage on the grounds that her dearly lamented Bertie would not have approved of a match between their daughter and a divorced man. The fact that she had taken a different stand two years before did not strike her as anomalous, but she was careful not to do her fighting herself. Having learnt during the Wallis Simpson episode how keen monarchists are to perform favours for royalty, she left most of the opposition up to her good friend the Marquis of Salisbury, a devout High Church Anglican as well as a member of the government. He, too, was adept at manipulating a situation to his advantage, and he threatened to resign from the government when it looked as if the marriage might receive governmental assent.

Faced with the implacable opposition of a member of his government, the Prime Minister Anthony Eden, himself a *divorcé* and recently remarried to Churchill's niece Clarissa, advised the Queen at Balmoral during a visit on 1 October that the government could not give its consent to the marriage. He pointed out that Margaret could wait another year, at which time she would no longer be subject to the strictures of the Royal Marriages Act. She could then give notice to the Privy Council of her intention to marry Peter Townsend. If she did so, however, parliament would most likely debate the application, and while they could not forbid her from marrying the man of her choice, they would most likely vote to strip her of her royal rank and her allowance under the Civil List. They might even advise that she live abroad, a prospect reminiscent of the fate endured by the Duke of Windsor, and one that filled both the Queen and her sister with dread.

When Princess Margaret heard the news, she became frantic. According to a friend of hers, she accused the Queen Mother and the Duke of Edinburgh of plotting behind her back. While this was undoubtedly true of Elizabeth, there has never been any indication that Philip's lack of support amounted to a conspiracy to deprive Margaret of her Group Captain. Such opposition as there was was directed only at keeping Lilibet out of the fray, but Margaret did not care. She harboured deep feelings of bitterness towards both her mother and her brother-in-law and has never forgiven either of them for the part they played in 'depriving me of my happiness', as she said to her friend. She also resented the passivity of her sister, feeling that Lilibet could have taken her side more actively, instead of standing on the sidelines, allowing everything to happen around her.

In a tirade of wounded feelings, Margaret got her own back by telling Lilibet all about the goings-on at the Thursday Club and Baron's studio. She described how Philip was spending his time, and when she stormed out of the room, slamming the door, she and Lilibet did not exchange another word for a year. Margaret's romance with Peter Townsend had ended. So, too, had the romance in Philip and Lilibet's marriage.

CHAPTER TEN

The Plateau of Tolerance

Fundamental changes do not take place in any marriage without pain and suffering, and Lilibet and Philip were typical examples of this truism. It had long been a matter of conjecture within royal circles that Philip had never been in love with the Queen, though Lilibet undoubtedly was besotted with him. While all the evidence pointed to him loving her as opposed to being in love with her, no one who knew them well could fail to notice how genuinely wrapped up in each other they had been, and how emotionally attached he was to her. When Lilibet discovered what everyone else in the royal circles had heard about, to have the moorings of the central relationship in each of their lives loosened like that, was shattering for both of them.

Lilibet's initial reaction was disbelief. This is a classical defence mechanism, but one which only the foolhardy can maintain over any length of time. As anyone who knows anything about the Queen will attest, she is anything but dumb or self-deluding, and once the news seeped in, she evidently confronted Philip.

Like most men, Philip was not about to admit to flirtations that were meaningless and insignificant in themselves and that would never have amounted to anything but harmless diversions had news of them not got back to his wife. He therefore assured Lilibet that there was no fire in the smoke-filled room. He had not done anything he should not have. He had never been disloyal. He had remained true to her.

Like most women in love who are confronted by an issue that threatens to destroy the very foundations of home life, Lilibet was only too happy to accept Philip's assurances. Margaret, naturally enough, remained out in the cold during this period. Lilibet could hardly believe that her dearly beloved little sister could have been the bearer of such distressing news, and for the first time in their lives they remained studiously distant from one another.

96

While Philip and Lilibet were going through the phase of assurances, she continued being as busy as she had been since her accession. Philip's official position also remained unchanged. He still had too little to challenge him, and time still lay heavy on his hands. It is hardly surprising, therefore, that he continued to fill his time as he had done before. Baron's studio and the diversions it offered persisted in being central to his activities, as did his friendship with such exotic females as Hélène Cordet.

Had Philip changed his habits, Lilibet might never have had cause to turn over his denials in her mind. However, her ear was now close to the ground. Surrounded as she was by a wealth of courtiers, many of whom disliked Philip, it was only a matter of time before she questioned the merit of how her consort was conducting that part of his private life that he was not sharing with her.

Coming to such a painful juncture was cataclysmic for Lilibet. She had worshipped Philip since she was thirteen years old. She had believed he loved her as wholeheartedly as she loved him. The knowledge that he had a more masculine approach to matters of the heart 'shattered her', in the words of one of her mother's courtiers. Ever since her marriage, she had co-existed with her handsome prince on a cloud of passion and principle. He was loving, attentive, protective, assertive. She was his perfect foil, gentle, tender, yielding and obsessed. Furthermore, they were more than lovers and a married couple. They were companions and cousins, royals together in a world of commoners. They were also best friends, tied as much by the loyalty and affection of two passionate people sharing the same goals and hopes as they were by the pleasures of the marriage bed.

For Lilibet, the pain of discovering that her marriage possessed dimensions of which she had known nothing was only part of the picture. Another significant part was the knowledge that she had been humiliated in front of everyone who mattered to her. Like many wives, she had been the last to hear the talk, and the mere thought that her personal life had been the stuff of gossip was enough to drive her into a frenzy of anguished indignation. While she might just have been able to salve her wounds had she been an ordinary person, because she was not one, and because she took the role of queen so seriously, the indignity done not only to her but also to Her Majesty The Queen was so loathsome as to bring her to a point of no return.

When most couples reach a point of no return, they part. This, however, was never an option for Lilibet. No matter what happened between Philip and herself, they could never take the paths of either separation or divorce. They were tied together for the remainder of their natural lives, and, irrespective of how they might feel about one another, or what form their lives might take in the future, they could never present anything but a united front to the world at large.

Being Queen, Lilibet could not take time off to have a quiet nervous breakdown. The affairs of state are relentless, and, regardless of her emotional state, she had to function. Nevertheless, human beings can only cope with so much without cracking up. Lilibet had none of the means of letting off steam that are open to most of us. She could not take tranquillizers, as she needed her faculties for the daily and unremitting demands of sovereignty. She was not tempted to turn to drink, for much the same reasons as why she could not take prescription drugs, plus the fact that she knew only too well that a tendency to alcoholism ran in both sides of her family. She was too considerate of others to throw temper tantrums, too dignified to rant and rave, too aware of her position to give way to her emotions and let herself down. It was clear, however, that she was as close to the edge as it was possible to be without going over it.

What was the solution? Despite appearances to the contrary, Lilibet has never been narrow-minded. Conservative and cautious, yes, but she is from too sophisticated a world to harbour many of the prejudices to which her less illustrious subjects might be partial.

The first step Lilibet took towards putting herself back together was to seek psychiatric help. This was not as radical a course of action as it might appear to some people. Her Aunt Marie (Princess George of Greece) was one of the world's most eminent lay psychoanalysts, so she could not have failed to be aware of how useful therapy can be at times of stress or distress. No one, however, has ever been able to discover the name of the doctor who treated her, for she did not go to him. According to a relation of the Queen, he went to her, at the Palace, as often as she needed to see him.

The need for secrecy was twofold. At the time, psychiatry was already an accepted form of therapy in the United States. Americans understood that life sometimes deals such painful blows to healthy individuals that their psyches need medical assistance to revert back to normal, in much the same way as their bones need to be reset professionally if they break an arm or a leg. The average Briton, however, was not as enlightened then. Psychiatry was regarded as a very suspect form of treatment used only by crackpots and nutcases. That, undoubtedly, was responsible for some of the extreme secrecy surrounding Lilibet's treatment, though she had always been private by inclination and would also have felt naked if news of her needing such a radical form of support had leaked out.

While Lilibet was trying to paste back the shards of her life into a cohesive unit, Philip was also picking up his broken hopes. He had been significantly more dependent emotionally upon her than was popularly believed, but no matter what he said or did, the time for returning hand in hand on to the cloud of dreams was past. The romance had left his marriage, and Lilibet did not, could not, allow it to return. He therefore had no choice but to accept a situation that he also found exceedingly painful. Yet again his childhood pattern of the uncertainties of an unstructured existence replacing the securities of a well structured life repeated itself.

There was nothing for Philip to do but face his fate, and this he did with the courage for which he is justly renowned. The emotional price was high, though. When he emerged from this phase of his life, his personality had altered, and it is generally agreed that this change was not for the better. Such even-temperedness as he had possessed had disappeared. He remained capable of kindness and compassion, especially to women and the underdog, but his explosions became the stuff of legend. For someone who was temperamentally prone to impatience and intolerance, against which Kurt Hahn had warned him, this was not a harbinger for personal happiness or harmony, and thereafter, his family life would be blighted by his ferocity.

To Philip, this ferocity was not a problem even though it would alienate the three sons born to Lilibet during their marriage. 'His mother was fierce,' Michael Parker claims, but her ferocity had not bothered him. Some people who know the Duke of Edinburgh reasonably well attribute this to insensitivity caused by intellectualizing or denying much of what he feels, but others who know him even better diagnose the cause as over-sensitivity denied to himself and masking as insensitivity, a mechanism commonly known in psychological circles as denial resulting in overcompensation. Whatever the reason, Philip undoubtedly has two qualities, which are only too rare in a world where courtiers and other acolytes have raised duplicity and insincerity into a fine art: he has integrity, and he is sincere. He may rant and rave, swear and curse, laugh and cajole, charm and beguile, but he is always true.

Philip is undoubtedly a passionate man. Whether he is speaking about the World Wide Fund for Nature or flirting with a pretty girl, you can see how fully engaged he is emotionally. Like many passionate people, he is given to extremes of expression, though the words he uses are often balanced and reasonable. If you meet him socially, he is surprisingly down-to-earth and charming but never for a moment do you doubt that this is someone who feels things acutely. This makes him gritty as well as appealing, especially to men who share his point of view and to women. There is no doubt that he is a fascinating man, and if his personality promises excitement rather than comfort, at least he will never be boring.

One of the immediate virtues of the profound change that occurred in the marriage was that Philip had more freedom to pursue professional interests without being stymied. The court knew all about what was going on more or less as it happened, for Buckingham Palace is a warren of gossip and intrigue, in which few secrets remain unknown for long. Now that they did not need to fear a diminution of their influence over Lilibet as a result of Philip's influence over her, the Palace clique no longer felt the need to thwart him at every turn.

Philip had always been interested in mankind, destiny and the environment, in a way that few members of his generation were. This was entirely due to the influence of Kurt Hahn and Prince Max of Baden's concept of the modern leader as a man following in the traditions of Ancient Greece. By Philip's own admission, 'In an ideal world, I would've preferred to make my career in the navy,' but now that this was no longer an option, he decided to use his new-found freedom to pursue interests that would profit humanity. His work with the environment and conservation, in the shape of the World Wide Fund for Nature, and with the enlightenment of his fellow human beings through shared experience and exposure to life's fundamentals, under the guise of the Duke of Edinburgh's Awards scheme, really owe their fruition to this period of his life. It is ironic to consider that such invaluable work might never have been allowed to flourish had Philip and Lilibet's marriage not undergone fundamental difficulties, and that the ecological movement in Britain, of which Prince Philip is the father, might still be viewed as the ravings of a crank (which is what the press and public believed in the fifties, sixties and seventies).

It is also interesting to note what foresight and intelligence Philip did indeed possess. He spotted a need and a remedy long before the experts even realized there was a problem. Possibly the courtiers should have let him get along with the business of updating the monarchy, instead of resisting his efforts at every turn. Had they done so, some of the more recent problems might never have arisen, though it would have been inconceivable for them to allow anyone to reform them out of existence. Which is precisely what Philip would have done.

By 1956, Philip and Lilibet were leading separate lives. It therefore made sense for them to perform as two separate parts of one team rather than as a double act. Philip had been asked to open the Olympic Games in Australia. The restless and pragmatic prince had the idea of putting the journey simultaneously to several different uses. One was to visit the residents of the farthest outposts of the Empire, thereby showing subjects who would not otherwise see the face of monarchy what their Queen's consort looked like.

Accompanied by Michael Parker, Philip flew out to join the royal yacht *Britannia* for a cruise, which not only included Australia and New Zealand but also Napoleon's place of exile, St Helena, and Ascension Island, where the inhabitants were thrilled to get their first glimpse of a living member of the Royal Family. Ecology was the second use to which Philip put this trip. Boarding the research ship, *John Biscoe*, he journeyed to twelve research bases throughout Antarctica.

On the way back home, the royal yacht called into ports where Philip could pump politicians' hands for Britain, or persuade for preservation in the interests of mankind. One such stop was in the Gambia, in January 1957, but as soon as *Britannia* departed, yet another marital crisis evolved when Michael Parker's wife filed suit against him for divorce on the grounds of adultery. Privately, she was rumoured to be exceedingly bitter against Philip, whom she regarded as having been a catalyst for many of the problems within the marriage, but publicly she remained silent. Margaret-style, she had issued the *coup de grâce*, for Parker had to resign.

Both men were upset by the turn events had taken, for they had been the closest of friends since their youth. But neither Philip nor Parker was prepared to put his personal desires before his duty, and both men knew that their first obligation was to the monarchy, not to their friendship.

By the time the royal yacht reached Gibraltar, where Philip was due to remain for eight days before flying to Lisbon to meet the Queen, there was a fully blown scandal. Newspapers in the United States and on the Continent were openly speculating about problems within the Queen's marriage, and while the British press displayed remarkable restraint at first, it was only a matter of time before they too jumped on the bandwagon. The upshot was that Buckingham Palace issued a statement asserting, 'It is quite untrue that there is any rift between the Queen and the Duke of Edinburgh.'

One result of the speculation was that Philip's full birthright was returned to him in an attempt to show that all was well. The Queen made him a Prince of the United Kingdom. And not just any old prince either. Henceforth, he was His Royal Highness The Prince Philip, Duke of Edinburgh. The 'The' was the most exact indication of Lilibet's attitude that the public would see. Had she made him His Royal Highness Prince Philip, Duke of Edinburgh, she would merely have been returning him to the rank he possessed at birth. But the 'The' was a style reserved solely for the children of monarchs, and by including it in Philip's title, Lilibet was sending out a clear message that their marriage was not a problem. Nor was this a message intended only for the general public. It was also directed at the royalists who occupy court circles and often cause more difficulties for the Royal Family, through their intrigue and backbiting, than republicans do. They would understand the significance of that extra 'The', which indicated Lilibet's support for her errant spouse more eloquently than any proclamation could have done.

Although Lilibet's generosity in elevating Philip in rank was partly pragmatic, appreciation for the loyalty he had shown her was also a factor. Throughout their difficulties, Philip had never once deviated from the posture of protection towards his monarch, which he had first adopted as a husbandly gesture of affection. Loyalty had always been one of his most striking qualities, and so it has remained throughout their marriage. No matter his mood or the state of their lives, he has never embarrassed the Queen nor sought to promote himself at her expense. The position of Queen has invariably come before his, or indeed Lilibet's own, desires and self-interest.

By appreciating this loyalty, Lilibet set the ground for a working partnership, which has weathered many a storm in the several decades of its existence. She and Philip share a deep and abiding affection based on trust and respect. They might have little in common in terms of interests or temperament, but this reservoir gives them the tolerance to endure what they see as one another's failings. Lilibet has patience with Philip's irascibility, while he suffers what he calls 'her passivity' in what passes as relative silence for him.

Before they reached the plateau of tolerance, however, Lilibet and Philip had many an adjustment to make. But the late 1950s, they no longer bothered to pretend that they were leading separate lives, except to the general public. Both of them were busy. Philip now had a plethora of official duties, many of which were an outgrowth of his patronage of organizations and causes relating to the environment and the disadvantaged in society. His schedule was planned around his athletic activities, chief of which was his passion: polo. He also sailed, with friends such as Uffa Fox, and could be found every year overseeing Cowes Week, the nation's premier sailing regatta, from the deck of the *Britannia*.

Lilibet, meanwhile, remained tied down with her monarchical responsibilities, though she was now sufficiently familiar with them to have found a way of ekeing out time for her private life. Her main pleasure was racing, and, between receiving ambassadors, visiting heads of state, crown officials and the prime minister, she made time to study the *Bloodstock Breeders' Review*, the results of the races of the day and the performance of her horses. Whenever she could, she would get up at dawn to look at her horses taking their early morning exercise.

Through racing, Lilibet met many of the people who would become her lifelong friends. One of these friendships which deepened as a result of Lilibet's interest in racing was her acquaintanceship with Lord Porchester. Tall, strapping and handsome, with the toothy grin of the Herberts, Henry George Reginald Molyneux Herbert was the heir of the Earl of Carnarvon, himself a famous figure in the racing fraternity. Married since 1956 to Jean Margaret Wallop, the daughter of the Hon. Oliver Wallop of Big Horn, Sheridan County in the state of Wyoming, USA, he was two years Lilibet's senior. He was also the father of one young son, Geordie, and would soon become the father of another when his wife produced the 'spare' named Henry but thereafter called Harry.

Lilibet had known the family for much of her life, firstly through her racing-mad mother, and secondly because the Carnarvon family lived near Windsor, at Highclere Castle in Berkshire. There they had housed many of the Egyptian treasures that the late Lord Carnarvon, the renowned underwriter of the Carter discoveries, had amassed. These included *objets* from the tomb of the boy-king Tutankhamun, which the family sold to the Metropolitan Museum in New York after the unfortunate earl succumbed to blood poisoning in 1924, thus giving birth to the tale of the curse of Tutankhamun.

It was only a matter of time before Lord Porchester, himself an owner and breeder, was giving Lilibet advice on her bloodstock. Breeding is very important to anyone who is interested in racing, but it is a long-term venture, as you cannot know the outcome of your experiment until the horse runs as a two year old. Nor was it easy for Lilibet to find a confidant she could trust, for the variabilities of human performance were as inconsistent as those of the animal kingdom. Nevertheless, Lilibet grew to respect Lord Porchester's opinions and to trust him. Being the sort of woman she was, she was soon consulting him as frequently as she could, and, as their relationship grew, he became her valued confidant.

Travel was now a large part of any royal's duties, and 1959 began as it would continue, with many of the Royal Family scattered to the four corners of the globe. Queen Elizabeth the Queen Mother took off for Uganda and Kenya, while the Duchess of Kent and Princess Alexandra headed south of the border to Latin America. Princess Margaret prepared to visit the Caribbean while her Uncle Harry and Aunt Alice (the Duke and Duchess of Gloucester) made plans to visit the politically troubled nation of Nigeria, which was agitating vociferously for independence. Lilibet, meanwhile, was going over details with representatives of the Foreign and Commonwealth Office as well as with her dressmakers, Norman Hartnell and Hardy Amies, for two forthcoming trips. One was scheduled for June and July to Canada and the United States, the other for the autumn to the territory that was then known as the Gold Coast but is now called Ghana.

While Lilibet remained at home preparing for these trips, her peripatetic husband was off on yet another of his extended tours, this time of three months' duration, to the Indian subcontinent and the Far East. Lilibet was due to celebrate her thirty third birthday on 21 April, and romantic royal-watchers, not realizing the state of play, hoped Philip would break his journey and spend the happy occasion with his wife. However, he went straight from one side of the world to the other, arriving in Bermuda for the celebrations of the 350th anniversary of that island's settlement by the British. Only afterwards did he return to Britain, for what was a brief stopover of a few weeks before setting off again with Lilibet to Canada and the United States.

Just before her departure, Lilibet received confirmation that she was pregnant. This caused consternation in the Royal Household. Lilibet did not wish to alter any of her immediate plans. The trip to Canada continued, though that to Ghana was postponed.

In Canada and the United States, Lilibet and Philip performed as the two seasoned and dedicated royal troupers that they were. There was no indication of any strains and stresses in their lives. Lilibet, however, was suffering from morning sickness, and her schedule was so punishing that she was ordered by her doctor, Surgeon Captain D. D. Steele-Perkins, to take a day's rest before a flight to Edmonton. At the end of the tour, she was so exhausted that she flew straight back to London instead of sailing home on *Britannia*. She headed northwards for rest and recovery to Balmoral, where the announcement of her pregnancy was made.

That summer Lilibet played hostess to her sister and Margaret's lover. Life had moved on since the bitter breach in 1955, and while the consequences of Margaret's revelations had been too momentous for forgetfulness to enter the frame, now that both women had satisfactory lives, they were able to resume the even tenor of their relationship. Lilibet, of course, was married to Philip and also had Lord Porchester whenever she felt the need of a confidant with whom she had much in common. Meanwhile, Margaret had found herself Antony Armstrong-Jones, a successful photographer who had, ironically enough, once been Baron's assistant. Theirs was a torrid romance, which was typical of the Windsors, and they wanted to be married. Once more Lilibet, who so studiously avoided controversy wherever possible, found herself at the centre of a potential sensation. The difficulty was not the photographer himself, but the marital taboos and customs with which the Royal Family were surrounded.

First of all, Tony Armstrong-Jones was neither royal nor aristocratic. While that problem could be solved by the simple expediency of bestowing a hereditary peerage upon him, Lilibet feared resistance from the court or the cabinet. The last Princess of the Blood Royal who had married a commoner had been Princess Patricia of Connaught in 1919. She had been made to renounce her royal rank and status. It would be cruelly paradoxical if Margaret's second choice of husband should result in her losing the very status for which she had given up Peter Townsend.

Furthermore, Tony Armstrong-Jones was from a broken home. His mother, the famed designer Oliver Messel's beautiful sister Anne, was now the Countess of Rosse. She at least had a title, which was some consolation to the snobs at court, but his father, Ronald Armstrong-Jones, QC, was married to a former air hostess who was only one year older than her stepson.

Fortunately for all concerned, Harold Macmillan, Anthony Eden's successor, had rather more compassion than the discredited and divorced ex-premier had had. He ensured that the cabinet gave the marriage their blessing by taking a lead that brooked no opposition. It was a salutary lesson in how decency could prevail against prejudice and hypocrisy, and one for which the pregnant Queen and her impassioned sister were grateful. Nevertheless, the possibility of an adverse public reaction could not be ruled out, so the decision was taken to announce Margaret's marriage after the birth of the Queen's baby.

The Queen is not an inconsiderate or an unkind woman, and, with another baby due, she sought to mollify her husband. She therefore approached Harold Macmillan during one of their famous Tuesday meetings at the Palace and asked him to set the ball in motion so that the issue of her grandchildren's names could be raised once more. As with Margaret's wedding, Macmillan took a firm lead in the cabinet discussions. The result was a decision that placated everyone and especially pleased Philip's vain uncle, Earl Mountbatten of Burma. The Queen was therefore able to announce in Council that:

> While I and my children shall continue to be styled and known as the House and Family of Windsor, my descendants, other than descendants enjoying the style, title or attributes of Royal Highness and the titular dignity of Prince or Princess, and female descendants who marry and their descendants, shall bear the name Mountbatten-Windsor.

Eleven days later, on 19 February 1960, Lilibet gave birth to her second son. Once more Philip was mollified. According to royal custom, the baby was named after ancestors of the Queen and her husband: Andrew in honour of Philip's father, Albert after hers, Christian in honour of their common ancestor the King of Denmark and Edward after her great-grandfather.

Baby Andrew was kept under wraps as no other royal baby has been before or since. The world received no glimpse of him, not even when he was christened, for there were no official photographers present to record what is normally a happy semi-official occasion shared by the Royal Family and the public alike.

In public-relations terms, such secrecy was a disaster, which would have long-term repercussions. Coming on top of society's knowledge that Philip and Lilibet's marriage had become nothing more than a viable but unromantic partnership, and that he had been absent throughout much of the period when she might have been impregnated, it only fed the fires of lurid speculation as to whether Philip was actually Andrew's father. So prevalent did these stories become that Philip's cousin Queen Alexandra of Yugoslavia went out of her way to answer them when she wrote a *Family Portrait of Prince Philip*. Royalty normally do not comment, even obliquely, on their own sex lives or those of anyone else, especially other royals, yet Alexandra hinted at carnality when she said that Philip returned from his three months round-the-world trip to spend 'an unusually long weekend' with Lilibet.

If Alexandra hoped that her disclaimer would douse the flames of speculation, she was mistaken. As Andrew grew up, he did so surrounded by people who had heard the rumours. It did not help that he bears an uncanny resemblance to Lord Carnarvon, as Lord Porchester became upon the death of his father in 1987, and that similarity goes beyond the facial. Unlike the other males in the Royal Family, who are slender like Philip, Andrew is chunky like Lord Carnarvon and the two sons born to his marriage. Nor did it help that Andrew was the apple of his mother's eye and not close to Philip, despite being, of the three sons born to Lilibet, the closest in personality to the kind-hearted, abrasive and self-confident Duke.

What has also aided the gossip mongers was Lord Carnarvon's steady rise in court circles. The Queen appointed him her Racing Manager in 1969, a post that he has held despite patchy results on the turf for sometimes extended periods. Lilibet also knighted him not once but twice – in 1976 and 1982 – and there is no doubt to anyone seeing them together that they have a touching comfort with one another, which has been born of many shared and meaningful experiences.

I had no idea just how widespread the rumours about Andrew's paternity were until I visited Ireland for the launch of *Diana in Private*. I had always assumed that what I had heard was confined to the narrow circle surrounding the Queen, her court and her cousins, but, to my consternation, Terri Keane of the prestigious *Sunday Independent* asked me if I could confirm whether it was true that Prince Andrew was Lord Carnarvon's and not Prince Philip's son. I mumbled something diplomatic and unquotable, hoping to sidestep the issue as gently as possible. I was therefore astonished to pick up the paper the following day and read a graphic description of the whole encounter, which left no doubt in the readers' minds regarding Ms Keane's views on the subject. These rumours, which have followed Andrew into adult life and caused him much distress, are obviously only rumours and as such must be viewed in that light.

Despite the talk about her marriage, Lilibet was besotted with her son. She breastfed Andrew, and while she was doing so, much concerned with domestic life, Hélène Cordet was preparing to branch out professionally. 'I wanted to get out of the restaurant business,' she says. 'I was looking around for something else to do when I went to a club in Paris with good music. That gave me the idea to simplify things with our restaurant, to open up a place with good music that served only simple food like hamburgers. So I opened up the Saddle Room Club, which became the first discothèque. It opened on 4 October 1961. It was also on Hamilton Place off Park Lane, near to the restaurant, which had been at number six. It was a great success.' By now the Night Club Queen of London, Hélène Cordet remained one of Philip's closest friends. But she was having to share him with other friends as well.

CHAPTER ELEVEN

A Royal Antidote

*I*ronically, the person responsible for enlarging Philip's circle was Princess Margaret. Although there would never be a true *rapprochement* between them after the Townsend débâcle, and to this day they cannot abide each other, royalty have to put a good face on private dislike. This they managed to do to the extent that Philip even gave Margaret away when she married Tony Armstrong-Jones at Westminster Abbey on 6 May 1960. Thereafter, the two couples mixed frequently and civilly. Tony Snowdon and Philip had little in common, for the former's interests lay in the arts while the latter's lay on the playing fields, but they had one invisible bond. Both had a feeling for the handicapped: Philip as a result of growing up with a deaf mother, and Snowdon because he still had a limp from a bout of polio as a youth.

By the mid-sixties, Margaret's marriage was heading towards shallow water. She and Lord Snowdon had a volatile union, which was characterized by rampant reconciliations following sudden eruptions. Margaret was very much in the Windsor mould, as motivated by her passionate nature as her father and sister had been. As a result, when the Snowdons were happy, there was no more delightful couple, and their apartment at Kensington Palace became one of the world's focal points for an intriguing and amusing collection of friends from the diffuse worlds of the arts, the entertainment industry and the aristocracy. The Margaret Set had always been glamorous; now it became renowned for how fascinating and scintillating it was. It consisted of such diverse couples as the Jocelyn Stevenses (he owned the magazine that is now called *Harper's & Queen*; she is a lady-in-waiting) and Peter Sellers and his actress wife Britt Ekland. The late comedian used to say that he and Margaret had had an affair, but the Sellers contribution to royal pleasures was altogether more significant. It was through him and his voluptuous Swedish wife that another show business couple, the director/

producer Bryan Forbes and his actress wife Nanette Newman, entered the life of Princess Margaret. And she introduced them to Prince Philip and the Queen.

Peter Sellers had been in love with the nineteen-year-old Nanette Newman before her marriage in 1958. The fact that he was years older than her was not the impediment, for Bryan Forbes was thirteen years her elder. But she loved Forbes, and when she married him she managed the imposs- ible, for she kept the notoriously touchy Sellers as a friend.

By the time Nanette Newman met Prince Philip at Princess Margaret's, she was approaching thirty and at the full flower of her beauty. She is also a charming and agreeable woman, with few pretensions, so it is hardly surprising that he was struck by her. Indeed, so beguiling did he find her that he became her most ardent fan.

It was a short step from introduction to inclusion. Mr and Mrs Bryan Forbes became a part of the royal circle, an honour that neither of them has ever sought to abuse. To become a royal confidant(e) is one of the highest accolades a royalist can achieve. All that is required is that the person concerned does not ever publicly speak about his or her relationship with the royals, nor does the spouse if he or she is married. Being a royal confidant(e) is not only a great privilege but also a great honour, and one moreover that protects the royal and non-royal parties. The structure, which has evolved over the years, means that each participant cannot embark upon behaviour that can be construed as dubious, unacceptable or dishonourable. Once a confidant(e), that person and the spouse remain members of the charmed inner circle even if the original nature of the relationship undergoes a change. This remains true as long as they remain discreet and do not let the Royal Family down in public, but if they do so, they are peremptorily dropped.

Over the years, Bryan Forbes and Nanette Newman have retained their hallowed positions. They have been entertained at Windsor Castle and Buckingham Palace, at the Royal Lodge in Windsor Great Park by Queen Elizabeth the Queen Mother and at Kensington Palace by Princess Margaret. Their behaviour throughout the various phases of their relationship with the royals has been impeccable, though Bryan Forbes, not being a member of the Establishment by birth, has never received the public acknowledgement that aristocrats in similar positions have done.

While Prince Philip was enjoying the fruit of an enlarged circle, and enjoying the pleasures of his show-business connection, Lilibet was preoc- cupied with her youngest child. Prince Edward was born on 10 March 1964, four years after Prince Andrew. The four years between the births of the two princes saw their mother's life assume the shape it would possess for many years to come. These were years of quiet change and settlement as well as of stability, for Lilibet was now one of the most experienced heads of state in the world. She was justly revered by British politicians for her perspicacity, her wit, her dedication and her conscientiousness. There was no more punctilious or co-operative constitutional monarch anywhere on earth, and she was beginning to acquire the reputation she now enjoys.

From the point of view of her personal reputation, Edward's birth slipped by unremarked, and he was generally acknowledged as being Prince Philip's son. This must have come as something as a relief to the Queen, for no one derives pleasure from having the paternity of their progeny picked over like the fleece of a shorn lamb.

This was a time of deep personal fulfilment for Lilibet. Not only did she now have another son to add to her brood, but she had also acquired a new confidant who would prove to be the closest friend she would have for the following eleven years. Patrick Terence William Span Plunket was the 7th Baron Plunket. As with Lord Carnarvon, formerly Porchester, Lilibet had known him for much of her life, although in this instance the childhood links were deeper and more far-reaching. Patrick's parents had been close friends of King George VI and Queen Elizabeth, and when they died tragically young in a plane crash in 1938, Bertie and Elizabeth treated the children more as wards than as the mere offspring of friends. The result was that Patrick and his two younger brothers were virtually raised at court, and the King made the young Lord Plunket, his equerry in 1948.

In 1954, Lilibet appointed this bachelor who was more like a cousin than a friend to the prestigious post of Deputy Master of Her Majesty's Household. As Patrick Plunket was only thirty years old, the appointment reflected the high regard his sovereign had for his ability and his integrity. It is a testament to his performance as well as to her judgement that he thereafter gave nothing but satisfaction in a post that called for tact and sensitivity. By 1955, Lilibet was so grateful for his help and efficiency that she rewarded him with an MVO, which is an honour within the personal gift of Her Majesty.

As a result of being Deputy Master of the Household, Patrick Plunket was in daily contact with Lilibet. He was privy to the innermost workings of the Household as well as to the gossip. Like everyone else, he knew all about the difficulties that had arisen in Lilibet and Philip's marriage.

For all Porchester and Lilibet had in common, the person to whom she was ultimately drawn was the sensitive and debonair Patrick Plunket. They shared many personality traits, including conscientiousness, dedication, tact and humour. Humour is a quality that can be especially endearing when everything else is right in a friendship, and so it proved in the case of Lilibet and Patrick. She had long been susceptible to the joys of laughter, and he possessed the wit of the Irish. As a result, they laughed and joked and worked their way through many a situation, and by 1963 Patrick Plunket had replaced Lord Porchester as Lilibet's closest male friend.

Philip's friendships did not prove to be as settled as Lilibet's, but this was hardly surprising, for he was an altogether more thrusting and restless personality. He liked new battlegrounds to conquer, new fields on which to roam, and these he found surprisingly at Buckingham Palace, where the monarchy was becoming a less hidebound and traditionalistic institution thanks to the influence Philip exerted upon Lilibet. It was he who suggested scrapping the presentation of debutantes in 1958, he who suggested making the monarchy more accessible to a broader spectrum of the population.

This was achieved in a multiplicity of ways, from expanding the scope of official functions so that they included more humble events to instituting luncheons and dinners at the Palace, during which he and the Queen entertained a broad selection of the nation's achievers. This reduced the traditional accessibility held by the aristocracy and the gentry, but it opened up social life at the Palace in a hitherto undreamed-of way. Anyone the Duke of Edinburgh or the Queen wished to meet, they did, simply by issuing them with an invitation. No one was ever blasé enough to refuse unless circumstances made it impossible to accept, and when Prince Charles reached manhood, he followed this precedent and invited, among others, sexy actresses whom he wished to meet such as Susan George to the Palace. Once more, no one refused.

This policy of enlarging the royal circle was only one of the means by which Philip made desirable friends. With or without the Queen, he was often attending film premières or galas, at which he encountered just about every major or second-league star there was in the world. While few of these did become confidantes, one who did was the beautiful Anglo-Indian actress Merle Oberon. By this time, she was retired and living in sumptuous style in Mexico with her Italian industrialist, multimillionaire husband Bruno Pagliai. She travelled a lot, as did Philip, and they had discreet rendezvous in London and in Europe. Merle Oberon, however, was too much of a snob to let a feather in her cap like Prince Philip go unacknowledged, so when he paid a visit to Mexico, she entertained him regally at her Acapulco home.

Someone else Philip had a lightweight friendship with was Mrs Ronald Ferguson. Ronald and Susie Ferguson's marriage had gone downhill by the time their younger daughter Sarah, born on 15 October 1959, was growing up. Philip and Ronald were both active on and off the polo field, and it was there that the former Susie Wright met the Duke of Edinburgh. Theirs was a warm and affectionate friendship, conducted with the finesse that their breeding had instilled in them. It was generally accepted by their circle for what it was, but it was not a relationship that could be transformed into anything substantial. Susie, however, did not want the icing on the cake. She wanted the cake, and not just any old cake either. It had to have all the right ingredients, for she was a fully blown romantic, and when she found what she was looking for with Hector Barrantes, a recently widowed polo-playing chum of her husband and Prince Philip, she left both her friend Philip and her husband Ronald behind.

Although diversion is the most accurate way of describing Philip's friendships with Merle Oberon and Susie Ferguson/Barrantes, there was nothing diverting about the friendship he enjoyed with the Countess of Westmoreland. Jane Westmoreland was the daughter of a baronet, Lieutenant-Colonel Sir Roland Lewis Findlay. Married since 1950 to David Anthony Thomas Fane, the 15th Earl of Westmoreland, she was well known in court circles, her husband having been a lord-in-waiting to the Queen since 1955. Tall, imposing and forceful, the attractive Jane Westmoreland became Prince Philip's closest lady friend, the feminine equivalent to Lilibet's confidant Patrick Plunket.

Lilibet heartily approved of Jane Westmoreland, to such an extent that she honoured Lord Westmoreland with a knighthood (KCVO) in 1970. Thereafter, the Westmorelands were one of the most sought-after couples in royal circles. Esteemed as a result of their personal and professional closeness to the sovereign and her consort, and for the impeccable and discreet way in which they conducted their gloriously honoured lives, they appeared wherever the Queen or the Duke of Edinburgh were. Royal favour, moreover, did not limit itself to the couple but shone upon their children as well. As they grew older, they too became fixtures on the royal scene. 'Burghie' (Lord) Burghersh, the heir, escorted Princess Anne, while Lady Camilla Fane was trotted out to accompany Prince Charles in the hope that something would 'take'.

For several years Philip and Lilibet led relatively settled lives. Gone were the days of bitterness and rancour. They had become one another's most ardent supporters. Each of them was only too happy to oblige the other by doing what they could to make life more agreeable. Then in 1975 tragedy struck. Patrick Plunket died on 28 May at the relatively young age of fifty-two. The Queen was in the process of conducting official business when her private secretary brought her the news. She promptly burst into tears and had to terminate her meeting. Grief-stricken, she personally made the arrangements for her beloved confidant to be buried in the Royal Family's private burial ground at Frogmore. There he now rests, his grave surmounted by an elegant tombstone, which Lilibet herself designed.

Patrick Plunket's younger brother succeeded to the title, but not to the position of Deputy Master of the Royal Household. As he has no son to inherit the barony either, one day the title will pass to his younger brother Shaun. Tall and willowy, with the fine nose, generous lips and slightly frizzy hair of Prince Edward, the Hon. Shaun Plunket is a delightful man. His personal life has also been intriguing. Married three times, his second wife Elizabeth was the mother of Antonia de Sancha, whose affair with the Arts Minister David Mellor precipitated his resignation from the Conservative government in 1992. His third wife is the former Andrea Reynolds, the exotic Hungarian-American who was the close friend of Claus von Bulow. She is a remarkable woman and has been credited with spearheading the appeal that resulted in the Danish aristocrat being retried and found not guilty of the attempted murder of his wife Sunny. Both the present and the future Lord Plunkets remain on excellent terms with the Queen and all the Royal Family.

Patrick Plunket's death left a void in Lilibet's life, which no other friend has replaced. At first, she was virtually inconsolable at the loss of such a perfect helpmeet and confidant, but, gradually, time healed her wounds, and she learnt to live without her closest friend. This task was made easier by the loving support of the Duke of Edinburgh as well as by the compassion and sympathy of her Racing Manager, Lord Porchester (as Lord Carnarvon still was).

Lord and Lady Westmoreland, meanwhile, continued to enjoy royal favour, and in 1978 he ceased being a lord-in-waiting and became Master of the Queen's Horse. Inevitably, time evokes changes in the lives of us all, and the Westmoreland friendship proved itself unexceptional in that regard. It was replaced by yet another friendship in which both sets of spouses got along famously. In fact, Commander Robert de Pass and his wife Philippa got along so well with both the Queen and the Duke of Edinburgh that he became one of Philip's closest friends, and she became one of Lilibet's ladies-in-waiting. They are a charming, good-looking couple, with a virtue too seldom seen in the British upper classes. Cosmopolitanism and sophistication exude from their every pore, for Robert de Pass is British only by birth and has kept up a strong connection with his roots. Born into one of the grandest and most ancient Jamaican families, his mother was from an equally grand and even richer family than his father. The de Mercado family were partners with the Lascelles family centuries before Viscount Lascelles married George V's daughter Princess Mary, and he was privy to a world in which everyone lived as only the Royal Family now exist in Britain.

Royal favour sat lightly upon Philippa and Robert de Pass. Neither one of them has ever been indiscreet or boastful about their association with the Royal Family, or about Philippa being Philip's confidante, and when time wrought its changes to the relationship, they continued to be numbered among the Queen and the Duke of Edinburgh's closest friends.

Meanwhile, however, Philip also formed a friendship with another actress. Anna Massey was the niece of the Hollywood star Raymond Massey and was once married to the actor Jeremy Brett. Although not glamorous or conventionally beautiful like Merle Oberon, she is endowed with so much charm and intelligence that she becomes more and more attractive the better you know her. Moreover, she has a fine, slender figure, and she is generally acknowledged to be one of Britain's finest actresses. Like the Westmoreland and de Pass friendships, this had the royal stamp of approval, as the King of Spain told one of his cousins when he came to Britain on a state visit. Anna Massey's presence as Queen Elizabeth I in the gala organized by Colonel Michael Parker to celebrate the fortieth anniversary of the Queen's accession also bears this out, though by 1992 she had long ceased to be Philip's confidante and was just another old friend.

By then, the mantle of royal confidante had swung serenely to the shoulders of a distant cousin of Prince Philip's. The Duchess of Abercorn is a stately, imposing 46 year old in the ancient tradition, when duchesses were grand, self-possessed and somewhat removed from ordinary mortals. Handsome rather than beautiful, this wife of the fifth Duke of Abercorn was born Alexandra Phillips and has always been called Sasha. Her family's links with Prince Philip and his family go back to before her birth. Sasha's father was Harold 'Bunny' Phillips, for many years the lover of Philip's aunt Edwina Mountbatten, who wanted a divorce to marry him. However, he ran off instead with a greater heiress, Sasha's mother 'Gina'.

Georgina Wernher was heiress to Luton Hoo, one of the great stately homes of England, as well as to her father Sir Harold Wernher's Electrolux and South African mining fortune. But what made the family grand, and has accounted for their social success down to this day, is Gina's mother's antecedents. Lady Zia Wernher was the daughter of the Grand Duke Michael of Russia by his morganatic wife, Countess Torby. As such, she was a relation of Prince Philip's grandmother, Queen Olga of Greece, who was born a Grand Duchess of Russia.

There was actually a stigma attached to Countess Torby, and it is arguable whether her descendants would have made the splendid matches they did, had the Russian monarchy not collapsed in 1917. The Tsar, Nicholas II, exiled his cousin Michael when he married the Countess, because 'the woman is a Negress and not fit to be part of the Imperial Family.' So the Grand Duke and his morganatic wife moved to England, where they were residing when the Revolution swept away Imperial Russia. As we know, one daughter Nadeja, known as Nada, married George, Marquis of Milford Haven. The other daughter, Zia, married Sir Harold Wernher.

Between them, Sir Harold and Lady Zia Wernher had enough of this world's blessings to live in regal style. His money and her royal blood were maximized to such effect that they were among the Queen and Prince Philip's closest friends. Each year the royal couple spent their wedding anniversary at Luton Hoo, a custom which continued even after Sir Harold and Lady Zia had died, and Sasha's brother Nicky had succeeded to the family fortune.

As a result of these family links, Prince Philip knew Sasha when she was a little girl. Little girls, however, grow up to become women, and fewer had greater appeal than Sasha. After marrying Jamie Abercorn and producing their heir, James Harold Charles, Marquis of Hamilton, on 19 August 1969, as well as the spare and a daughter, Sasha's marital duty was complete. She and Jamie Abercorn settled down to an equable and traditional marriage, and by the mid-seventies she had become the object of oil magnate Algy Cluff's veneration in a completely honourable way. For two years they became the closest of friends, and Algy was regularly entertained by the ducal couple.

Prince Philip has also had the benign hospitality of the Duke and his Duchess lavished upon him since the early 1980s, especially on the Bahamian island of Eleuthera, where they own a comfortable villa, Hamilton House. There they have informal pool-side parties, and so much a part of the family has Philip become, that he has been observed, drink in one hand, the other arm draped affectionately around the bikini-clad Sasha's shoulder, while they both talk to her banker husband, who is in the pool smiling approvingly. This is hospitality that Philip returns whenever he can, for instance in March 1993 when the Abercorns joined *Britannia* for a cruise. The one Abercorn residence Philip does not frequent regularly is Barons Court. Located at Omagh in County Tyrone, Northern Ireland, it is too near to the 'troubles' for any member of the Royal Family, especially a nephew of the assassinated Lord Mountbatten of Burma, to visit privately. Nevertheless, Philip would be very comfortable there. It has been done up, in true incestuous fashion, by David Hicks, the interior-designer husband of his first cousin, Lady Pamela Mountbatten.

Privacy, for people like the Abercorns, is no problem. They have enough money and access to sufficient landed estates to be able to conduct their lives in relative anonymity. Aside from their own homes, there are those of her sister Natalia, known universally as 'Tally'. She is married to the immensely wealthy Duke of Westminster, who owns the Grosvenor Estates. If they need other bolt-holes, they need look no further than within the family. Sasha and Tally's brother Nicky Phillips inherited Luton Hoo from their grandparents, and though he is now dead (he committed suicide in his BMW on the estate), his widow Lucy still lives there with their two children.

All in all, people like the Abercorns, the Queen and the Duke of Edinburgh lead charmed lives because they play by the old, aristocratic rules. Dignity, respect, discretion and civility are the touchstone of their existence, and certainly in the case of Philip and Lilibet it has brought them public privacy and private independence. Philip and Lilibet remain devoted to one another, though they continue to lead lives of quiet individuality. Only occasionally is this put to the test. For instance, in the latter years of the 1980s, when Prince Philip developed a friendship with Patricia Kluge, the wife of the billionaire John Kluge, former owner of the American entertainments complex, Metromedia.

Although the depth of the friendship has never been gauged outside the royal circle, Mrs Kluge's entertainment of Philip and of the Waleses caught the eyes of gossip columnists. There was constant attention drawn to the fact that the Queen refused to meet or greet the Baghdad-born socialite, but none of the columnists ever hit upon the reason for her exclusion. This was due to the fact that the Queen did not like an addition to her circle who is as rich and lavish as she is, but who had the additional disadvantage of an exotic past, which discomforted Her Majesty, upset her view of the world and therefore rendered the addition, in Her Majesty's eyes, unsuitable for any confidential relationship with any member of the Royal Family.

Over the years, Philip has perfected the art of ignoring the shackles with which not only the Palace clique but also the Queen once sought to chain him down. He often sleeps at his club in preference to retiring to his own bed at Buckingham Palace. White's is the premier gentleman's club in the country, and he can have absolute privacy whenever he wishes to entertain guests to dinner at their splendid quarters in St James's Street, which is handily near to Buckingham Palace. Or he can make off to the relative anonymity he enjoys as a guest of his confidante and distant cousin Sasha Abercorn.

Lilibet, meanwhile, remains true to a less gregarious nature. After a long day attending to matters of state, or meeting strangers, she enjoys the peace and quiet of a solitary supper on a tray in front of the television in her suite of rooms at Buckingham Palace. Then she turns in to bed, alone.

Theirs might not be an ideal marriage in terms of Hollywood-style romance, but it has been a durable, supportive union, in which both partners have contributed extensively to the good of the nation and humanity. More surely cannot be asked of any individual, nor of any couple.

CHAPTER TWELVE

A Reluctant Lothario

*T*he children of troubled marriages often grow up to have troubled unions themselves, and this has in fact proved to be the case with the Prince of Wales, the Duke of York and the Princess Royal.

A child's first experience of marriage is its parents'. As it grows up, it accepts as normal whatever its parents are doing. This establishes the boundaries of expectation as well as of acceptable behaviour. Because no child can escape the consequences of its environment, this first taste of marriage becomes crucial, especially in later life, when patterns are already established, and that first marital example comes back to haunt sometimes, like a ghost.

Royal children are undeniably different from ordinary children in social terms. From a very early age they are brought up as celebrities, expected to perform upon the world stage as mini-adults who bring credit to their parents, their royal house and the nation, with good manners and impeccable decorum. Beneath the formality, however, royal children remain subject to the same desires as ordinary children. They, too, want to be loved by their daddies and mummies. They, too, base themselves upon their parents and seek to emulate them, becoming little versions of the parent with whom they most closely identify.

Because royal children are reared by nannies while their busy parents are otherwise occupied on official duties, they usually have a far greater inclination to hero-worship their parents than would ordinary children. This was certainly true of Prince Charles when he was a little boy. He adored his father, who was always off doing something exciting or seeing somewhere exotic. To Charles, Philip was more than just a glorious action man. He was a figure of perfection, a standard to which he should aspire. Because he never spent enough time with his father to develop a critical perspective, Charles did not see Philip as a fallible human being, and later, when the scales fell from his eyes, the pendulum would swing too much in the opposite direction.

By then, however, the die was cast. Charles was very much his father's son in many respects, not the least of which were two important areas of his personality. Superficially, Charles grew into an athletic action man in the Philip mould. This helped to give him a taut physique, accounted in large measure for his appeal with women and made him into a dashing media star. But it was the deeper aspect of Charles's personality that had an even more lasting effect upon his intimate life. Through his father, he developed a traditional, almost chauvinistic approach to women.

The negative effects of this trait were exacerbated rather than alleviated by Lilibet's influence upon her eldest son. From his mother, Charles inherited a shyness and a reserve, which would rule out a whole segment of women to whom a more outgoing man might have been drawn. In the final stages of his evolution into manhood, this trait was so pronounced that it actually crippled the Prince of Wales. The point is best made by Michael Thornton, who was a friend and contemporary of Lucia Santa Cruz, Charles's first girlfriend, at King's College, University of London, where they both read history.

'Lucia told me that the Royal Family were so concerned by Charles's late development with the opposite sex that it was more or less arranged between the Queen and her great friend, Victor Santa Cruz, that Lucia should give him a "kick start" into the art of personal relations. She did so, but told me that she found it an extremely difficult task and that Charles was very far from being an accomplished lover.' This took place in the late sixties, when Charles was a student at Trinity College, Cambridge, and Lucia was working as a research assistant on the memoirs of the Master of Trinity College, Lord Butler.

Nor would Charles ever get over this tendency towards diffidence. At the height of his bachelor days in the 1970s when he was dating Fiona Watson, Lord Manton's buxom daughter, he stopped calling her because she was not able to accept one of his invitations.

Charles's great-aunt, Princess Alice, Duchess of Gloucester, opined that he is 'possibly too sensitive for his own good', and there is no doubt that he can function effectively with women only when the environment is nurturing. To a large extent, this is because he was an emotionally deprived child, though his own genetic structure cannot be discounted entirely. His mother and her father before her were both shy and diffident socially, though Lilibet and Bertie were spared the youthful cross of sexual diffidence thanks to their passionate, obsessive natures.

Why Charles was so diffident bears some inspection. His natural predilection was undoubtedly exaggerated by interrupted bonding with his mother. Even before George VI's death, Lilibet was sent away on tours, replacing her father, and, after 1952, her work schedule increased dramatically. Whether she was at home or away on tour, she had little time in which to see Charles and Anne. As a result of being the hardier of the two, Anne was less affected, though she too has never exhibited the warmth or affection that a well-loved child naturally possesses.

What also heightened Charles's tendency towards diffidence was the treatment handed out to him by his grandmother. Queen Elizabeth the Queen Mother was a magical figure in his life. In his words, 'She has been a source of infinite fun and love.' She was also, by all accounts, far more partial to Charles than to Anne or any of her subsequent grandchildren. Some people who know her well attribute this to the fact that Charles was born to be King, while others mark it down to an old-fashioned and flirtatious grandmother's prejudice towards the first-born grandson. Whatever the reason for her attitude, it had an effect. Thereafter, Charles was predisposed to strong, decisive and powerful women who would make a big deal of him while he sat back and basked in their adulation. He never became forceful like his father or obsessive like his mother. At the very best, he overcame his diffidence just enough to be tentative. This was hardly the stuff of which Lotharios could be made, but the position of the Prince of Wales has infinite appeal to most women who whirl in that orbit, and by the time Charles had left university, he was on his way to gaining a reputation as a ladies' man.

Charles's tragedy is that he missed the opportunity when the ideal woman entered his life. Camilla Shand was the girlfriend of his sister Anne's former boyfriend, Andrew Parker Bowles. She was sensible, down-to-earth, warm, witty and vivacious. Although not pretty or beautiful, she was so sexually appealing that men saw her as an attractive woman.

When Charles met Camilla, her opening remark captivated him. 'My great-grandmother was your great-great-grandfather's mistress. How about it?' How about it indeed. Charles and Camilla were soon out and about when he had time off from the navy, and before long they were deeply in love. Engaged upon a full-blown love affair, they were bound together as much by their passion as by their interests. Both of them possessed a profound love of the country, a lust for hunting and polo and compatible temperaments. They were a perfect match.

Traditional without being stuffy, Camilla had one goal in life: to get married. Charles, however, was only in his early twenties. His great-uncle, Lord Mountbatten, had recommended he sow his wild oats until about the age of thirty before considering settling down. Taking this advice to heart, he prevaricated.

True, Camilla possessed the ideal human qualities. True, she was from a good family. True, her great-grandmother Alice, the Hon. Mrs George Keppel, had been the mistress of his great-great-grandfather, King Edward VII. But her father was Major Bruce Shand, a mere wine merchant, though also a master of hounds, and her mother Rosalind was only the daughter of Lord Ashcombe of the Cubitt family, which had constructed Belgravia for the Duke of Westminster's Grosvenor Estate. Camilla's family, though good, was not especially grand or particularly ancient. Nor was she beautiful. Charles's age aside, there were other factors militating against so precipitate a step as an early marriage, for he had been reared to expect the best, and Camilla, while wonderful in many ways, simply was not the *crème de la crème*. And one didn't know what the future held in store in the way of more suitable girls for the eventual role of Queen.

While Charles dithered at sea, wondering whether it was better to wait and see if someone more appropriate would come along, or whether he should settle for Camilla, Andrew Parker Bowles took up the slack on land. A captain in the Household Cavalry, his social situation was akin to Camilla's. He, too, was from a good family. He, too, had connections far more illustrious than himself. The lookalike 11th Duke of Marlborough and Earl Cadogan were both cousins. Comfortably off rather than rich, entertaining, easy-going and sociable, the tall and handsome Andrew would give any woman lucky enough to become his wife a pleasant and agreeable life. So when he proposed, Camilla accepted.

In 1973, Camilla became Mrs Andrew Parker Bowles. She and Charles remained close friends, and when her son was born, he became godfather. Thereafter, while her position as *première confidante* to the Prince of Wales gained her more and more prestige, Camilla stood by quietly and saw a plethora of beauties come and go. Some, like Lady Jane Wellesley, Davina Sheffield and Anna Wallace were more serious romances than others, such as Jane Ward, Susan George or Sheila Ferguson.

One fancy who figured prominently between 1977 and 1978 was Lady Sarah Spencer, a highly strung, anorexic redhead whose nerve snapped under Charles's dilatory attentions. Ambitious, proud and competitive, Sarah hoped to knee-jerk Charles into paying more constant attention to her by announcing to the world that she was not in love with him and would only marry a man with whom she was in love. Her ploy misfired, for rather than rising to the challenge, Charles cut her out of his personal life, though they remained on sociable terms.

It was through the loquacious Sarah that Charles met the girl who would become his wife. The venue was Nobottle Field on the Althorp Estate in Northamptonshire. The time was November 1977. The occasion was a shooting weekend, which Sarah's father Earl Spencer was hosting for the royal beau. The sixteen-year-old Diana Spencer was up for the weekend from her boarding school, West Heath, near Sevenoaks in Kent, and the meeting was fleeting. Sarah introduced her baby sister to her boyfriend, he greeted her, and they passed on, leaving her to her own devices.

Later, at dinner, Charles was not seated anywhere near Diana, and afterwards, when the kind-hearted prince suggested out of his well-known sense of duty that the teenager show him the 115-foot picture gallery, the possessive Sarah interceded. Sparing her boyfriend the sort of chore he was always undertaking with the young or the disadvantaged, she offered to be his guide, and socialite Lady Freyberg, who was there for dinner, says, 'I was not aware of Prince Charles noticing Diana in any special way.'

Contrary to later claims, neither love nor perfunctory interest had struck. This was hardly surprising, considering that Diana was a podgy neophyte whose ambition was to marry Prince Andrew, and Charles was the most eligible bachelor in the world, with women everywhere throwing themselves at his feet. To say that she was the antithesis of everything he prized in womanhood would not be putting the case too strongly. His taste ran to sophisticated women of the world, and she was still a giggly if charming schoolgirl.

After that meeting, and Sarah Spencer's misguided attempt to bring Charles to heel, his path did not cross Diana's until January 1979. In the interval, the Spencers gained an invaluable foothold in the court when Diana's 21-year-old sister Jane married the Queen's Assistant Private Secretary in April 1978. The wedding was a grand affair at the Guards Chapel, followed by a reception at St James's Palace. After the honeymoon, the couple took up residence in Kensington Palace, which confirmed Diana's inclination towards grandeur. 'It would be wonderful to live at KP', she told a friend after visiting her sister in her new home. But Charles was not the man she had in mind when she had thoughts of nesting there. It was his brother Andrew with whom she pictured herself.

Diana's brother-in-law, 36-year-old Robert Fellowes, had spent most of his life in the bosom of the Royal Family. His father had been the Queen's Land Agent at Sandringham, and his courtly manners, while comforting to the sovereign, did not affect his ability. Renowned for the sharpness of his mind and the effectiveness of his tongue, he also possessed charm and the prim but sharp-witted Jane settled down to a life of marital bliss. This was enhanced in no small measure by the knowledge that she had bagged a social catch, for though Robert Fellowes was not a great aristocrat and would never inherit a stately home or a great estate, his position at court gave him social parity with many a duke and all marquises.

It was through Jane's husband that Diana next encountered the Prince of Wales. In January 1979 Robert Fellowes arranged for his two sisters-in-law to be asked to stay at Sandringham for a shooting weekend. Much has been written about the special closeness between Diana and her father, and it is therefore useful to note that on the very day she was hobnobbing with the royals at Sandringham, her father was being released from hospital in London, after a stay of several months due to a severe stroke.

After the weekend, Diana returned to London and the Vacani Dance

School, where she was training to become a dance teacher. Her head was a muddle of conflicting ideas. Charles had been kind to her the way he usually is with everyone whom he encounters. He is also surprisingly appealing in person, with the intense physicality of a sportsman. And, of course, he was the most eligible bachelor in the world.

From earliest childhood, Diana's family had raised her with the notion that one day she would marry Prince Andrew. This, of course, was ambition on their part rather than an actual arrangement struck with the Royal Family. Hundreds of other well-born young ladies had also been reared on a diet of royal hopes, but Diana, unlike most of her contemporaries, truly believed that this was her destiny. She kept a photograph of Prince Andrew in a locket, which she wore around her neck at all times, and also had a photograph of him beside her bed, even when she was at school. The prospect of switching allegiance from the second to the first son had definite appeal. However, one had to be careful, for no one got a second chance with the royals, as sister Sarah had learnt to her cost. Nevertheless, the seed had been planted in Diana's fertile imagination, and she told Simon Berry on a skiing trip, 'It would be nice if I could become a successful dancer – or the Princess of Wales.'

By the time Diana received her second royal invitation, in July 1979, she had given up all hope of becoming a dancer. She was too tall, and, rather than settle for a career as a dance teacher, she left the Vacani Dance School. This invitation also came once more as a result of her brother-in-law Robert Fellowes. This time, however, it was for Balmoral. The idea was not to cultivate Charles, but to keep Diana within scenting distance of Andrew, in the hope of sparking his interest. It was not a bad plan, for Diana had been a playmate of Andrew when they were both children at Sandringham, but Diana would give it a novel twist.

Once more, nothing much came of this visit. Diana got along well with Charles and Andrew, but there was no spark of interest from either prince, though they were both friendly to her and enjoyed her company. She returned to her new flat at Coleherne Court and her pleasant but lack-lustre life in London full of ambitions to be either the Princess of Wales or the Duchess of York, as everyone in royal circles knew Andrew's wife would become. She had a glimpse of royal life, with all the attendant luxury, attention, pomp and circumstance, and she liked what she saw. It was exciting, but, even more important, it made one feel important. It was stardom without having to dance, and the young and romantic Diana, whose daily diet included at least one Barbara Cartland romance, saw herself cast in the heady role of heroine.

A marriage with Charles, however, seemed very unlikely. He was considering the prospect of marrying his cousin the Hon. Amanda Knatch-bull. She was the granddaughter of his beloved 'honorary grandfather' Lord Mountbatten and the daughter of Lord and Lady Brabourne, the former

Lady Patricia Mountbatten. Even though they were not in love, it was Lord Mountbatten's dearest wish. Moreover, she would make a good Princess of Wales and eventual Queen, and they were deeply fond of each other. It might not be a Hollywood-style romance, but it would be a traditional royal union, characterized by affection and accommodation.

The month after Diana's visit to Balmoral, Lord Mountbatten was assassinated in Ireland. This not only scuppered any chance of Charles marrying Amanda Knatchbull but also plunged him into a deep depression. He had loved the older man. Isolated because of the eminence of his position, Charles had relied upon his Uncle Dickie for the loving ear and disinterested advice he could get from few people. He had long since given up trying to speak to his irascible father, who had no patience for his son's hypersensitivity or tendency towards prevarication.

Recovering from his depression, in November 1979 Charles began a torrid romance with Anna Wallace, a wealthy Scots landowner's beautiful daughter whom he met while hunting. She was called the Whiplash because of her fiery disposition, not because of her skill at wielding a whip, and this soon had scope for display. Charles was as dilatory as he had ever been, even though he fell passionately in love with Anna and proposed marriage to her. By this time, however, she was heartily sick of the cavalier way in which he often treated her, so she refused. In case Charles might tempt her to return to a relationship that she had decided would ultimately bring her little satisfaction, she hurriedly married the Hon. Johnny Hesketh.

Losing Anna Wallace plunged Charles into another deep depression, which gave Diana Spencer the toe-hold she might never otherwise have had. That was all she needed, for Diana Spencer was no ordinary nineteen year old. Beneath the gentle and demure exterior lay a strong and determined personality that possessed a whole array of contradictory traits, which she took care to conceal from even her nearest and dearest. Not everyone, however, was blind, and she left rather more of a trail than she intended to leave.

Top: The whole Royal Family putting on a happy and united face for the marriage of the Duke and Duchess of York.

Above: At polo, The Queen and her consort's body language give the lie to the rumour that they have absolutely nothing in common.

Below: The true royal angel: Prince Philip's mother, at the wedding of Princess Sophie of Greece and Prince Juan Carlos of Spain.

Right and Below: Windsor passion brooked no opposition, as both Elizabeth of Glamis (pictured at her marriage to Prince Albert, Duke of York, in 1923), and Wallis Warfield Simpson, (pictured after hers to the Duke of Windsor) could testify.

Above: A truly happy family:
King George VI, his enchanting
Queen Elizabeth, with their
beloved and protected
daughters, Princess Elizabeth
and Princess Margaret Rose.

Left: Still coquettish at ninety,
Queen Elizabeth The Queen
Mother enchants Luciano
Pavarotti.

Above: Security was a new sensation for the former Prince Philip of Greece, photographed with his ecstatic Duchess by his close friend Baron at the christening of his son, and England's heir, Charles.

Right: The Queen and the child of her heart: her second son, Prince Andrew.

Left: The Queen's racing manager and close friend, the Earl of Carnarvon, whose toothy grin and good looks enhance his considerable charms.

Above: Andrew was a one-off, the Prince who grew into a hunk with movie-star looks.

Left: Turfites together: The racing-mad Queen, her equally obsessed mother, and her racing manager, the Earl of Carnarvon.

Top: Despite having nothing in common, Prince Edward gets along better with Prince Philip than Charles or Andrew.

Above: Patrick Plunket, the Queen's childhood friend who grew up to become her most enduring companion and the Deputy Master of the Royal Household.

Above: Patrick, Lord Plunket's youngest brother, the Hon. Shaun Plunket, (with his wife, the former Andrea Reynolds), whose coincidental resemblance to Prince Edward is a taboo topic of conversation in royal circles.

Above: A besotted Princess Margaret inspects the troops attended by her love, Group Captain Peter Townsend (left) and Earl Mountbatten of Burma.

Top: The Windsor passion brought Margaret and her husband Antony Armstrong-Jones, later the Earl of Snowdon, together, but too many fireworks then blew them apart.

Left: Her marriage over in all but name, Princess Margaret sought comfort with her toyboy, the gentle and charming Roddy Llewellyn.

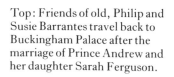

Top: Friends of old, Philip and
Susie Barrantes travel back to
Buckingham Palace after the
marriage of Prince Andrew and
her daughter Sarah Ferguson.

Above: The Duke of Edinburgh
has enjoyed friendships with
some of the world's most
beautiful women, including the
late screen goddess, Merle
Oberon.

Right: The Duchess of
Abercorn (right) had
supplanted the Countess of
Westmoreland (left) as the
Consort's closest female friend
by Royal Ascot 1982.

Top and above: The aristocracy and royalty have never been afraid of the odd swap, as Charles (photographed with Lady Sarah Spencer at the height of their romance) and Diana (who had expectations of marrying her childhood friend Andrew), proved.

Above: Charles would have
married the Duke of
Wellington's daughter, Lady
Jane Wellesley, but she did not
want a goldfish bowl existence.

Right: Had his mentor, Earl
Mountbatten of Burma, lived,
Charles most likely would have
married his great-uncle's
granddaughter, Amanda
Knatchbull.

Top and above: Diana never
warmed to either Dale or
Charles's other pre-marital
confidante, Camilla Parker-
Bowles, but she sensibly waited
until the engagement before
making a stand.

Left: Prior to his marriage, one
of Charles's closest confidantes
was his old girlfriend, Dale
'Kanga' Harper, later Lady
Tryon.

Right: Before the separation, Diana could count on the uncritical support of her sister, Lady Jane Fellowes (second from left with her mother, Frances Shand Kydd, far left in sarong), but since then, only her sister Lady Sarah McCorquodale has remained unequivocal.

Above: One of Diana's closest counsels before, during and after her separation was her brother Charles, photographed with her at the Birthright Ball.

Right: Diana personally orchestrated a public show of solidarity for her former flatmate Carolyn Bartholomew, though this created dissatisfaction at Buckingham Palace.

Top: James Hewitt taught Diana's sons to ride and gained his own private trophy as her most enduring confidant.

Above: James Gilbey was the beau from her single days who returned to provide a shoulder to cry on and a body to comment upon.

Left: The Princess of Wales alleviated her loneliness with an inappropriate companion, Private Detective Sergeant Barry Mannakee.

Right: In the early days of their marriage, Anne and Captain Phillips had many physical pursuits to bind them together.

Below: By the time Anne gave birth to Mark's son Peter, the marriage was under a strain.

Bottom: Happy at last, Mrs Timothy Laurence with her ideal companion at her second, history-making marriage in 1992.

Top: Sarah with the man who gave new meaning to the term, financial adviser, Johnny Bryan.

Above: Sarah Ferguson captured Prince Andrew's heart from the first playful punch, and he has remained her most ardent admirer since.

Left: The Queen liked the delightful American-born actress Koo Stark, but Andrew's romance with her became untenable when the tabloids labelled her a soft porn actress.

Top: Contrary to later claims, Diana was happy with an attentive Charles in the early days of their marriage.

Above: Charles's and Diana's marriage was dead by 1986. Thereafter, the only thing to flourish between them was hatred.

CHAPTER THIRTEEN

Opportunity Knocks

*D*iana Spencer was born into a family that was exceedingly ambitious. For two and a half centuries they had pursued royal associations with a tenacity that was exceptional for even the staunchest of courtly aristocrats. They happily accepted unofficial and illegitimate positions when their official and legitimate aspirations were spurned. Throughout that time, however, they had a goal: to marry into the Royal Family as soon as they could.

The first move towards making a Spencer into a royal took place over 250 years ago, when Sarah, Duchess of Marlborough, offered King George II's heir Frederick, Prince of Wales, the phenomenal sum of £100,000 (worth over a hundred times that amount today) to marry her favourite granddaughter, Lady Diana Spencer. The prime minister refused to consent to a union that was, for those days, an outrageous proposition, and Poor Fred, as the prince was called, was married off instead to Princess Augusta of Saxe-Coburg.

Thereafter, the Spencers helped to serve the Royal Family. Sometimes they did this officially, becoming equerries like Diana's father, who served King George VI, or ladies-in-waiting like Diana's grandmother Cynthia, Countess Spencer, who was a Lady of Queen Elizabeth's Bedchamber. Sometimes, however, their service assumed altogether different proportions, as was typified by the Duchess of Devonshire, born Lady Georgiana Spencer. She was a mistress of the Prince of Wales who became King George IV, and even went so far as to produce progeny in confirmation of that fact.

All this ambition and closeness to the seat of power reinforced the Spencers' strong belief in their own greatness. The result was that generation after generation of Spencers possessed forceful, domineering personalities, often masked by a thin veneer of charm. Diana's father Johnnie and her grandfather Black Jack were renowned for their vicious, violent tempers, although they could be as nice as they were nasty. Getting their own way was a family characteristic, as was spouse-battering, and by the time Diana's grandmother Cynthia died, death seemed a welcome relief to her after a lifetime of brutalization in the midst of splendour.

It is easy to get a distorted concept of your true worth if you are encircled by great people and great surroundings. This accounted in large measure for the Spencers' perceptions, for they were never as great as they thought they were. Nevertheless, they did possess one of the most beautiful houses in England. Althorp House was filled with the finest eighteenth-century furniture as well as a collection of pictures many museums would envy. It boasted twelve Van Dycks alone, aside from works by masters such as Andrea Sacchi, Reynolds, Kneller, Rubens and Gainsborough. Dating from 1508 and improved by Henry Holland, the Prince Regent's architect, it was situated in a 600-acre park on a 13,000-acre estate and had an airy and imposing façade of white brick.

The fortunes of the family, however, were due to undergo a downward spiral before Diana's marriage into the Royal Family restored their direction upwards. The first lurch in the wrong direction was after Diana's mother left her father. Frances Burke Roche was herself from a noble Irish family. Her mother Ruth, Lady Fermoy, was one of Queen Elizabeth the Queen Mother's closest friends as well as a Woman of her Bedchamber. Her half-American father Maurice, Lord Fermoy, had been one of King George VI's closest friends and was the heir to the Work stockbroking fortune.

Married at eighteen, Frances lived to regret making a match that seemed so advantageous at the time. Johnnie Spencer was not only a self-centred and self-satisfied bore, but he also had a violent temper. When Frances got tired of being a punching-bag, she looked for a way out of her misery. Peter Shand Kydd, heir to a wallpaper fortune, became her ticket out of the marriage and into notoriety, for Johnnie opposed Frances's application for divorce on the grounds of his cruelty and managed to present himself as the injured party. Frances thereafter was stuck with the label of adulteress, though in truth she had been more sinned against than sinner.

Diana was six years old when her mother left her father. Only weeks before, in September 1967, Sarah and Jane had been sent to boarding school. Frances took Diana and Charles, the youngest child and heir, to London, where they lived happily until she made the mistake of taking the children back to the family home for Christmas. Johnnie was not yet Earl Spencer, as Black Jack still flourished at Althorp House. Johnnie was Viscount Althorp, and the family home came through Frances. Park House, on the Sandringham Estate, was owned by the Queen and had actually been leased by Frances's father from King George V. Despite the amorality of seizing both a woman's family house and her children, Johnnie dug his heels in that Christmas. He refused to allow Frances to take the children back to London and made no move to vacate Park House.

Faced with an obdurate husband, Frances had no choice but to fight Johnnie through the courts. He won, not because right or even the law was on his side, but because he was an unscrupulous liar who used his social position against his wife. It is a sad reflection on some of the friends in their circle that they took Johnnie's side, not because he was the innocent party, but because Frances had run off with a mere wallpaper merchant while Johnnie was due to be the next Earl Spencer, would inherit Althorp House and had the toehold on the Sandringham Estate, having retained Park House.

Friends, however, were not the only ones who took Johnnie's side. Frances's mother Ruth, Lady Fermoy, took Johnnie's side in the custody battle. She even testified in his favour, adopting the high moral tone of her royal friend Queen Elizabeth the Queen Mother, who was well known for disapproving of divorce.

This débâcle marked Frances as well as her youngest daughter for life. Old enough to know what was going on but too young to be sent away to boarding school, Diana was torn between her parents and would later blame her father for much of the misery through which he put the whole family. When she got married, she would go through a standard process that all of us go through, which psychologists call the process of transference. At that juncture, she would transfer much of the unconscious hostility she felt for her father to her husband, with devastating results to Prince Charles, her marriage and her own life. For what this episode between Johnnie and Frances established in Diana was an emotional pattern of fear and expectancy where marriage was concerned, with propelled her into duplicating the very circumstances she dreaded.

Despite the underlying tragedy of a young woman destroying her own marriage due to the childhood trauma of her parents' divorce, Diana had one advantage when her subconscious triggered off the very pattern of behaviour that had made such a deep impression upon her psyche. Her parents' battles had been uncivilized. But the differences between the Prince of Wales's parents had been resolved with civility and decency. This gave her an unwitting advantage over Charles, for Diana had learnt how to fight from her father. And when her own marriage hit the rocks, she applied the lessons he had taught her as ruthlessly as he had done.

Like many divorced parents, Johnnie and Frances embarked upon a contest for their children's affections. If parents wish to rear happy, well-adjusted adults, love without discipline is meaningless, for children need to know that there are boundaries beyond which they cannot stray. For the Spencer children, however, there was little forbidden territory beyond good manners. As long as they said please and thank you, they could do almost as they chose. And they did.

Sarah became a tearaway who brought her horse into the drawing-room for tea, drank to excess and was expelled from West Heath, the boarding school to which she, Jane and eventually Diana were sent. Jane was quieter, but she, too, was not above ruthless execution of her will, as she showed by refusing to speak to her stepmother Raine, or in any other way acknowledge her existence, for the first two years after her father's remarriage in July 1976. Diana, for her part, started off as an overt rebel who threw one nanny's clothes away and locked another in the lavatory. By nature, however, Diana was not a leader. She was more a people-pleaser whose hostility and aggression lurked beneath an agreeable façade.

Learning the value of presenting a sweet and innocent face to the world, Diana used the lesson to especial advantage when she was sent away to boarding school, to avoid whatever rules she did not wish to abide by. She had a compulsion for cleanliness and not only snuck a shower every day, despite being allowed to do so only every other day, but also washed her hair daily, though this was only allowed once a week. The fact that she successfully got away with breaking a rule she regarded as ludicrous for several years shows that she possessed dexterity from an early age and was far cleverer at outwitting the powers-that-be than they thought.

At school Diana did not like academic studies. On the other hand, she loved to read fiction, especially Barbara Cartland romances. Her school work suffered when every term she took back scores of that author's books, adding them to an already vast pool, which then circulated among other romantic novel aficionados throughout the term. She read these books late into the night after lights out with the help of a torch, or hid them behind her school books during study periods, when she was meant to be doing her homework. The outcome was that she was always at or dismally near the bottom of her class, and when the time came to take her 'O'-level examinations, Diana failed every subject.

Lack of parental discipline allied to a wilful disposition resulted in more than academic failure, however. Diana was already somewhat spoilt, and while she could be very sweet and charming and had a gentle manner, she was also renowned at school for her temper and self-indulgence. She found it hard to deny herself anything, even food, and used to start the day with three, four or sometimes even five helpings of cereal at breakfast. Luckily for her, she was intensely athletic and very competitive, so she worked off the food she ate, playing games such as tennis and hockey or swimming. She also spent hour after hour perfecting her dive, so that she would become diving champion of the school, and while this showed application and adherence to goals, it was also an early indication of a rather obsessive personality.

After leaving West Heath at the age of sixteen, Diana attended a finishing school, the Institut Alpin Videmanette near Gstaad, Switzerland, for one term in early 1978. That Easter, she started living in London, first at her mother's home, then at her own flat in Coleherne Court, Earl's Court, which was bought for her upon her eighteenth birthday with money inherited from her American great-grandmother Fanny Work.

Diana had the typically full social and personal life that upper-class girls in the pre-AIDS late seventies had. Contrary to later claims, there was a wealth of boyfriends, including Rory Scott, James Gilbey, Adam Russell and the Hon. George Plumptre, with whom she dined, danced and went away for skiing trips and country-house weekends. Diana was very much the popular girl-about-town. Diana the Saint had not been born yet.

According to her version of events Diana's first, tentative step towards rebirth as a pure and regal saint took place at Petworth in July 1980 at the West Sussex home of Commander Robert de Pass and his wife Philippa. Diana was staying for the weekend as a guest of their son Philip, with whom she had become friendly as a result of her brother-in-law's position at the Palace. It would be fair to say that she was now seriously cultivating anyone who could keep her within reasonable proximity of either the Prince of Wales or Prince Andrew, for Diana, like Camilla Parker Bowles and her sister Jane before her, was a traditional girl who wanted nothing more out of life than a wedding ring and the requisite two or three babies. But she wanted this from a prince if she could get one.

On the Sunday, the houseparty went, as it often did, to watch the family's good friend the Prince of Wales play polo at Cowdray Park with his then team, Les Diables Bleux. After the game, Charles returned to the de Pass house for a barbecue. It was no secret in royal circles that he was in a state of despondency due to the break-up of his relationship with Anna Wallace, coming so close after his beloved 'honorary grandfather's' assassination.

During dinner, Diana went and sat next to Charles on a bale of hay. Keen to convey a good impression and make some impact on the man she had ambitions to marry, she raised the subject of Lord Mountbatten's assassination. This was a shrewd move, which could hardly pass unnoticed, for Diana already knew the power that sympathy has over the vulnerable. Although only nineteen, she was proficient at dealing with children, old people and the infirm as a result of compulsory visits to them during her years at West Heath, where community work was on the curriculum. Indeed, so skilled was she in this field that it brought her the only accolade she ever received at school, the Leggatt Cup for Helpfulness. So, according to a friend of Charles, keen to set the record straight, she said to him, 'When I saw you walking up the aisle at Westminster Abbey, I thought it was the most tragic thing I had ever seen. You looked so desolate and alone it made my heart bleed for you. I thought what you need is someone to understand you, to be there for you, to take care of you.'

According to Diana, it was at that moment that her relationship with the Prince of Wales changed from a distant friendship into something more substantial. She claims and has done for some time that her sympathy so engaged him and inflamed him with ardour that he thereafter pursued a pure and reluctant Diana until he wore down her resistance.

Aside from the unlikelihood of any depressed person casting off their shadows so suddenly and for such little reason, this picture of the prince is not one that he or anyone who knows him recognizes. There is his well-known diffidence to consider. There is also the anomaly of Diana's own contradictory claims. On the one hand, she now wishes the world to believe that her sympathetic nature was what motivated the prince to behave against character, while on the other hand she claims that she 'had no interest in him from the first time I met him in Nobottle Field. I thought he was the saddest man I ever saw.' Why any woman who had no interest in a man would deliberately go out of her way to cater to the very quality she found unappealing is the one question she has never addressed, but it does reveal one of the methods she used to capture his interest.

Although Diana's version of events has scrambled the positions of chaser and chased, it does possess a kernel of truth. She undeniably used Charles's need for empathy and understanding to win his affection and regard. Despite his reputation as a lady killer with a history of derring-do, Action Man was still as hypersensitive as the little boy who had hungered for his mother's attention and his father's approval, and whose happiest times had been spent in the loving aura of his enchanting, infinitely sympathetic but stern grandmother Queen Elizabeth the Queen Mother. He still wanted to lead his life with people who shared his values and temperament and was still looking for the one woman who could be helpmate, companion, best friend and bedmate. With Charles, passion was triggered more by a compatible personality than by good looks, though he was not blind to the charms of feminine flesh either.

Since childhood, Diana had had the ability to court affection to a remarkable degree. She was a people-pleaser, and, like most of her kind, could be a chameleon, instantly empathizing partly out of genuine feelings for others and partly to earn her the regard she sought. Where she differed from the average charmer, as the world would soon learn, was in the remarkable degree of her aptitude.

This should not have been as surprising as it was, for Diana was undeniably bright, without being intellectual. Moreover, her brightness was typical of both sides of her family. Her brother and three sisters had excelled academically, as had her mother, and her grandfather Black Jack's intellectual prowess was much admired by his peers. She would therefore have had to be a complete mutant not to have inherited at least some of the family brains. In fact, Diana possessed intelligence as well as the personal qualities of the Spencer and Burke Roche families. Particularly, she was an amalgam of her two sisters, and Jane's determination and level-headedness allied to Sarah's charm and good looks would help her to succeed with the Prince of Wales where the more straightforward and overtly highly strung Sarah had failed.

•   •   •

Contrary to Diana's version of events, Charles did not immediately begin to hound her after the encounter on the hay bale at Robert and Philippa de Pass's house. The resourceful Diana, however, asked her childhood friend Lady Sarah Armstrong-Jones to get her invited on to the royal yacht *Britannia* during Cowes Week. Using the sea as an excuse to exhibit her ample physical charms, Diana was forever diving in the Prince of Wales's direction without effect. Though Charles may or may not have noticed, he nevertheless took care to be as pleasant and polite to his young cousin's friend as he invariably was with any of the Royal Family's guests.

By this time, the romantic Diana had convinced herself that she was in love with Charles. Undeniably, she was in love with love and with the Prince of Wales, though not necessarily with Charles the man. Stephen Barry, Charles's valet, was only one member of the Household who was convinced that Diana would never have been drawn to Charles Windsor had he not also been the Prince of Wales. This fatal blurring of lines would cost her and the British monarchy dear, but first all she wanted was to charm him into her arms.

Towards this objective Diana continued to manoeuvre, once more benefiting from her family's courtly connections to advance her cause. This time, it was her grandmother Ruth, Lady Fermoy, who managed to secure the invitation for her. So in September she headed for Birkhall, the Queen Mother's house on the Balmoral Estate, where she once more pulled out all the stops in trying to entice Charles. She followed him around, laughing at all his jokes, evincing interest in all his interests, displaying a shared love for the countryside and all its pursuits. She threw caution to the winds, shrewdly realizing that a kindly and sensitive man will not spurn open adoration.

As, indeed, Charles did not. He was touched, the members of the royal party charmed, and all but the Queen openly approving of the romantic sparks that now began flying through the air. Only too soon, these ignited into a fire of passion, for Charles, though a ditherer in matters of the heart, was also a Windsor, and once Diana had aroused physical desire in him, she had him hooked. Thereafter, she did turn the tables on him, and the chaser did become the chased, but her method was not purely the nobility of her sentiment.

For the next six months, Charles pursued Diana as he had pursued countless women before her. He blew hot and cold. He dithered. For instance, when he went away to India, he did not rush back home, as a man in love would have done. Instead, when the official part of the visit was over, he took a trek through the Himalayas. To this and every other set-back, such as Charles not telephoning her immediately upon his return, Diana reacted with exemplary patience. She did not lose her temper with the prevaricating prince the way Anna Wallace had done. Instead, she left her telephone off the hook. This sparked his interest even further, for Charles, like many other men, became enchanted by what threatened to elude him.

During this period, Diana conducted herself with extraordinary presence of mind. The press had turned its beady eye on to her, making her daily attempts to drive from her flat at Coleherne Court to work at St George's Square, Pimlico (a distance of about three miles), into a latter-day version of running the gauntlet.

Diana behaved towards the press with as much circumspection and finesse as she did with Charles. Striking the right note between friendliness and aloofness, she took care not to shoot off her mouth the way her sister Sarah had done, and on the one occasion that she did, when she confessed to Roger Taverner of the Press Association that her real ambition was to get married, Diana promptly and brazenly denied her admission. This was the first glimpse the world would see of her gift for presenting herself simply as the injured party when she was partly the guilty one.

Conducting a romance in the full glare of the public eye is not an easy task, but Charles knew how to work his way around the limitations imposed with skilful employment of the discreet encounter. He had bought Highgrove House in Tetbury, Gloucestershire, from Viscount and Viscountess Macmillan of Ovenden that August, and this became a convenient meeting place, especially as the press knew it was not furnished and therefore concluded it would not be fit for occupancy. They were wrong, of course, as it had all the furniture any courting couple needed: a bed.

Stephen Barry used to drive Diana there for overnight assignations. These invariably ended at dawn, when the valet would drive her back to her flat, from which she would set out for work as if she had been there all night. Charles also had an obliging network of friends and relations, such as Queen Elizabeth the Queen Mother, who lent him their houses for visits of a few days' duration with Diana.

As Charles got to know Diana better, he grew fonder and fonder of her. Idealistic rather than romantic, he could scarcely believe his luck in having finally found an almost perfect girl. Diana was everything he had ever wanted, aside from her inability to engage in deep discourse. She was warm, loving and sensitive. She was passionate, fun-loving and entertaining. She loved the country the way he did. She wanted a harmonious family life the way he did. She was soft and kind and gentle, patient and easy-going rather than pushy or strident the way some of his previous girlfriends had been. She allowed him to be himself. She did not try to change or improve him, the way Anna Wallace had done, nor did she shy away from the press attention, the way Lady Jane Wellesley had done. All in all, he could hardly believe he had found such a marvel. Gradually, it became apparent that he had, for she did not change the better he got to know her. So he decided that she was genuine and sincere and allowed himself to fall in love with her.

Charles's thoughts now turned to marriage. He knew Diana wanted marriage. So, too, did the country. And his father. The only two people who were not enthusiastic were the Queen and his Private Secretary, the Hon. Edward Adeane. Lilibet thought Charles and Diana did not have enough in common to sustain a lifelong relationship. She also felt that Diana did not have the right character for the job as Princess of Wales. 'She has never stuck to anything she has ever undertaken,' she told her heir, rightly warning against the possibility of ultimate failure and Diana's flight when things did not turn out the way she wanted. Edward Adeane also had reservations about Diana's character, though neither Charles's mother nor his private secretary belaboured their opposition.

In January 1981, Charles went skiing in Switzerland. He returned to London on 2 February. This time he promptly got in touch with Diana and asked her to dinner à deux at the Palace. He proposed, she accepted, and the die was cast for one of royalty's greatest marital fiascos since the misalliance between Princess Caroline of Brunswick and the eighteenth-century Prince of Wales who fathered Lady Georgiana Spencer's bastard and later became King George IV.

On 24 February 1981, Buckingham Palace announced the engagement of the Prince of Wales and Lady Diana Spencer. That evening Diana did not sleep at Coleherne Court, but at Clarence House, where it is popularly believed she then resided until her marriage. This, in fact, is nothing more than a diplomatic red herring, for after sleeping under the Queen Mother's protection for one night, she moved over to Buckingham Palace to a suite of rooms with easy access to Prince Charles's.

The good times, such as they had been, were about to end for Diana. This was not because Charles was the callous and heartless cad that he has subsequently been portrayed as being, or because he was still as close to Camilla Parker Bowles as he had once been. He and Camilla were nothing more than innocent friends at that point, and Charles was deeply committed to making his marriage work. But Diana was constitutionally incapable of making a positive adjustment to her new circumstances. This, of course, is deserving of sympathy and not a matter for condemnation, but it nevertheless caused problems, which reverberated within the Royal Family and still have the potential to affect their standing for many years to come.

The trouble began right after Charles and Diana gave their first media interview as a couple. They went inside, turned on the television to watch themselves, and Diana froze with horror. 'My God, I look so fat,' she commented.

It is true that the blue Cojana suit, which she had selected from Harrods with her mother's help, made her look podgy and squat. This was quite an accomplishment considering that she was six feet tall in her two-inch heels, but Charles said, 'It's just the television. Don't worry about it. You look fine.'

Had that been the end of the matter, the whole course of the recent history of the monarchy might have been different. But it was not. The following morning's newspapers made Diana look as chubby and squat as the television cameras had done. Then and there, she decided that she was going on a diet. 'I'm not walking up the aisle waddling like a duck,' she declared, displaying the wit for which she had always been known around dinner tables.

Because every man knows that many brides go on diets to lose a few pounds before their big day, Charles was not worried. Had he known what time has revealed, however, he would have climbed the walls with anxiety. Always prone to excess, Diana promptly embarked upon a starvation diet, which she fell off after three days. Ravenously hungry, but intending only to pick when lunch was put before her, she polished off the lot. Diana had always had a voracious appetite, and she was still hungry, so excusing herself from the work she was doing in the office at the time, writing thank-you notes, she went across the road and bought some bars of chocolate from the candy and souvenir shop opposite the side entrance at Buckingham Palace. According to her version of events, recounted to the person with whom she was working at the time, she took these back to her room, ate one, then another, then another, until disgust got the better of her. Resolved that this lapse would not damage her goal, she went to the bathroom, bent over the lavatory bowl and made herself sick.

Although she did not realize it, Diana had taken the first step down the destructive road to bulimia. Initially, her novel method of dieting did not seem to be a problem. She lost the weight she wanted to shed, while still managing to satisfy her more uncontrollable bouts of hunger. She was even quite funny about it, as proved by the occasion when a member of her future husband's staff stumbled in as she was getting up from the lavatory bowl. 'I'm fine. It's nothing,' she said reassuringly. 'I've discovered this great way of dieting. Eat all you want, then aagh,' she continued descriptively, opening her mouth and pointing her finger downwards.

Between the announcement of the engagement in February and the wedding ceremony in July, Diana was kept busy writing letters of thanks for presents and good wishes, selecting her trousseau, updating her wardrobe and learning to behave as a royal.

Oliver Everett, a high-flying diplomat who had been once seconded from the Foreign Office to become the Prince of Wales's assistant private secretary for the standard two-year contract, was then recalled from his posting in Madrid and offered by Charles a lifetime sinecure as private secretary to the future Princess of Wales and comptroller to her Household. He was specifically targeted because Charles knew he was young, easy-going and personable as well as efficient and capable. Charles was sensitive to the fact that Diana was young and inexperienced, and that she must be surrounded by compatible and understanding staff. For that very reason, Lady Susan Hussey, who was a lady-in-waiting to the Queen and a close friend of hers as well as of Charles's, was also delegated to put Diana through her paces so that the whole business of public appearances and dealing with the press would not be daunting.

Between them, Oliver Everett and Susan Hussey gave Diana as much valuable instruction as any other royal bride has ever received. She was a willing and co-operative student in every regard bar one. She managed to avoid looking at any of the recommended reading matter, which included books on the constitution and biographies of previous royals.

It was easy to let that slip, for she was busy, though not so busy that she did not invite her former dance teacher and accompanist from West Heath, Lily Snipp and Wendy Vickers, to give her dance lessons at the Palace. Diana loved to dance, and she remained as athletic as ever, but gone were the days when she could take exercise classes at Covent Garden. She therefore spent hour after hour perfecting her tap routine in the ballroom at Buckingham Palace, went for long swims in the pool downstairs and roller-skated up and down the passages, a Sony Walkman playing her favourite pop music clamped to her ear.

What with the physical exertion and her bulimic method of dieting, the weight just fell off Diana. She also became isolated from her old friends, as Kinty Waite Walker from Young England Kindergarten, where Diana had worked as a childminder prior to the engagement, observed. Diana, however, was happy. With each passing day, Charles became more and more besotted with her. He could hardly believe his luck in having met such an agreeable companion. Aside from being beautiful on the inside, she was also beautiful on the outside. He had no clue about her incipient problems with bulimia or about the underlying emotional disturbances from childhood, which would be exaggerated once her novel dietary method took hold, precipitating an explosion that would rend asunder first their relationship, then the monarchy itself.

As the date of the wedding approached, and Charles and Diana melded more and more into what he thought was a cohesive unit, the first signs that all was not well with Diana became evident. On one occasion when he had to carry out an official engagement, she burst into tears when they were saying goodbye. This seemed touching rather than worrisome, however, and the incident went unnoticed as nothing but an indication of a young girl so in love with her prospective bridegroom that she did not wish to be apart from him for even a moment. Then just a few days before the wedding, she was watching Charles play polo when she burst into tears again. This was marked down to the strain of the impending nuptials, but hindsight reveals that these were early warning signals that Diana's bulimic method of dieting was starting to make inroads into her health.

According to psychologist Dr Gloria Litman, bulimia nervosa affects sufferers physically and emotionally. The act of vomiting rids the body of essential minerals and nutrients. As the bulimia nervosa takes hold, the sufferer induces the vomiting more and more constantly. This is because they become hooked on the chemicals that the body only releases after vomiting has taken place. These give a high, and this spiral of frequent vomiting has the effect of sending the system into overdrive, for the body embarks upon the futile task of achieving a pH balance, which the next bout of vomiting will thwart. Physical chaos induces emotional chaos, which exacerbates the underlying emotional disturbance that caused the eating disorder in the first place, and, as the condition takes hold, the bulimic becomes more and more emotional, prone to mood swings and subject to anxiety and depression. If the condition persists, as it usually does, over a period of time the bulimic becomes increasingly irrational, unbalanced both physically and emotionally, destroying first their relationships, then their health and, if left untreated, finally their lives.

Diana was not the only member of her family to suffer from an eating disorder. Her sister Sarah had been anorexic during the late seventies, including the period when she was dating the Prince of Wales. She and Diana exhibited many of the same personality traits, which underlay their illnesses. They were both intensely competitive, vain, determined, highly strung, self-willed and insecure. Sarah, however, was more open to the opinions of others than Diana, so when friends sought to help her with her problem (the Prince of Wales included), she allowed them to do so, instead of denying it, as Diana did for years.

Nor were Diana and Sarah the only members of their family to suffer from emotional disorders. Their father had had a serious drinking problem towards the end of his marriage to their mother. His monumental rages and violence were also indicative of a deeply disturbed personality, one which he shared with his equally vicious and violent father, Black Jack. And their mother's side of the family was no monument to emotional balance either. Frances's brother Edmund, who was the current Lord Fermoy, suffered from manic depression and would blow his brains out with a shotgun in 1984.

It says a lot for the criterion by which the Royal Family approve of potential spouses for their progeny that they allowed the marriage to take place at all. Such an unhappy emotional history had to indicate a genetic predisposition to imbalance, which did not bode well for the future. Happy marriages, however, had never been the primary goal of royal marriages. The aim was to produce offspring of eminent lineage. And if their marriages did not bring lasting personal satisfaction, as they seldom did, that did not matter particularly either. Not when both partners could do as they pleased, as long as they did so with discretion and presented a united façade to the world at large.

Contrary to royalty's traditionally pragmatic attitude towards marriage, Charles did have high expectations for his own. He genuinely believed he had found his body and soul mate. For someone who was as emotionally deprived as he had been as a child, the chance to create a family life with all he had once lacked was of crucial importance.

The care Charles took with the arrangements for the wedding was indicative of his feelings. It was he who selected the location, St Paul's Cathedral, contrary to royal tradition, which favoured Westminster Abbey. It was he who chose the hymns and music. It was he who approached the Director of the Royal College of Music, Sir David Willcocks, and arranged for three orchestras to take part in a feast to the soul and the senses. There was not one detail of the whole day to which the prince was not privy. He wanted a magical and moving occasion to celebrate the most important day of his adult life.

Charles achieved it, too. On 29 July 1981, hundreds of millions of people all over the world agreed that the wedding was the most magnificent event in living memory. Moreover, it was as moving as it was beautiful.

The bride also made a huge impression upon her worldwide audience. She looked gorgeous, like a fairy princess brought to life. Her face was incandescent, her figure sylphlike, her tiara spectacular, her wedding dress romantic. When Diana walked down the aisle to become the Princess of Wales, fairy tales did seem capable of coming true. She looked so beautiful, so pure, so radiant, so in love. She seemed so sincere, so unassuming, so natural. Charles was as convinced as the hundreds of millions of viewers that he was getting himself a bride in a million. They were all right, of course. They simply did not know that there was a twist to the tale.

CHAPTER FOURTEEN

A Bed of Roses

The marriage began well enough.

After the wedding ceremony, there followed a wedding breakfast at Buckingham Palace for 118 guests who included the Royal Family, foreign royals such as Princess Grace of Monaco, close personal friends, Royal Household staff and, more particularly, all the members of the Prince and new Princess of Wales's staff. Significantly, neither Andrew and Camilla Parker Bowles nor Anthony and Dale Tryon were at the Palace. Nor was Barbara Cartland, Diana's step-grandmother-in-law and the donor to her of countless romantic novels over the years.

In her first show of strength and jealousy, Diana had put her foot down and crossed all them off the guest list. 'I'm not having that woman at my wedding,' she informed Michael Colbourne, a member of the Royal Household, in the presence of others of the Prince of Wales's staff when she came to Barbara Cartland's name. 'I don't intend to have her upstage me.' She remained unmoved by the embarrassment she would cause someone who had only ever showed her kindness, when the news got out. Not even the intercession of Lord Mountbatten's former Private Secretary, John Barratt, could budge the stubborn and competitive Diana, and when the snub became public, it did indeed create a fuss.

Charles kept out of that needless battle so that he could fight effectively the one that mattered to him. When Diana had come to the names of Charles's two closest women friends and their husbands, her face had contorted, and she had silently crossed them out. Charles, however, was not about to let her publicly humiliate people who had only ever shown him loyalty and supportiveness. He knew that Diana was jealous of Camilla and Dale because he had foolhardily answered questions about women who had once mattered to him in a moment of intimate frankness. Even though he assured her that these

136

relationships had undergone a metamorphosis from the moment he realized he loved her, Diana could not forgive either of them for having been involved previously with Charles.

To Charles this was ridiculous. Diana was inviting men with whom she had conducted full relationships, so why should there be one set of rules for her and another for him? He reinstated the Parker Bowleses and the Tryons on to the list, though, in a spirit of compromise, he did relent on having them at the sanctum sanctorum. They were only asked to St Paul's, not to Buckingham Palace. It was a slight, but only a minor one, and while the press were not blind to it and did make the expected comments, honour had been maintained all round, and everyone could claim to be happy.

Diana's power plays before the wedding did not diminish their joy on the big day itself. After it was over, the royal couple headed by train for Broadlands, the late Lord Mountbatten's home in Hampshire. The Queen and the Duke of Edinburgh had also spent the first part of their honeymoon there, and, ever keen to keep up agreeable royal traditions, Charles also began his marriage there. Both he and Diana were exhausted by the events leading up to the wedding, however, so for the two days of their stay, when they were not making love, she rested while he fished on the River Test.

Leaving Broadlands, they flew to Gibraltar, where the royal yacht *Britannia* awaited them for a cruise of the Mediterranean. This was meant to be the high point of their honeymoon, but it also proved to be the apex of their marriage. They saw an array of exotic places including the Algerian coast, Crete and other Greek islands such as Santorini, as well as Sicily and Tunisia. When they were not ensconced in the new double bed in their cabin, they lounged sybaritically in the sun. Sometimes this was on deck, sometimes on a deserted beach, which they had selected for an impromptu picnic. Always it was sensual, and there was no doubt to every onlooker that Charles and Diana, who could not keep their hands off one another, were deeply in love.

Trouble, however, was around the corner. As the yacht steamed towards the Red Sea, the prince and princess broke their journey in Port Said. There they were joined for dinner by the President of Egypt and Madame Sadat. Throughout the evening, the only contribution the normally witty Diana could make to the conversation was to repeat, over and over again, how much she liked mangoes. Charles marked this down to Diana's youth and made a note to ask her private secretary, Oliver Everett, to suggest reading material that would expand her mind and enable her to conduct informed conversations with the world leaders she would thereafter be encountering. However, in keeping with the royal tradition of not barking when you have a dog to do so for you, Charles himself said nothing to Diana. This was just as well, for she had never been known to take kindly to criticism of even the most constructive variety, and it would undoubtedly have blighted what remained of a blissful time.

The first stage of the honeymoon was nevertheless coming to an end.

Charles and Diana were due to fly back to Scotland on an RAF VC10. As Anwar and Jehan Sadat waved goodbye to them from Murghada military airfield, Charles and Diana would have been surprised if someone had told them that the remainder of their time together would be one long trip downhill. And they had only been married a couple of weeks.

The trouble began in earnest as soon as the royal couple arrived in Scotland. Diana immediately began agitating for a change in their schedule. She, who had claimed previously that she loved country life and could well understand why Charles preferred Balmoral to any other place on earth, now whined that she was bored, stuck in the middle of nowhere. This was quite a volte-face and a disturbing and important one to boot, for it went right to the heart of Charles's favoured lifestyle.

He had married Diana believing that they both wanted the same way of life, yet here she was, less than a month after the wedding, telling him that she did not. Even worse, she was not content to respect his wishes and co-exist in a spirit of accommodation. She wanted him to change to suit her and began exerting pressure upon him to give way to her. No amount of discussion, no amount of appealing to reason, of asking her to consider the effect that abandoning the schedule would have upon their relationships with the other members of the Royal Family made any difference. Every time Charles thought he had talked the issue through to an agreed conclusion, Diana let it slide until the next time. And there was always a next time, which always came too soon for his comfort.

Pressure, however, was not the only unwelcome guest at Balmoral Castle during the honeymoon period. Turmoil also showed its ugly face. Annoyed that the husband who professed to love her refused to facilitate her in the simple matter of forsaking the countryside, Diana began issuing tests of that love. Often, when Charles tried to do something without her, she complained, 'If you loved me, you'd want to be with me.'

On one notable occasion she tried to get him to stand up to his mother. When he rightly refused, she chased after his Land Rover shrieking, 'Yes, dump me like garbage. Leave me on my own again. Run off and have lunch with your precious Mummy.' Undoubtedly, her behaviour was connected to her bulimic condition, which no one yet suspected, but it was also indicative of a warped concept of the male/female relationship, which went right back to her early childhood. This, of course, was small comfort to the notoriously peace and harmony loving Charles, whose favourite saying was 'anything for a peaceful life', and soon he was wondering whether he had done the right thing in marrying Diana. Where had the agreeable and compatible paragon of perfection gone?

To make matters worse, Diana displayed remarkable resistance when Oliver Everett approached her with a view to broadening her knowledge prior to beginning her official duties at the end of the honeymoon. Although she and the easy-going Everett got along well, she was adamant that she was not going to do any of the reading he suggested. 'I didn't leave school to do homework,' was only the first of her comments.

This was more serious than it might appear at first sight. With regard to briefings, all official visits contain material that is crucial if the royal is going to be capable of holding up his or her end. All conversation has to be initiated by the royal, so if he or she does not know the salient points, he or she cannot even ask pertinent questions, much less make relevant asides. The visit then becomes a photo-opportunity at which everything but the purpose of the visit is discussed, for an unbriefed royal either remains silent, or talks about trivia.

As revealed in *Diana in Private*, from 1981 to 1987, Diana's approach towards her responsibilities was so slapdash that she never had anything to say except how wonderful everyone and everything was. At first, people were charmed because she was so young and so approving, but as the years passed and expectations rose, the complaints started flooding back to the Palace. Even then, she did not bother to improve her performance until she realized that approaching her official duties conscientiously would enhance her reputation and make life easier for herself and everyone else. Only then did she begin to look at her briefings, though even then the staff had to distil pages of information into a few concise paragraphs of highlights.

While Diana was able at official visits to fake her ignorance behind a stunning smile and flirtatious looks, she was not able privately to con her way through her refusal to improve her mind. She had known before she married Charles that he was a genuine intellectual who delighted in intelligent and informed conversation. Certainly she could be witty and even risqué, but the icing on the cake was not a substitute for the cake itself. Diana, however, refused all blandishments from Oliver Everett and Charles to read anything but Barbara Cartland and her ilk. 'You solve the problems of the world,' she once told her husband. 'I've got more important things to do.'

Had that incident been isolated, it would not have been worthy of attention. However, it was but one of many typical incidents. She made it clear to Charles and Everett that she was perfectly happy with her intellectual development, and if they were not, that was their problem. When Charles made the point that he wanted a companion with whom he could discuss what was important to him, she informed him, 'The whole world thinks I'm fine just as I am. That ought to be enough for you.'

Charles, however, was not concerned with what the world thought. His only concern was what was happening between Diana and himself. They had only been married a matter of weeks, and here the whole fairy tale was unravelling in his hands. He could hardly believe what was happening. He had married one person and woken up to another. It was every man's nightmare come true.

The Queen and the Duke of Edinburgh were also worried. Already their rows could be overheard by everyone at the Castle, and both the Queen and Prince Philip raised the delicate subject with him. There was no prospect of the heir to the throne ever being divorced – or so they thought at the time – so the marriage had to work. They counselled patience and indulgence of Diana's wishes and whims in the belief that she was experiencing growing pains and would soon settle down. Philip did point out that he could one day begin leading an independent private life if the marriage did not work out, but neither he nor the Queen ever countenanced the thought of the heir to the throne not doing everything in his power to make his marriage work.

Nor did Charles. He desperately wanted a happy home life, with a warm and loving wife with whom he could have a mutual and reciprocal relationship. He hoped, as his parents believed, that Diana was just going through a phase of adjustment and that she would soon revert to being the lovely person she had been prior to this.

There is no doubt that international celebrity and marriage into the Royal Family turned Diana's head. Among her friends, she had always been known for the high regard she placed upon herself. Contrary to the popular image of Shy Di, she was anything but. She was full of confidence and firmly believed that she was a special person, by virtue of all that she and her family represented. Now she had the adulation of the world to ratify her own private estimate of herself, her self-adulation became so pronounced that she tilted over into arrogance.

Nevertheless, Diana was a young woman in a new environment, and parallel with this arrogance went all the insecurities and uncertainties that adjustment brings. The result was that her personality began fracturing, thereby exacerbating all the underlying problems caused by her childhood conflicts, lack of discipline and bulimia nervosa. Nor were her weaknesses the only contributory factors. She was a strong, forceful personality. Like her father and grandfather before her, she had no compunction about creating a stir. She also had a compulsion about having her own way. Even at West Heath she had been notorious for throwing her weight around. While this side of her personality showed only if her standard method of inducement, seductiveness, failed, it was nevertheless an aspect that was already pronounced by the age of fourteen.

Diana saw nothing wrong with her behaviour. In her opinion, all she was doing, she was doing in the name of love. That therefore made it all right. Bearing in mind that she was only twenty, and that her head was filled with the stuff of Barbara Cartland romances, it is possible to excuse her. Yet there are those who say that the name of her game was always subservience, and if she did not get it, she fought until she did. Everything else was technique and consequence.

Subservience, on the one hand, was antipathetic to Charles. He had been subjected to a curious amalgam of experiences, which made subservience impossible. First, there was his childish hero-worship of his critical father. This had led to an almost complete breakdown in their relations, and while Charles now admired his father's interests and accomplishments, and had even emulated them, he no longer liked him as a person. Second, there as the bullying to which Charles had been subjected during his years at Cheam and Gordonstoun. At the latter school, this had grown so bad that he never emerged from a rugby scrum without some mark from the latest bully who walked away saying, 'I punched/kicked/squeezed the balls of the future King of England' or some such juvenile variation on that theme. Charles had so hated the constant abuse that he resolved, once he left school, that he would never succumb to it again. This resolution had been reinforced by the way the courtiers and his friends treated him, especially after his investiture as Prince of Wales. He was granted respect and deference and quickly grew used to them. Even though he soon exhibited signs of selfishness, this was more a reflection of the way his life was run than a malicious disregard for the feelings of others.

It was hardly his fault that the system surrounding any VIP is geared towards his job, his activities, his schedule, his time, his convenience, and while he took full advantage of that to squeeze in the extra polo match or an additional day's hunting, he always made a point of asking those whose lives he was affecting if they minded. To one and all, he remained kind and sensitive, decent and conscientious. If he did not like something, he said so, but he was not one for brawls or scenes. Nor was he one for being pushed around or manipulated. Beneath the sensitivity and the consideration lay someone who refused to be dominated or bullied. He had had too much of it in the past, and now that he had grown into a man whose main concerns were for the spiritual secrets of life and the betterment of all humanity, he would no longer tolerate infringements upon his rights.

The irony of such a disastrous marital mixture is the part played by Queen Elizabeth the Queen Mother. She liked Diana, not only because Diana was the granddaughter of her friend and lady-in-waiting Ruth, Lady Fermoy, but because she saw something of herself in the girl. The warmth, the desire for a cosy family life and the pliability were all characteristic of the young Elizabeth. Both women were ultra feminine. Both were naturally flirtatious. Both were gentle of manner. Both were eager to please and could charm and seduce anyone into doing anything they wished. On the other hand, the determination, the domination and the manipulativeness were also present in both women, though it is doubtful that Elizabeth would have acknowledged that to anyone, herself included, until Diana's fate was well and truly sealed.

Despite the similarities, there were substantial differences in both women, for Diana was a more troubled and alienated version of the Queen Mother. Throughout her long life, Elizabeth had remained a firm team player, batting for the family into which she had married. Whatever her personal failings, she had remained a force for good, within her immediate family, the Royal Family as a whole (the Windsors excepted) and the nation at large. Once the wedding ring was on Diana's finger, however, she wanted to change the rules of the game.

Diana was quite prepared to continue batting for the Royal Family, to further their interests, whether in a private or public sense, but the price of doing so was that they must better understand her needs. This attitude was an early indication of a demanding young woman who was floundering under the weight of her insecurities – about herself and her new role as Princess of Wales. The mere scale of what she was up against was breathtaking, if you stop to think that Diana had married into one of the greatest families on earth, and that she gained from them the platform that had already brought her so much adulation and exposure.

These problems simmered away, bubbling to the surface from time to time, but not yet recognized for what they really were. All that everyone in the royal circle knew was that the marriage was not going particularly well. Then, just as the honeymoon was coming to an end, Diana announced that she was pregnant. This was a surprise to Charles, who had wanted to wait until he and Diana had solidified their relationship properly before having children. She, however, wanted children and saw motherhood as a way out of the official duties at which she was so successful, but which she found difficult.

Once Diana's pregnancy was known within court circles, everyone seized upon it as the explanation for her unstable conduct. This was good news indeed. Not only would the line of succession soon be secured, but it also explained why she was so hysterical and vomiting constantly. Everyone accepted the diagnosis that she was suffering from morning sickness, though it stopped as soon as her pregnancy began showing, and she was no longer worried about dieting to keep her figure.

Coinciding with the cessation of morning sickness was a most peculiar but welcome occurrence. As the pregnancy entered its sixth month, Diana gained weight and reverted, more or less, to the person she had been before her marriage. Once more she became easy-going and loving. 'The bat from hell disappeared,' one of Charles's cousins told me. But it was too little too late to reverse the process of deterioration within the marriage. That would have been possible had Diana been interested in developing her mind and Charles prepared to take a step towards her, to extend a helping hand to her in the wilderness of her isolation. They could then have regained their respect and regard for each other. But Charles had retreated too far from her, so much so that he avoided being in the same room as her whenever possible.

'I have nothing to say to her,' the normally loquacious Prince of Wales would say to his staff whenever they encouraged him to spend time *à deux* with her. And for her part Diana would not budge from her defensive exile.

Despite Charles's boredom, Diana did not realize she was alienating him. She actually thought her behaviour was getting her the marriage she desired. This, along with an improved diet and no more vomiting, doubtless helped restore her munificence, for Charles, in an effort to make the marriage work, was giving her her own way to a remarkable degree. He still refused to allow her to get away with manipulating him into cancelling plans as a show of love, and he still would not give up his sporting activities so that he could sit beside her while she watched television or read *Cosmopolitan*. But he did give her areas of influence.

If you stop to consider that Diana was not yet twenty-one and that Charles was a man in his mid-thirties, the amount of control he turned over to her was remarkable. Kensington Palace and Highgrove House were both being done up by Dudley Poplak, her mother's South African interior designer, and Charles gave Diana more or less a free rein, with only the merest of consultation. She criticized the way he wore his hair and how he dressed, telling him, 'You look like a stiff. You embarrass me in front of my friends.' So he obligingly changed tailors and gave up his barber in favour of a hairdresser. She even embarked upon the process of replacing the staff, which he had assembled during the decade and a half since leaving school, with choices of her own. Already she had got rid of her private detective, Chief Detective Paul Officer, because he was not deferential enough. The fact that he had once risked his life to save Charles's, and that Charles liked him, made no difference. Nor did she bother to factor Charles's feelings into the equation when she turned her attention to his valet, Stephen Barry. All she cared about was that Barry knew more about her husband's past than she did, and that he had once stopped her from barging in on Charles prior to the marriage when he was busy working on a speech, and she had wanted to indulge in lovetalk.

Control and jealousy were themes that would continue to dominate the Waleses' marriage until it would break under the strain. Diana had always been jealous and competitive, as her schoolfriends from West Heath attested. But Lady Diana Spencer had never had the power or size of platform that Her Royal Highness the Princess of Wales did, so she had had to keep her jealousy and competitiveness in check. However, Prince William's birth on Monday, 21 July 1982 changed all that. Diana was now the mother of the future king, as she never failed thereafter to remember, or to remind those who forgot, Charles included.

Ironically, William's birth also signalled halcyon days within the marriage. Charles took time off work to stay home and become a hands-on father. He and Diana bathed the baby, changed him, played with him, rendering the nanny, Barbara Barnes, all but redundant. They finally had something they could talk about, and their relationship improved significantly. Had Diana been able to maintain her equilibrium, the marriage might even have worked.

However, as soon as she stopped breastfeeding William, Diana set about losing weight. Within weeks, the 'bat from hell' was flying about Kensington Palace again. The weight fell off between bouts of famine and feast and her constant resort to that ancient Roman institution, the vomitorium. As it did, her moods swung from loving to hateful and back again with the suddenness of a sandstorm in the Sahara. In a characteristic display of aristocratic language, well known to be colourful, she demanded, within earshot of a member of the Royal Household, 'Why the fuck can't you go to work like every other husband and get out from under my fucking feet? You're stealing my baby from me.' Ten minutes later, she would rush up to him and wonder why he was withdrawn. 'If you loved me, you'd be more affectionate.'

As William got older and exhibited a preference for his father over his highly strung mother, Diana became convinced that Charles and their staff were conspiring against her so that William would prefer his father to his mother. 'I'm his mother,' she would say time and time again. 'The most important person in a child's life is his mother. He should love me more than anyone else. Your staff is organizing all sorts of duties for me so that you can have him to yourself.' She became insanely jealous of Charles, and when she forced him to retreat – an act much appreciated by Prince Philip, who was not in sympathy with any man taking time off work to spend it with babies – she discovered she had won a Pyrrhic victory. William simply shifted his affection to his nanny.

From then until Harry's birth, Diana had Barbara Barnes firmly in her sights. In the meantime, she did target practice with other members of the household. The difficulty was that no one could ever predict when she would go off someone. Oliver Everett, to whom she was close, became a case in point. One day she simply woke up and decided that she no longer liked him and had outgrown him. Thereafter, she refused to speak to him. No matter what he said or did, irrespective of the importance of the topic under discussion, she would pretend that he was not there. Charles tried speaking to her, pointing out that he had guaranteed the former diplomat the job for life. Diana remained unmoved, so Everett was removed to Windsor Castle, where a sinecure was found for him as Deputy Librarian. It was an ignominious derailment to what had been a hitherto brilliant career.

By this time, Diana's behaviour had become so erratic that she had fallen into deep despair. She could still be the sweet person the world saw when she did her official duties, but Charles and the staff were finding it more and more difficult to reconcile the 'bat from hell' with the other Diana. 'The actress,' as they called her, refused to believe that she had a problem with bulimia nervosa or that her behaviour was irrational and destructive, and whenever Charles arranged for her to see doctors, she declined to go. 'You're the one with the problem,' she would scream so loudly that she could be overheard by members of the Royal Household. 'You're the lunatic. You're barking mad.'

In a classical act of projection, Diana was firmly convinced that Charles was jealous of her because of her popularity. This was not so. Indeed, in the early days of the marriage, he had been proud of her success. What had altered his attitude was the gradual discernment that her public courting of popularity was tinged with competitiveness. It was as if she were trying to supersede him, which struck him as unhealthy where their personal relationship was concerned and damaging where the monarchy was. He, after all, was the heir to the throne. She was merely his consort. Not even his vain grandmother Queen Elizabeth had tried to usurp the special position that ultimately devolved upon the actual or potential sovereign, though his grandfather King George VI had always pushed his wife to the forefront.

On Saturday 15 September 1984, Diana gave birth to her second son. Harry turned out to be everything she had ever wanted in a baby. He loved her more than his father or his nanny, and Diana was ecstatic with that. She had still not forgiven Barbara Barnes for 'stealing Wills's love,' however.

Lord Glenconner, better known as Colin Tennant, hosted a party on Mustique in December 1986, at which Princess Margaret, Raquel Welch, Mick Jagger, Jerry Hall and Barbara Barnes, who had been nanny to the youngest Tennant children and was a close family friend, were among the guests. It was a grand and glamorous affair, reported in all the most fashionable papers and magazines worldwide. Barbara Barnes, as royal nanny, received prominent coverage. This was too much for Diana. It was one thing for her to steal the affection of Diana's elder son, but quite another to make off with headlines that rightfully belonged to the world's favourite cover girl. So, as soon as the sun-bronzed 'Baba' set foot in Kensington Palace, Diana informed her that she was accepting the resignation she had not yet tendered.

Wielding power and soaking up the adulation of the international media are scarcely ways to achieve peace of mind or fulfilment, but Diana did not seem to appreciate this. By the time Harry was a toddler, her marriage was over in all but name. She and Charles were no longer sleeping together, nor were they doing any of the myriad things that married couples normally do. Being the Prince and Princess of Wales, their lives together did still have a common purpose at times, such as on certain official duties or on such private social occasions as weddings, dinner parties and dances. But Charles, fed up with his wife's bullying and antics, had begun avoiding Diana as much as possible since shortly after Harry's birth, when Diana did all in her power to keep him away from the baby.

The disintegration in the Waleses' marriage came as no surprise to anyone but Diana and her family, to whom she increasingly turned. Her sisters Jane and Sarah and brother Charles were her closest companions, though she also confided in her mother and her father. Earl Spencer was supportive, even though the issue of Raine and the sale of treasures from Althorp would continue causing problems until his death in 1992. But this was a period of deep distress for Diana, and they all rallied round.

This was also a period of deep distress for Charles. He had entered the marriage with high expectations. For years he had hit his head against the brick wall, but finally he too succumbed to despair. Nothing he had done had made any difference. He simply could not get through to Diana, to make her realize that her behaviour was driving him away. They just didn't get on, no matter how they tried. Fed up with returning home to a shrew who sought to rewrite Shakespeare and tame him, he did what most other men would do. He returned to old friends. In particular, he began seeing more and more of the Tryons and the Parker Bowleses.

People seldom comprehend what living with an emotionally unstable person actually involves. They do not appreciate that these individuals do not act or react as normal, healthy people would. They create problems when none exist, exacerbate them where they do and always manage to turn a drama into a crisis and a crisis into a full-blown tragedy. Living with the emotionally unstable is like trying to walk on constantly shifting sand. This becomes a very wearying exercise, and the healthier partner often comes to the conclusion that they must take a break or be dragged into the mire beyond the point of no return. Charles, however, could not take the break he needed due to the prominence of his position. So he did the next best thing. He withdrew from Diana and turned to old friends.

It was a solution of sorts, but served only to infuriate Diana and trigger her jealousy. Despite her irrational and childish behaviour she wanted her husband there for her. She loved him in her way, unbearable as it was. She became firmly convinced Charles wished to return to the former intimacy he had once shared with Camilla and Dale, and for a while their names could not be mentioned in front of her without making her explode with anger. Incredible as this may now seem to those who have heard of the Camillagate tapes, at the time Diana was wrong. Charles had no intention of returning to anyone from his past. However, her jealous behaviour allied to Camilla's understanding proved an inflammatory mix, and within a matter of months he and Camilla were once again the truest of companions.

Diana is nothing if not instinctive, and she quickly felt her way to the relative positions of Dale and Camilla. Once she realized that Dale was not going to be restored to the position of confidante, and that that honour was reserved exclusively for Camilla, she knew who she should have within her sights.

It was not long before Diana was putting her plan into action. One foray was to set up a photo-opportunity in San Lorenzo, where she and Dale were photographed having lunch. This was an insecure attempt to reduce Camilla's status in the eyes of the world by boosting Dale's stature, and while it did indeed accomplish the latter objective, it did not succeed with the former. A more direct tactic, however, was to cross-examine Charles as to his comings and goings.

Such antics only had the effect of driving Charles further and further away. Nor did Diana's family help. Rather than finding out what the problem truly was, they encouraged her to consider herself the victim. As often happens in families, the Spencers fed Diana's interpretation of what was causing the problems, instead of rectifying it, so their support was ultimately of little practical use to her.

Within the Royal Family, the state of the Wales marriage was a source of never-ending concern. Diana still got along with her father-in-law and still enjoyed cordial though correct relations with the Queen, but the people to whom she was closest were Prince Andrew and Prince Edward. She had known both brothers since her childhood days at Park House on the Sandringham Estate, when they used to play with each other and attend each other's birthday parties and go swimming together in the pool that Diana's father, then Viscount Althorp, built.

Through her friendship with Andrew, Diana's life was due to change. But, first, she changed his. Despite his image as Randy Andy, Andrew's personal life had been unsatisfactory since the end of his affair with Koo Stark. Diana, however, had made friends with the daughter of Charles's polo manager, Major Ronald Ferguson. Sarah Ferguson was fun. She was always good for a laugh. She was loyal and kind. But most important of all, she knew how to behave in royal circles. Having spent much of her life in them, she was not daunted by illustrious hosts, nor did she become over familiar. She trod the perfect line between naturalness and formality, while remaining what socialites call 'excellent value'.

In June 1985, Diana arranged for Sarah Ferguson to be invited to Windsor Castle for the Royal Ascot races. At lunch prior to the meeting, she was seated beside Andrew. Over the profiteroles, they discovered an attraction, which soon carried them into marriage.

For Diana, Fergie's coming had a profound effect. Fergie is a kind-hearted, warm-spirited, life-enhancer. Popular, with a wide circle of worldly friends, she could no more contemplate life without companionship than without breathing air, and she breezily reintroduced the element of friendship and warmth that Diana, with her new responsibilities, had found herself cut off from at the time of her marriage. Quite soon, Diana began seeing her old friends and made new ones with some of Fergie's. Kate Menzies, for instance, became even closer to Diana than she had been to Fergie.

While Fergie blew a fresh breeze into the stuffy corridors of Diana's life, the main cause for Diana's despair remained the state of her marriage, which she wanted desperately to work. Andrew knew the eminent astrologer Penny Thornton through his closest friends, photographer Gene Nocon and his wife Liz. He knew that Penny Thornton was no ordinary star-gazer, but a thoughtful and spiritual woman who took a scientific view of astrology, using it as a guide by which her clients could develop their potential and guard against weaknesses, which might otherwise destroy them. So he gave Diana her number, Diana telephoned her, and the two women met for the first time at 4 p.m. on Thursday, 6 March 1986.

At that first meeting, and at the many subsequent meetings Diana and Penny Thornton had, they discussed ways that Diana could lift herself out of the black hole of despair. She attributed many of her problems to Charles, and their failure to relate, but Thornton, being an astute professional, recognized that the answers lay in what Diana did with herself, not in the outcome of her marital relationship. She therefore steered Diana in a spiritual direction, convincing her that the way to happiness and satisfaction lay in what she did with her life. Work was still a big problem, so Thornton convinced Diana to change her attitude towards it. Instead of her official duties remaining a chore, which 'The actress' managed to fake her way through, Thornton gradually got her to see them as a platform through which she could express herself. It was the beginning of Diana the Good.

As she reaped the dividends of a different approach towards her work, Diana came to believe in her 'specialness'. She was Diana the Healer, Diana the Sufferer, Diana the Martyr who had a mission: to touch the suffering and gain the admiration of the world. Charles was surprised by this latest development. He respected Penny Thornton, and on one occasion even credited her with keeping Diana from departing when she had already packed her bags. He soon discovered, however, that Diana was seeing other, less spiritual, more conventional astrologers, ones from whom she sought a revalidation of her ego. Debbie Franks became a regular, giving standard briefings, which counteracted Thornton's more spiritual approach and appealed to Diana's heightened sense of her own worth. It was a slippery slope of self-delusion for her.

Hungry for appreciation and attention, Diana had by 1986 discovered that there was a large segment of humanity ready and waiting to respond to her. The male sex, which she had found so appreciative of her charms prior to her marriage, was as eager as ever to share the delights of her company.

She was, after all, a young woman, in need of the attention and admiration of a man. Charles was too much a part of the problem to be able to help her there. So she took a leaf out of Princess Anne's book and looked no further than her immediate circle, selecting as her confidant Sergeant Barry Mannakee, her private detective. He started out as a friendly shoulder to cry on and ended up as a source of deep comfort, which brought her all the satisfaction she yearned for. A tall, burly, handsome man in the prime of his life and safely married with two children, he was so personable and charming that he fitted in wherever he went.

The role of the private detective in a royal's life is worth looking at. He goes everywhere his charge does. Whether it is to a wedding or the lavatory, he is always at hand. It is imperative that guard and guarded be compatible, for they share so much time and so many activities that life becomes intolerable for both of them if they cannot strike up a genuine rapport. Usually male royals and their detectives become firm friends, as do female royals and their bodyguards.

When the sexes mix, however, there can be a spark that transcends friendship, as happened with Princess Anne and Peter Cross. This can be a fortuitous event, for a royal is never meant to be without her detective, and there is therefore no cause for unseemly suspicion if they make off together on solitary acts.

This is how Diana and Barry Mannakee managed to establish such a firm friendship. She was bored and lonely for much of the time she was in the company of her husband and his relations, especially when they stayed at Balmoral or Sandringham. No one therefore thought anything of her taking off for long drives in the company of her private detective. Even the normally suspicious photographers who trail the royals used to see them making off into the distance without a second thought.

As Diana became more and more reliant upon the comfort that Barry Mannakee provided, her marriage continued on its downward path. Such joy as she received from her private detective's companionship did not distract from her jealous obsession about Camilla Parker Bowles, nor did it inspire her to stop the more dramatic expression of her feelings to Charles. She knew she was losing him and could not cope with the loss. She dealt with it by overcompensation. For one long year Diana, assuming the posture of righteous indignation, never missed an opportunity to flay or berate Charles. But the status quo was about to change.

One afternoon in July 1986, Charles came home unexpectedly. According to an ardent supporter of the Prince of Wales, Charles, to his horror, stumbled in upon an intimate discourse his wife was having with her confidant. He was outraged to witness his wife, the wife of the Prince of Wales, Her Royal Highness The Princess of Wales, sharing confidences of a personal nature with a private detective. It was one thing for her to have a gentleman whispering in her ear, but for her to allow someone to do so who was not even a gentleman, and worse, a servant of lowly rank, broke every precept of ladylike as well as royal behaviour. Some things just were not done. And this above all was one.

Charles promptly stormed out of the room, rang his private secretary, informed him that Sergeant Barry Mannakee was to be relieved of his duties forthwith and transferred from the Royal Protection Department back to ordinary police duties. He then returned to Diana and moved the few remaining possessions he had in their marital bedroom at Kensington Palace into his dressing room. Thereafter, the marriage was at an end. It was dead. Finished. Over. Diana had broken the cardinal rule. She had humiliated her husband. And while Charles the man might have forgiven her, Charles the Prince of Wales never would.

CHAPTER FIFTEEN

Adrift in an Icy Sea

Seldom has a corpse taken so long to be interred as the Waleses' marriage. For six years and five months it remained on view, putrefying until its stench became a public scandal threatening to engulf the whole monarchy.

There is no doubt that in the days immediately following Charles's withdrawal from Diana, she remained emotionally engaged. She could not believe what had happened. It was something that in a stronger relationship might have been mendable, but in her own marriage she knew in her heart to be the end. Nevertheless, when they went on holiday in Majorca that August with the King and Queen of Spain, she hoped to make Charles jealous by flirting with Juan Carlos. At least somebody likes me was the message. Can't you? Charles, however, was now beyond the reach of such emotions, and while the exercise boosted her ego and helped her to get over the loss of her private detective, it did not restore her husband's interest.

Kings, however, are not good prospects for anything more substantial than in-depth holiday flirtations. They have too many demands upon their time and too many restrictions upon their mobility to make good confidants. What Diana needed was someone closer to hand, who could give her the time and attention she needed. As 1986 came to a close, and 1987 dawned, Diana was drawn in two opposing directions: trying to revitalize Charles's interest and looking around for a more suitable confidant then the one who had got her into such trouble.

Charles, meanwhile, struck out on the overtly independent lifestyle of which he had never quite let go and which he would never relinquish thereafter. It was no way to run a marriage, except into the ground. He shot from August to January, hosting shooting parties at Sandringham or joining friends such as the Duke of Westminster on their estates for overnight shoots. Two or three days a week he hunted, often with the Quorn or the Belvoir, frequently with Camilla. He had long had an abiding interest in such subjects as the architecture of churches and the execution of watercolours. Now he started going on special-interest trips related to those subjects, touring the country looking at churches with Candida Lycett Green or spending time in Tuscany with Bona Frescobaldi, the elegant Italian marchesa whose daughter was erroneously linked with him.

It did not take Diana long to get the point. His absence, one of the early bones of contention between them, made it clear that there was no longer any room in her husband's life for her. He would no longer court her, pander to her desires or placate her. Their interests had always been different and while in the past he had made some effort to incorporate her into his life, now he gave her the unspoken message: there is no room in my life for you.

Frozen out of Charles's life, Diana remained desperate and despairing until early 1987, when she met Philip Dunne. The son of the Lord Lieutenant of Hereford and Worcester and godson of Princess Alexandra, Dunne was a tall, handsome merchant banker with Warburg's. He also had an established girlfriend, Lord St Just's daughter, the Hon. Katya Grenfell. He did not allow this to cramp his style as he took Diana to lunch at Ménage à Trois in London's fashionable Beauchamp Place. Nor did it deter him from joining Diana and Charles for a skiing holiday in Klosters, which silenced the rumourmongers who were saying that Charles did not approve of Diana's friendship. In fact, Charles had made what Diana did a matter of complete indifference to him, as long as she maintained his and her own dignity. He was too wounded and proud to do otherwise.

Diana's exhibitionistic streak and inexperienced eye for the established parameters of royal conduct, exacerbated by the intolerable position partly of her own making, were bound to trip her up before long, however, and later that year they did just that. The venue was the dance following the wedding of the Marquis of Worcester to actress Tracy Ward. Charles and Diana arrived together, but that was the only thing they did jointly for the whole evening.

While Charles was huddled in conversation with Anna Wallace, saying how much he regretted having married Diana and what a misery she had made of his life, she took to the dance floor with Philip Dunne. As record after record was played, the princess who had once wanted to be a dancer gave the assembled company an exhibition of her more than adequate skills. These were not limited to the latest dance steps, however. Flushed with the joy of indulging in an exercise that gave her pleasure, she ran her hands through Dunne's hair, whispered in his ear in the real, not the figurative meaning of the phrase, and pecked him on the cheek.

Although naturally one might not impute anything but the purest and most innocent of motives to such conduct, it had a profound effect upon the onlookers. They were shocked that the Princess of Wales, their Princess of Wales, could behave in such an overtly flirtatious manner. Diana, after all, was not just a human being. She was also royalty, and, as the Princess of Wales, the living embodiment of the monarchy, so everyone was surprised at her conduct, even people who are normally laissez-faire. When Diana added further fuel to the fires of gossip by remaining behind while Charles went home, the die was cast for a scandal. Sure enough, within a matter of days everyone in royal circles knew about the 'Matter of the Worcester Wedding Dance'. It was a short hop from there into the gossip columns.

Publicity is the death knell of most relationships between royals and their confidants. As soon as the press began speculating about Philip Dunne, he received a telephone call from Buckingham Palace. He was asked to desist from seeing the Princess of Wales. Being a gentleman, he did as he was asked.

How Diana reacted to the termination of her friendship with Philip Dunne is indicative of a sometimes ignored, manipulative side of her personality. After giving vent to her rage in verbal as well as actual terms, including sailing a lamp across the room at Charles, she asked Katya Grenfell to lunch – an honour no one would ever refuse – and made sure the photographers were on hand to record the event. She wanted to relay a message to the world: all speculation about me and Philip Dunne has been unfounded. It has to be so. Look. I'm having lunch with his girlfriend. She wouldn't be having lunch with me if I'd been flirting with her boyfriend, would she? I'm an innocent, promise.

Innocence or its loss was not the only preoccupation to perturb Diana that summer of 1987. In July, her former confidant Barry Mannakee was killed in a motor accident in east London. He was riding pillion on a Suzuki motor-bike when a Ford Fiesta car driven by seventeen-year-old Nicola Chopp came out of a side street. The police officer swerved; Mannakee was thrown and though neither driver was hurt, he was killed. Rumours immediately began to rage that Mannakee had been in the process of selling the story of his relationship with Diana to the press. Diana not only believed them but was soon going around telling friends that she was positive that Barry Mannakee had been wiped out to silence him. The fact that he had died almost immediately and that the accident involved a novice driver did not influence her conclusions, and while there is no doubt that she sincerely holds that belief, it is a hard one to sustain.

Fortunately for her, as Diana became more distraught, more needy of the confirmation of her own specialness and bounty and more affected by the disapproving reactions of the officials surrounding her, she now had her own circle of friends on whom she could rely. These included Catherine Soames, the wife of Charles's good friend the Hon. Nicholas Soames; Sabrina Guinness's sister Julia Samuel; and Major David Waterhouse, the Duke of Marlborough's nephew and her bridge partner. She was photographed on three separate occasions that autumn with Waterhouse, when the press noted that she and Charles had spent a total of six weeks apart. The private split within the marriage was becoming too public for everyone's comfort, and the

Queen called Charles and Diana to Buckingham Palace for a late-night meeting during which she counselled a greater display of unity. Diana was only too happy to oblige, for she still hoped against hope that Charles would give her another chance to re-establish their marriage. Having never gained satisfaction from it, however, Charles was only prepared to abide by appearances.

Adrift in a sea without particular male admiration, Diana continued to rely upon the platonic attentions of David Waterhouse, a very distant cousin. He was not as close a friend as the media supposed, and it is likely that Diana was using him not only as a shoulder to cry on but also as a means of gleaning information about Charles's activities. His elder brother Michael is the best friend of Camilla Parker Bowles's brother Mark Shand, though that is not a fact any outsider would have known.

Unknown to Diana, however, admiration and appreciation were around the corner. And the form it took was unexpected, to say the least.

Riding was a sport that she had dreaded since a childhood accident, but in 1988 it brought the most enduring of her confidants into her life. Major James Hewitt was an ace equestrian. The dashing and handsome athlete gripped a horse like a dream and played such a mean game of polo that few women could watch him in action without inflammatory thoughts. But he was more than a captivating sight. Witty and entertaining, he could beguile children as well as their parents, and when the Prince of Wales asked the army to recommend someone to teach his heir how to ride, they sent over James Hewitt, who was posted at Combermere Barracks near Windsor Castle. First William and later Harry took to the dashing Guards officer immediately, and soon their mother was as firm a fan of the delightful James as they were.

So began the most enduring of Diana's friendships with the opposite sex. Hewitt gave her everything Charles did not. He listened to her problems, provided her with the intense admiration and absolute attention she required and made her know that she truly was a special person. In every respect he was the ideal companion, and above all he was suitable as a confidant due to his standing as a gentleman.

This time Diana had learnt to remain within the parameters of royal conduct, and, as the relationship flourished, so too did Diana. Soon she was even taking riding lessons herself, which was quite a switch for someone who had always claimed to be terrified of horses.

Like many army officers, James Hewitt's actions were closely watched by his valet/groom. Quite why William Leete should claim that he became suspicious of Hewitt and Diana when they should have remained above suspicion remains a mystery, but he does make the claim, and he did decide to see for himself what they were up to in the course of those riding lessons Diana dreaded so much. One bright autumn day in 1988 he therefore followed them into the riding-school arena where a lesson was taking place. Although Leete does not say so, I imagine that bees must have been loose in the vicinity, for he saw Hewitt's hands going up the back of Diana's blouse, which was outside her breeches. She was also embarked upon a similar mission of mercy, and Leete sensibly slipped away before anyone got stung.

When the lesson was over, and Diana came out of the arena, Leete observes that Diana's exertions had left her looking flushed and dishevelled. Only the horse seems to have been spared the arduousness of being threatened by bee stings. Fear must have lowered its body temperature, for it was cold to Leete's touch, despite having been party to a lesson of an hour's duration.

With her personal life in better shape, Diana had a spring in her step when she attended a party given by Julia Samuel in the summer of 1989, which would have unforeseen repercussions in her life that have not ended yet. A fellow guest was an old boyfriend of hers. Diana had known James Gilbey since she was seventeen, when she had been sufficiently keen on him, prior to her relationship with Charles, to pour a mixture of flour and egg over his treasured Alfa Romeo when he stood her up on a date. This paste had set like cement, causing him no end of trouble and damaging the paintwork of the car.

Time and Diana's eminence had wrought their magic for Gilbey, however, and the car-dealing scion of the Roman Catholic gin family let bygones be bygones. For Diana, the attentions of yet another tall, handsome and attentive swain could not have come at a better time. Her relationship with James Hewitt soon hit a rough spot when she started to worry that its existence might become public. She therefore terminated it and was relieved that Gilbey's presence meant that she did not have to tolerate transitional gaps and do without the support that she needed.

Diana's relationship with Gilbey, however, was less powerfully motivated than that with Hewitt had been, for she was never as drawn to Gilbey as she had been to the polo-playing Major. Nevertheless, Diana found Gilbey appealing enough company to allow him to play host to her on a regular basis, as a friend of mine, who lived at Lennox Gardens where Gilbey had a flat, was soon reporting to me. She saw Diana driving away on a regular basis in the early hours of the morning, and indeed on one occasion Diana was stopped by the police at 6.45 a.m. *en route* to Kensington Palace.

Gilbey's re-entrance into Diana's life was not only timely but also fortuitous and would have dramatic repercussions for the Royal Family as a whole and the institution of the monarchy in particular. Her brother Charles, who married Victoria Lockwood that year, also became a fast friend of the car dealer. Both men were of the firm opinion that they could offer Diana no greater support than encouraging her in her quest for self-realization.

By this time, Diana had conceived the incredible idea of leaving Charles. She knew as well as everyone else in the world that the Royal Family believed that the marriages of the sovereign and the heir to the throne were sacrosanct and must remain inviolate, but Diana could not care. Her marriage was shot to pieces, and she had to escape from the pain of it.

However, Diana wanted to depart with her privileges intact. This might no longer seem so surprising now that Charles and Diana are separated, but in 1989 it was an incredible undertaking, and she needed to move very carefully and appeal to rather than alienate public sympathy for her predicament.

Charles Althorp, as he then was, had worked as a journalist for several years. He understood the power of persuasion and the power of the press, and he sympathized with his sister's desire to marshal those forces in her favour.

As Diana and her advisers were laying the ground for a public-relations coup that would create waves of support for her and hopefully help to secure her position, she received even more substantial help from someone in the security forces. He felt compassion for Diana, who only wanted her husband back. Difficult as this was, in the pain of her rejection she believed she could do it. For some time now Diana had been saying that she wanted real proof that Charles was being unfaithful to her with Camilla Parker Bowles. All she needed to help her put her marriage right, she claimed, was the evidence that her suspicions were well founded. A compromising photograph or tape-recorded conversation to wave under Charles's nose would do the trick.

Taping a telephone conversation was considerably easier than capturing the confidants *in flagrante delicto*, so Diana's friend, believing that her motives were only to preserve her marriage, and never thinking that they might also serve to destroy her husband's reputation, obliged her. He locked on to Charles's mobile telephone, whose number he knew, with a call tracking device. This is a standard though sophisticated piece of software, which allows anyone to tap into a telephone conversation, without either party to it knowing that they are being overheard. The manufacturers do not sell such equipment over the counter, however. It is available only to authorized firms, government bodies, the security services – and royal protection departments. It took several attempts before he acquired a sufficiently compromising conversation, but each attempt was recorded. Then on 17 December 1989, he struck pay dirt when he locked on to the telephone call that later became known as Camillagate.

In it, Charles and Camilla are trying to make arrangements to meet before Christmas for one last night of passion. They exchange the usual intimacies of people who are in love and at ease with one another. Their language is never lewd or louche, simply intimate and easy, and they both give vent to their wit with jokes about him living in her trousers and coming back as a pair of her knickers or a tampax. They repeatedly say how much they love one another and spend a good part of the six minutes of the tape saying goodbye but being so happy talking to one another that neither one can quite hang up. It is harmless, endearing stuff, the sort of conversation no one would consider remarkable, except that it involved the Prince of Wales.

Diana's obliging friend saw the sense behind her reluctance to associate herself with a tape obtained in so furtive a manner. It was better if it looked as if the tape had fallen into her hands. After all, she didn't want Charles getting cross with her, not when her objective was to use it to save her marriage.

The difficulty was now: How could Diana hear about the tape? The answer was simple: Rebroadcast it and get a radio buff to happen upon it and send it to Diana. The ostensible reasoning behind the scheme was far-fetched indeed, for Charles was not a fool and would never have fallen for so harebrained an explanation. However, Diana's obliging friend, who was totally on her side, did. And on 18 December he broadcast the tape for it to be picked up by a radio buff. When one didn't, that did not present a problem because they already had the tape in their possession and could simply claim that it had been sent to them. One giveaway concerning the tampering of the tape, however, is that Camilla alludes to her son Tom's birthday being 'tomorrow', when in fact it took place on the day the tape was broadcast.

Armed with the ammunition, Diana then confronted Charles. He could hardly believe that any wife of any man, much less a wife of his, could resort to such a cunning scheme to win back the affections of a reluctant spouse. He refused to bow to her ultimatum for a separation unless he gave up Camilla and allowed Diana back into his heart. Not for the first time in their marriage, however, he underestimated her, and her determination to get him back, and when he brushed her aside, he was fortunate enough to have advisers who treated this latest development more seriously.

That Christmas, when the Royal Family congregated at Sandringham, the security services were ready and waiting. They turned the tables on Diana's sad scheme, capturing her conversation with a confidant named James on New Year's Eve by tapping her landline and recording the conversation. During it, Diana reveals a hostility and self-centredness that are at some variance with her public image. James encourages her in this, congratulating her for being unnecessarily rude to the Bishop of Norwich, who was quite obviously only being polite to her, when he asked her what her secret was when she dealt with the infirm. She complains about the Queen Mother looking at her, and when James suggests that she take issue with her, Diana backs off and explains that the old lady is merely fascinated with her.

Her self-admiration knowing no bounds, Diana also speaks about Fergie contemptuously, even though they are meant to be friends, and every time James tries to steer the conversation away from Diana on to some of the people they know, she resolutely yanks it back. He does not seem to mind this, however, and keeps on telling her how much he loves her. Her response is decidedly lukewarm, and the only ardour she manages to summon up is to tell him that he is the nicest man in the world. They even touch upon James Hewitt, whom she says she kitted out from head to toe. Once more, she reveals the insecure calculation behind even her generosity, for she then gracelessly comments that outfitting him cost her a fortune. They blow kisses to one another, though James the confidant is always the one initiating such affection.

When the Squidgy tape was broadcast in summer 1992, several minutes were missing from it. Those minutes are hot stuff, according to two respected journalists who have heard the entire tape in the *Sun's* possession, as well as a member of the Royal Household, who has heard the complete, unexpurgated version, which not even the *Sun* has. Far more explicit than anything on the Camillagate tape, James the Libran car dealer suggests to Squidgy, who is tense due to being with her husband and his family, that they make love over the telephone. Squidgy, mistress not only of James the Libran car dealer but also of the put-down, gets in a pot-shot about how her husband is dead below the waist, before she recounts how scared she recently was that James the Libran car dealer with the living penis might have impregnated her.

This revelation is a source of yet more sympathy and solicitation from the solicitous James before it emerges that her fear was unfounded. Then they get down to the serious business at hand. James the Libran car dealer suggests they masturbate. Squidgy responds by asking him if he is touching himself down there and claims that she has never masturbated in her life. So he spends the rest of the time leading her through a masturbatory exercise. Graphically, he tells her to touch herself down there, to fondle herself, to stroke herself. He becomes so caught up in what he is doing for his Squidgy that he quite forgets to give himself any pleasure. Not once thereafter during the long and sizzling conversation does he mention himself, and nor does the unnervingly self-centred Squidgy.

It strikes one as understandable why an egotist like Squidgy would need someone like James the Libran car dealer, for he makes his needs totally subservient to hers, and she remains the focus of attention even during the sex act.

Having struck pay dirt, the secret services next turned their attention to Fergie. The Royal Family knew that she and Andrew were having marital troubles and suspected her of encouraging Diana in her desire to depart. This was both unfair and untrue, and they were never able to capture Fergie encouraging Diana or doing anything more offensive or explicit on the telephone than rowing with Andrew.

The British secret services are among the most sophisticated in the world. Once they had the Squidgy tape, they also rebroadcast it in emulation of Diana and her friend's tactic. However, they did so repeatedly over the next fortnight, on at least three separate occasions, for they wanted radio buffs to hear and possibly tape it. Then they sat back and waited while Cyril Reenan, a radio buff, taped it and took his version to the *Sun*. Although the

157

newspaper bought the tape, it did not run the story immediately, as everyone now knows. Instead, it sent reporters round to accost James Gilbey outside his flat in Lennox Gardens. He turned white and started to shake when he heard what the tape contained. The *Sun* then received confirmation that the tape was genuine, after which it sat on all of it for nearly three years. Even now, at the time of writing this, that paper has suppressed the segments of the tape that are most damaging to Diana, though other branches of the Murdoch press elsewhere have been assiduous in revealing all about Charles and Camilla.

After James Gilbey's confrontation, Diana was alerted to the fact that the *Sun* had a copy of the compromising conversation. She now found herself in a predicament that looked very much like a Mexican stand-off. She could not use the evidence she had amassed against Charles without damaging both of them. This naturally caused her grave frustration and distress, leading to even more rows. Using her reputation as the excuse, Diana had to end her association with Gilbey and readmit the other James, James Hewitt, into her life.

However, Diana did not want to exclude Gilbey as she still had some feelings for him. Besides she needed him as a friend in case the *Sun* ran the story. And if it did not, she was still better off with him on her side. Especially when he was in possession of such dynamite information, which, if revealed, could badly damage her and any last-ditch attempts to win back her husband. So Gilbey became a listening post and adviser, a role that he continued to fulfil happily with the enthusiastic co-operation of her brother Charles, who became such a good friend of Gilbey's that he regularly entertained him at Althorp, and they even went away on holiday in foursomes.

With the passage of time, Diana became less worried about the tape getting out. She realized the *Sun* must be afraid of using it, or that suppressing it must serve the Murdoch organization's interests better than revealing it. She therefore returned to finding a way out of her unhappy marriage, though she exercised great care lest the sword of Damocles fall off the *Sun*'s shelf and cut off her head.

CHAPTER SIXTEEN

The War of the Waleses

While Diana and her advisers thought of ways and means of extricating her from her marital misery, Diana was fending off her ever increasing despair. She was engaged in a full and satisfying friendship with her confidant, took advantage of the support of her former confidant, her brother and friends such as Carolyn Bartholomew and even sought help through Dr Maurice Lipsedge for her novel way of dieting. Her former flatmate Carolyn Bartholomew had finally got through where Charles had been stymied. Perhaps it was easier to take advice from those she was less close to. By this time, Charles and Diana were leading completely separate private lives. They never saw one another unless they had to. He lived at Highgrove House in Gloucestershire during the week, she at Kensington Palace in London. Only at weekends did they see anything of one another. She would arrive with the children on Friday afternoon and promptly take to her room, as much as she could. After lunch on Sunday, she departed for London. In September 1990, this regimen varied slightly after William was taken away from his school in London and boarded at Ludgrove School near Wokingham in Berkshire. He joined the battlefield for weekends whenever he was allowed out. Otherwise, only Harry was privy to the scenes.

Like any conscientious father, Charles was deeply worried by the effect of his and Diana's problems on his children. He had been raised in an atmosphere of harmony and civility, whatever its failings, and he was convinced that the conflict the boys witnessed must be affecting them detrimentally.

Moreover, Charles himself now found living in such an atmosphere increasingly disturbing. He remained the man whose favourite maxim was 'Anything for a peaceful life,' but Diana could not permit him to adhere to it. More than ever, in her frustration and grief, she had become anything but the sort of woman a man could ignore or placate. So Charles retreated to his walled garden, to which only he had a key. It was not really helpful to do this but a way that he could cope with his own disappointment at the failure of his marriage. If that did not work, there was always Balmoral or Sandringham to which he could flee for a few weeks. It was hardly a way to lead a life, but he could not see any other option. As far as Charles was concerned, he was wedded to Diana for the remainder of his days on earth, and the best he could do was to make his intolerable marriage tolerable.

With that in mind, Charles pursued his own life during the week while Diana remained in London. He entertained at Highgrove House as if he were a bachelor. Camilla Parker Bowles often came over from Middlewich House at nearby Corsham in Wiltshire to act as his hostess. This, of course, upset Diana and made her jealous, but Charles, for his own emotional survival, had long since passed the stage where he could care about her feelings. She had to be as good as dead to him.

However, Diana was the quick, not the dead, and as proof of that, Charles had to contend with her unhappy public competitiveness. She had decided to wage a popularity war with him, with the objective of compounding the natural affection of the world outside. Maybe then he would want her and if not the Royal Family would have to grant her the separation she required. Out of compassion, at least, they could not do otherwise. One way of achieving this goal was to steal Charles's thunder whenever she could. This was easy enough to do, for their offices were housed under the same roof, and her staff was actually a part of his household. So whenever she got wind of a major speech he had planned, she made sure that she, who had always shied away from public speaking, spoke on something even more topical and newsworthy. As most newspapers will always choose stories about glamorous and photogenic women over men, no matter how attractive or photogenic they may be, the result was that Diana knocked Charles out of the spotlight every single time.

It did not take long for Charles and his household to figure out what Diana was up to. Such ploys only made him withdraw from her all the more, for she was now tampering with his work and trivializing his efforts to improve the lives of the British citizenry. But no amount of reasoning with her about the damage she was inflicting made any impression on her. She was a woman with a mission, albeit lost and misguided. Indeed, she seemed to gain strength from harming him – getting her own back for the pain she felt – and any attempt on his part to get her to stop only had the effect of making her redouble her efforts.

Once more, the disintegration of the Waleses' marriage was spilling over into the public arena. This time, however, the flow would not be staunched the way it had been in 1987, partly because Diana wanted to involve the public. She felt that she needed all the help she could get. The limits to which she would go became very clear in July 1991, when she refused Charles's offer of hosting a thirtieth birthday party for her, knowing full well that the press would infer that he was snubbing her. This indeed is what happened, and the normally loquacious and friendly Diana made sure she did not rectify the mistaken impression with any of the many journalists with whom she was on chummy terms.

What happened next should have been a warning to Diana, for Charles's friends took it upon themselves to ignore his request that they remain above the fray and leaked the truth to the gossip columnists. Far from being the heartless husband Diana believed he was and wanted the world to share, he had offered her a party. But, she was the one who had refused it, not because there was a recession on, nor because she did not want to flaunt her wealth in front of the public. Her reason, as she told her friends, was simpler. She wanted to celebrate her birthday with her nearest and dearest friends, including James Hewitt. Charles, by then, offered her only upset and distress, a reminder of failure. But he had tried, and she had turned him down. It had become an emotional war, with neither side willing to disarm. Failing to understand the two sides of her marriage story, Diana's birthday machinations blew up in her face. She believed that Charles's friends had no justification in revealing their side of the story. She was angry that he had not stopped them and remained impervious to the fact that he could hardly stop them if he did not know their plans. So distressed was Diana that she was convinced that Charles was lying when he protested innocence. Nevertheless, cousins and friends of his, who have given me quite compromising information about him, have assured me that he has genuinely sought all along to keep his marital differences private.

Whatever the Waleses' marital strife, the publicity surrounding it was quickly overshadowed by the next royal story that went to press: the Duke and Duchess of York were going to separate. This, however, was not strictly true. They had been discussing the possibility of separation and had been granted permission to do so by the Queen if their discussions broke down, but they had not reached a definite decision. This Diana knew well, for she had been encouraging Fergie to proceed, saying that she would leave at the same time, too, though she had no intention of doing any such thing, as she confided to more than one friend.

Fergie can be far more straightforward than Diana and did not appreciate that Diana might be pushing her so that she could learn from Fergie's mistakes if and when she made her move. Diana herself didn't feel brave enough to end her marriage yet. In the event, Fergie's hand was forced by Diana leaking the possible separation to journalist Andrew Morton, as if it were a foregone conclusion, during the very week her private life was the focus of international attention due to revelations in *Diana in Private*. He wrote it up in the *Daily Mail*, which announced the news across its front pages. Fergie then found herself in the position of being forced to take a decision before she was ready to do so. Diana was on hand to offer her the benefit of her advice and counsel. *Leave. You may as well do it now. You want to. Do it. Take advantage of the situation. Leave. If you stay, you'll only look foolish.*

Confronted with an international mêlée, Fergie made up her mind to leave. So precipitate had events been, however, that she and Andrew continued to share the same bed throughout the early days of their separation. For Diana's part, the news of the York separation silenced speculation about the state of the Wales marriage and knocked the stories about Diana's private life out of the papers. The months between March 1992, when *Diana in Private* was published, and June 1992, when Diana's story by Andrew Morton hit the stands, was a period of intense stress for Diana. Which version of her life would the public believe? So much depended on whether she retained her popularity, on whose side the public chose in the War of the Waleses.

The first round went to Diana. This was partly due to the technical skills of News International Plc, the massive media empire owned by the famous republican Rupert Murdoch. Its most prestigious publication, the *Sunday Times*, had bought the first serial rights, the *Sun* second, to the Morton book. For Diana, *Sunday Times* editor Andrew Neil's promotion of Morton's biography was a bonus. She felt vindicated by the press she received. Charles, on the other hand, was outraged. Humiliated in the eyes of the world, misrepresented as the antithesis of the father he was and the husband he had tried to be, he could never have imagined when he had taken his marriage vows at St Paul's Cathedral eleven long years before that his marriage would bring him to this pass.

Personal feelings aside, Charles was also the Prince of Wales. He and his advisers decided upon a damage-limitation exercise. At a meeting with Diana, they proposed that she disassociate herself from the book and make it clear that Andrew Neil and Andrew Morton's claims that the book was written with her connivance were false.

Not only did Diana refuse to oblige Charles, she went to the opposite extreme. At the time, there was conjecture whether she would drop Carolyn Bartholomew and James Gilbey. Diana's response was to arrange to visit Carolyn Bartholomew at her Fulham house. She then organized for the press to be given advance warning of the time and date of the projected visit as well as the precise location of the Bartholomew residence. On the appointed day, Diana showed up as expected. She noticed that the photographers were a respectful distance from the house. This meant they would not get good photographs. So she circled the block, using her car phone to contact one of her friends to ask him to relay the message to them that they could come nearer the house. Only when they had done so did she pull up to the house and alight from the car.

The greeting was as staged as everything else. For ten minutes Diana, Carolyn Bartholomew, her husband William, and their child stood on the doorstep, kissing, chatting animatedly and providing the massed banks of photographers with a photo-opportunity *par excellence*. Making absolutely sure that the following day's papers had a wide selection of pictures to publish, their co-operation was so transparent that word of it soon got out.

Back at Buckingham Palace, Diana's behaviour caused consternation. It was bad enough that she had refused to come to the rescue of her husband's reputation. But conveying tacit approval to the world was treachery. Her brother-in-law Robert Fellowes was dismayed, to say the least. The prime minister informed her that he was aware of her dealings with the press. And the Royal Family, down to the last individual, turned against her.

In his straightforward way, the Duke of Edinburgh made Diana know in no uncertain terms that he considered her to be disloyal, and that she had a duty of loyalty to her husband and the family and institution into which she had married. The Queen agreed with her husband's assessment, but handled 'that dangerous, tiresome girl' more tactfully. She asked Diana what she wanted, and was astounded to hear her daughter-in-law recite a catalogue that could be summarized in one word: everything. Diana wanted an official separation, the right to continue performing her official duties as and when she saw fit, her own staff, household, palace. In the Queen's opinion, a separation would damage the monarchy and must therefore be avoided at all costs, and at a meeting between Diana and herself, Charles and Philip at Windsor Castle during Royal Ascot Week, she convinced Diana to wait six months before coming to a decision.

As for the rest of the family, the scales fell off the eyes of those who had hitherto been blinded by Diana's convincing charm and not seen her other all too human side. The Princess Royal had never been a fan, but Princess Margaret and Andrew and Edward had always been reluctant to believe that Diana might really be as difficult as rumour attributed her as being. The Queen Mother too had to come to the reluctant conclusion that Diana might never have been a suitable addition to the Royal Family, and this pained her, especially as she had encouraged Charles to marry Diana.

Even though all the family continued to treat Diana with scrupulous *politesse*, she knew they now despised her. She told friends she could see the hatred in their eyes whenever she walked into a room and found being in their company an ordeal. It had become survival of the fittest. However, although Diana wanted to survive, she had no plans to stay within the Royal Family's fold after the expiration of the six-month deadline in December. With the aid of her solicitor, Paul Butner, senior partner in the firm of Wright, Son and Pepper, she devised a strategy that would give her the separation she yearned for while protecting her privileges. In a nutshell, she had the means to hold the family up to ransom. They so dreaded controversy that they would agree to any of her demands in an attempt to keep her quiet. At that juncture, she wanted to remain married to Charles and to be crowned Queen when he succeeded to the throne. However, she also knew that the courtiers would renege on any agreement that did not suit the Royal Family once the settlement had been finalized.

This led to the prime minister making a statement to parliament, stating that she retained all the rights of a wife, including the right to succeed and be crowned as Charles's consort when the time came.

While Diana was dealing with her separation, the courtiers were plotting her demise. The second round of the War of the Waleses was about to be fought, and Charles would emerge the victor. The means they chose was to tarnish Diana's saintly image by a judicious counter-attack. The Squidgy tape was therefore sent to a variety of newspapers. Although the *Sun* had had it in its possession for nearly three years, it had never elected to utilize it until their competitors were in danger of doing so. The tape was doctored, and the incriminating masturbatory minutes were left out of it. Saint Diana still ruled, albeit with a tarnished halo.

Chastened and frightened about what else might emerge to sully her pristine reputation, the formerly victorious Diana now retreated behind a posture of compliance. She even agreed to honour her commitment to accompany Charles to Korea in October 1992.

Relations between Charles and herself were so dire that they could not bear to be in the same room as one another, but their fight was no longer over their personal lives. Charles still had Camilla Parker Bowles as his premiere confidante while Diana had James Hewitt to whisper in her ear. Moreover, she could entertain her friends away from the prying eyes of the courtiers. Her good friend Mara Berni, who owns the fashionable restaurant San Lorenzo with her husband, allowed her the use of a flat above the restaurant. This had been occupied by the socialite Solweiga Wallach for over fifteen years until 1991. Aside from the fact that it was discreet (Diana could be seen entering and leaving the restaurant but could disappear for hours on end without the press or public being any wiser as to her whereabouts), it also had several entrances, most of which were unknown to the papparazzi who stood on the doorstep to record Diana's arrival and departure.

For a few short weeks, Charles even allowed himself to hope that they were over the worst. Then he and Diana went to Korea, and his worst fears were realized. It was unavoidably obvious to the world how miserable she was with him and how happy without. Upon their return to Britain, he informed his mother that they would have no choice but to bite the bullet and agree to the dreaded separation.

Throughout November, Sir Matthew Farrer of Farrer & Co., acting on behalf of the Prince of Wales, and Paul Butner of Wright, Son and Pepper for Diana, conducted negotiations. The Duke of Edinburgh had been of the opinion since June that Charles would be better off to be divorced from Diana, and Charles was now coming round to that way of thinking. However, Diana still wanted to be Queen one day, and the Queen was still wary of the damage she might do to the monarchy. So they agreed to all her demands, including drafting a speech that the prime minister would deliver to parliament when the announcement was made in January.

Saturday 12 December had been earmarked for the Princess Royal's marriage to Commander Tim Laurence. On Tuesday, 8 December, Diana dropped a bombshell in Charles's lap. Unless the announcement of their separation was brought forward, she would personally announce it on the day of Anne's wedding.

Diana's motives were twofold. On the one hand, she now felt such a pariah within the Royal Family that she wanted to avoid having to spend any more embarrassing time with them – and Christmas, peak family time, was approaching. On the other hand, Diane had never liked Anne. Stealing her thunder was an ideal way of settling an old score while incidentally satisfying her competitive lust for winning, making her feel better at this unhappy time. So John Major, who had been due to attend a meeting with the European Commission's Heads of State and Government in Scotland, had to alter his plans and remain in London to make the announcement to parliament.

Diana's reaction was a replay of her victorious stance during June, when her authorized version of the story was published. After the initial elation of winning her freedom, she was shaken to discover that neither parliament nor the people wished to have her as Queen. 'Fine,' she said, quickly recovering her equilibrium, 'I don't have to be Queen. I'll be the King's mother.'

Without even missing a beat and propelled by the hatred she now felt for Charles, Diana saw that she had a new objective: to deprive Charles of the throne, which she could no longer share, and hand the prize over to her son. She also decided she wanted the divorce that she had so resisted when the Duke of Edinburgh had floated the idea past her. However, she also wanted a royal title of her own to accompany it, so that she could remarry while retaining her position as a fully fledged senior member of the Royal Family. For his part, Charles was a very worried man as the year drew to a close. And he knew that his birthright was now at risk.

Sure enough, the month of January saw a flurry of tapes arrive anonymously at various newspaper offices in Britain. These bore the Camillagate recording, which could not have landed on the editors' desks at a worse time. The Calcutt Report on press abuse had just been published and was calling for curbs, so all the British publications to which it had been sent declined to run it.

The oldest journalistic trick in the book, however, is to run a story you want published in one country, then let it be picked up second-hand in your own country. The Rupert Murdoch group's Australian magazine *New Idea* published what its British brothers and sisters had been too afraid to carry.

The Murdoch group in Britain did not even need to publish the contents of the tape here to achieve the damage to the monarchy that the British Establishment feared it sought. The *Sport*, the *Mirror* and the *People* did, and just about everyone in Britain knew what Charles and Camilla had said to one another. The Establishment interpretation was that yet another nail had been driven into the coffin of the British Royal Family's reputation. The republic was that bit nearer. Charles's camp did not take this latest flurry of activity any more passively than they had before. The result was that January proved to be the month that damaged Diana's reputation as well. A letter from Lord MacGregor of Durris to Sir Robert Calcutt, QC, revealing how she had been manipulating the press, was leaked. This rightly upset her, for it was calculated to damage her reputation and succeeded in doing so.

In years to come, 1992 will be seen as the year during which Diana was relegated from the peak of public adoration to ever increasing obscurity. The courtiers are intent upon marginalizing and trivializing her. It is their declared intention to reduce her status and to delegate her to the royal backburner.

Like many a movie star who believes her own publicity and ends up destroying her career with unrealistic ambitions, Diana confused the worship that attaches itself to a symbol and believed that her greatness sprang from herself instead of from the role she represented. Admittedly she did a superb job in the execution of her public duties and earned the high esteem in which she was held. But seldom has anyone in the history of the world possessed so much and thrown it away in a quest for even more. Ultimately, her life is a latter-day version of a morality tale, with the awful warning of what hubris can do, especially when it is allied to an unhappy, unresolved life.

Doubtless the saga of the Waleses is a drama that will run and run and run some more. Both Charles and Diana remain in the public eye, though the Palace intend to wind down her public appearances and starve her of the oxygen of publicity. Whether she will go quietly, or pull a few more tricks out of her bag of goodies in an attempt to save her reputation, remains to be seen.

The Royal Family are adamant that the huge gulf between Charles and Diana will not succeed in destroying Charles's chances of succeeding to the throne. Rather than see that happen, they will use the opportunity to overhaul institutions and organizations, which are long overdue for a change. For instance, the prospect of a divorced King-to-be is not so untenable if there is separation of Church and State, and the Church of England is dis-established. Whether the Royal Family and their advisers keep their nerve remains to be seen. They will certainly need it if they are to succeed, for Diana is equally adamant that no one will wind her down, and she has an innate talent for protecting and enhancing her interests.

Insofar as the outcome of the marriage is concerned, the most likely course is a divorce after two years' separation. Following that, the Palace machinery will swing into operation and get in touch with the various charities and organizations that Diana supports. They will discreetly ask that her visits be low-key and without publicity, for the goal will be to whisk Diana's platform from under her feet. Deprived of the grandeur and stature of her position as a real member of the Royal Family, she will wither on the vine of celebrity. This process will be inexorable, whether she resists it or not. Ultimately, Diana is not more powerful than the monarchy. As the Establishment continues to close ranks in Charles's favour, she will be shunted aside.

Already she is *persona non grata* in the highest levels of British society, and if her opponents at court have their way, she will eventually become the Zsa Zsa Gabor of royalty. As for Charles, he feels that he has passed his nadir. The Camillagate tapes hung over his head like a sword of Damocles. They have been published. They have proved he is not dead beneath the waist. And he has survived. The belief at the Palace is that, as he beavers away working on behalf of the nation, the affection and regard in which he was held, before Diana's manipulations sullied his reputation, will restore him to the level of popularity he once possessed. The people will choose his side, not only because he is their future King and they owe him the loyalty that his endeavours on their behalf have inspired, but because he is a decent man, and they sense that fact.

Like any other couple who have children, Charles and Diana's break-up has affected William and Harry. Both boys were mortified, as all children are, to find themselves the centre of gossip. It is only to be hoped that they will learn the lessons of how harmful bitter marital failures are rather better than Diana did. She repeated the pattern of her parents' destructive relationship. With a bit of luck, her sons will learn that some things are better avoided than repeated.

The marriage of the Prince and Princess of Wales started on such a high note. It seems unbelievable that it could have ended the way it did. But fact really is stranger than fiction, and the most incredulous stories are not those that are invented, but those that are true.

CHAPTER SEVENTEEN

Rear Admiral

After the complications and convolutions of the Waleses' marriage, the Yorks' marriage is as refreshingly straightforward as the Duke and Duchess of York themselves. Every marriage, of course, is the story of the two people involved. How they relate, what effect they have upon each other, becomes the tale of their union, so it is impossible to trace what transpired between the Yorks without looking at them individually and collectively.

From the word go, His Royal Highness The Prince Andrew Albert Christian Edward was destined to be spoilt. He was adored by his mother from the very moment of his birth. Indisputably her favourite child, Lilibet had a bond with Andrew she has never had with any of the other children.

While Lilibet was falling deeper and deeper under the spell of her second son, Philip took a less enthusiastic view of the child named after his father. According to him, 'People want their first child very much. They want the second child almost as much. If a third child comes along they accept it as natural, even if they have not gone out of their way for it.'

Possibly to compensate for Philip's matter-of-fact approach to the birth, Lilibet lavished love on Andrew the way she had not been inclined or allowed to do with her two elder children. No longer as young or as inexperienced in her role as she had been when Charles and Anne were small, she was better able to juggle her schedule and manage her time to enjoy something of ordinary motherhood. Dedicating time to Andrew that had never been available for the other two, she discovered a joy and delight in motherhood, which had hitherto escaped her.

Flourishing under his mother's ministrations, baby Andrew also escaped the strict disciplinarianism of Charles and Anne's Nanny Lightbody. Mabel Anderson, who had been nursery assistant to Nanny Lightbody, was appointed Nanny. The indulgence of children advised by Doctor Spock was all the rage. This coincided perfectly with Lilibet and Nanny Anderson's predilections, for the former was by nature a soft and easy-going mother while the latter was more flexible than her predecessor.

The result was that baby Andrew grew into an unruly terror. By his own admission, he played football in the passages of Buckingham Palace and made the life of the servants a misery. He was rude, arrogant and full of his own importance, for, unlike Charles and Anne, who had been deprived of the knowledge of their high rank even as they were photographed at every turn, he was made aware of his from an early age. He would swan around the various royal homes ordering the staff about, snapping his fingers at them and generally making himself 'a bloody nuisance', according to members of his mother's staff. The Palace servants could not abide him, but no one said anything until one day he was so rude to a footman that he sailed Andrew across the room with a slap. Resignation seemed the only course open to him, so he duly proffered the necessary letter. Before he could depart, however, the Queen got wind of what had happened. 'He was quite right to slap him,' she said, instructing that the footman remain in his job.

The die cast, Andrew grew into the classic spoilt brat. Arrogant and overbearing, he had an uncontrollable temper. When he lost it, he did not always limit himself to raising his voice or cutting the object of his anger down to verbal size. Sometimes, he would become physical. By the time it occurred to the adults surrounding him that Andrew needed to be controlled, he was already so out of control that it was impossible to reign him back in. Not, it must be said, that anyone tried very hard. As with the Royal Family's Sandringham neighbours, the Spencer children, no one ever made a concerted attempt to impose discipline on Andrew, and he continued taking advantage of that to do as he pleased.

Allied to this lack of discipline was Andrew's natural energy and predisposition towards authoritarianism. His role model of masculinity was Prince Philip, who had a justly deserved reputation as a bully. Emulating the older man, Andrew lacked not only the age and authority, but also he did not possess Philip's charm, intelligence, energy or ability. This meant that he had all the failings of an oaf without the redeeming qualities, and even his mother was moved to reminisce acerbically, 'He was not always a little ray of sunshine.'

Under the circumstances, it is hardly surprising that Andrew was never popular at school. Sent first to Heatherdown School in defiance of the Battenberg tradition of educating its sons at Cheam, then later to Gordonstoun, he was so pompous and arrogant that he was soon the most unpopular boy in the school. The level of hostility he engendered is reflected in his failure to become guardian or head boy at Gordonstoun, as Philip, Charles and later Edward were. The other students would simply not have tolerated the appointment, which usually went to the royals by virtue of who they were, and he had to settle for the humiliating sop of being made head boy of his house, Cumming House. Indeed, so unpopular was Andrew that the headmaster had to select boys to watch out for him so that he would not be beaten up.

During Andrew's day, Gordonstoun was a lot gentler than it had been in Charles or Philip's time. The dormitories were heated, cold showers were followed by hot, short trousers had been replaced by long, and even the morning run was nothing more than a 200-yard dash. Sparta was a thing of the past, which was just as well, for Andrew liked his comfort.

Had his academic ability matched his gift for antagonism, Andrew would have gone far, but, as it was, he failed all but one of his O-level subjects at the first sitting and only managed the lowest passes in A-level English, Economic and Political Studies, and History.

Where he was more gifted, however, was in his appeal to the opposite sex. Gordonstoun was a co-educational school by the time he went there. Andrew was growing into a tall, burly, well-built young man with a toothy smile and good looks that were atypically Windsor or Mountbatten. The girls fell for him in droves. They did not mind that he was arrogant and overbearing. They liked the power of his dominating voice as much as the power of his rank. They did not despise him the way the boys did, for being a mother's boy. They liked the easy way he related to them, the way he lapped up all the love and attention they gave him and still came back for more. There might have been nothing sensitive about Andrew, but his needs were pronounced, and they inspired positive feminine reactions. He had several flirtations with Gordonstoun girls, including Cally Oldershaw, Jenny Wooten, Kirstie Richmond, who was his first big love, and Clio Nathaniels.

Being a royal prince, Andrew had a job waiting for him, as he so indelicately announced to his classmates when the subject of future careers was raised. He had developed a love for the air when he joined the Air Training Corps at Gordonstoun at the age of fifteen and had even gone on three years later to earn his wings on a course at No. 1 Parachute Training Centre, RAF Brize Norton. The RAF, however, was not perceived as being a suitable branch of the armed services for a prince of the blood royal, so Andrew killed two birds with one stone and became a cadet at the Naval College, Dartmouth, with the intention of qualifying as a helicopter pilot. This he did at twenty-one, after which he was posted as a pilot of Sea Kings for the 829 Naval Air Squadron on HMS *Invincible*.

At sea, Andrew was no more popular than he had been on land. He was ever mindful of the superiority of his royal rank and could not understand that his bluff attempts to make friends pushed away men of all ranks. There is one notable incident when he approached an admiral and said, 'You may call me Andrew.'

'And you may call me Sir,' his senior officer replied, putting the puppy prince in his place.

Despite the trouble he had earning the regard of his fellow officers, Andrew loved the naval life and relished being at sea for long stretches. He was comfortable being a man in a man's world. A jock by nature, he liked the company of men and enjoyed the exclusively male environment. Unlike some of the men, who found it difficult coping with the frustrations that being without women created, Andrew did not suffer from such deprivations. He was perfectly happy doing without feminine companionship as long as he had male companionship as a substitute. To him, it was the companionship that mattered, not the sex of the person whence it came. He was therefore ideally cast for a naval future.

In fact, the pressures for Andrew usually started when his ship returned to shore. Already he was being portrayed as Randy Andy in the popular press, but the reality was considerably less glamorous. True, he was as sexually motivated as all the other members of the House of Windsor. True, he enjoyed the catholic popularity his good looks and royal rank brought him. But he was a lot more simplistic and a lot less erudite than his reputation deserved. The rampant ladies' man was more a press invention than a fact, one that played well for the newspapers but also one that put a lot of pressure on a young man who was still discovering where his true interests lay. Moreover, the public image did not improve his relations with most of his naval mates, who could now add envy to the list of reasons why Andrew antagonized them.

In 1981, Charles married Diana, and Andrew's status underwent a profound change. Almost immediately, he learnt that he was about to be demoted from second to third in line to the throne. Diana was pregnant. Moreover, with his marriage the Prince of Wales had vacated the position of the world's most eligible bachelor. The mantle of that mixed blessing promptly fell on to Randy Andy's shoulders.

Because Andrew stood little or no chance of ever becoming king, he was not subject to the same rigorous rules of courting that had so hampered Charles. This was accepted not only by the Palace and the prince but also by the press and the public, who were dished up a veritable feast of nubile beauties. These included traditional gels such as Kirstie Richmond and Clio Nathaniels as well as less regal choices like Miss United Kingdom 1980, Carolyn Seaward and Royal Ballet dancer Karen Paisey. They confirmed the Randy Andy image, while also conveying the message that this prince did not need to marry an aristocrat or a virgin, or at least someone who could be palmed off on the public as one. While the public bought the image of the popular playboy prince, those who lived or worked with Andrew knew that the reality, both of his playing and of his popularity, was somewhat different.

Unexpected circumstances can radically alter the course or shape of someone's life. This applies equally to princes and peasants. And it happened to Andrew in 1982, when Argentina invaded the Falkland Islands. Mrs Thatcher sent the Task Force to reclaim the territory to which Britain possessed sovereignty. Prince Andrew's ship, *Invincible*, crossed the Atlantic with its royal helicopter pilot on board. The Queen was as worried as any of the other mothers or wives whose sons or husbands were involved in the fighting for, contrary to press reports, her favourite child was in the thick of it all.

Andrew's job was to fly his helicopter as a decoy, which pulled Exocet missiles away from the aircraft carrier. According to him, 'The idea is that the Exocet comes in low over the waves and is not supposed to go above a height of twenty-seven feet. When the missile is coming at you, you rise quickly above twenty-seven feet, and it flies harmlessly underneath – in theory.' In practice, it was one of the most dangerous jobs of all, and the prince acquitted himself so valiantly that first the navy, then the press, developed an admiration for him where previously there had been only contempt. General Galtieri had saved not only the unpopular Mrs Thatcher's political bacon but also the unpopular Prince Andrew's personal reputation. Thereafter, he would never be perceived as an arrogant boor, but as a courageous man of action whose bluffness owed more to resolution than to insensitivity. A hero was born. And for the first time in his life Andrew knew the meaning of the word popularity.

Andrew the oaf, however, had never been quite as thoughtless as everyone supposed. When a journalist said stupidly, 'Bet you wouldn't have missed the opportunity for the world,' he wisely retorted, 'I would have avoided it if I could. So would any sane man.'

Andrew returned to a hero's welcome and to the loving arms of Koo Stark. He had met her in February 1982 through socialite and public-relations consultant Ricci Lewis and her boyfriend of the time, Charlie Young, who was Andrew's best friend and had been since their days together at Gordonstoun. Always quick off the mark, Andrew was soon besotted with the petite, attractive, quick-witted and entirely charming Koo.

The daughter of Beverly Hills film producer Wilbur Stark, Koo rented the basement flat at socialite Scodina Dwek's spacious Chester Square, Belgravia house. To date, her life had been one of comfort, and her deportment confirmed that. When Andrew took her home to introduce her to his family, all of them were taken with her. The Queen was especially fond of her, which in itself was high praise, for Lilibet is a superb judge of character, as her pre-marital assessment of Diana proves. Koo fitted in perfectly.

As the romance 'hotted up', Andrew played host to Koo at whichever royal residence he happened to be staying. There were lingering romantic dinners at Buckingham Palace and weekends in the country. Koo was as deeply in love with Andrew as he was with her. She seemed tailor-made for the role of royal duchess, despite being slightly older than her prince, for she was a genuinely kind and decent person as well as an attractive girl with a sociable personality and brains. Indeed, her maturity was a positive benefit in dealing with Andrew. He was still as uncontrolled as ever. This deficiency extended beyond his temper to rather more personal matters, but she solved the problem by teaching him that he could distract himself. Her method was for him to count to ten, after which he would hopefully have broken the spiral of overwhelming excitement.

Andrew returned to the Falkland Islands for another tour of duty, but the three months he and Koo spent apart did not lessen their love for one another. So when he returned, they planned a pre-marital honeymoon at Princess Margaret's house on Mustique. They flew out as Mr and Mrs Cambridge, but, as luck would have it, Andrew was recognized by journalists on the flight, who were keen not only to share the news of the lovebirds' love nest but also Koo's compromising past.

Koo was an actress. At the age of seventeen, she had appeared topless in *The Adventures of Emily*, a film that the Earl of Pembroke produced under his professional name, Henry Herbert. It was hardly pornographic by today's standards, but once the tabloids found out about it, they labelled her a soft-porn actress and flogged the issue of Koo's suitability to death.

It mattered not whether she was a decent person, whether she had decorum and finesse, whether she would make a good royal duchess. All that mattered was that they could exaggerate a youthful indiscretion and turn it into a stigma to disqualify her from marrying the man she loved. Meanwhile, in Mustique the love nest turned into a target for an army of long-range lenses, and Koo and Andrew were compelled to lie low and never appear out of doors. By the time they flew back to Britain they were suffering from seige mentality, and Prince Edward rightly observed, 'He came back from that holiday more drawn, more tired, than he did from three months of war.'

Upon their return, Andrew went straight to see his mother, and Koo went straight home. The Queen was mortified that the press could have vilified her son the way it had done, or that they could behave so cruelly to a young woman she had liked. Prince Philip, on the other hand, saw the practicalities only too clearly and advised Andrew to give up the first great love of his life. Duty involved sacrifices, some of which were personally painful, but Andrew did not have a choice unless he wished to damage the monarchy. So Andrew bit the bullet and gave up Koo.

The manner in which Andrew made his sacrifice did not reflect well upon him. Emulating his great-uncle David, who dropped Freda Dudley Ward without so much as a perfunctory goodbye, Andrew instructed the telephone operators at Buckingham Palace that the next time Koo called she was not to be put through. One can take a charitable view and say that he was still so in love with her he was afraid his resolve might weaken, but the sad fact is that he was no hero off the battlefield.

Returning to the merry-go-round as Randy Andy, the Queen's second son set about rebuilding his shattered personal life. He was happy for the refuge the navy provided, but it was not the only one. Koo had encouraged Andrew's fledgling interest in photography, and, under the wing of the internationally famous photographer Norman Parkinson, Andrew developed a passion for the art as well as a close friendship with Parkinson's Filipino printer Gene Nocon and his wife Liz.

According to Gene Nocon, 'We were certainly very, very friendly with

Prince Andrew – still are. It goes both ways. He would come and see us. He was very much a part of the family.' Gene Nocon did all of Andrew's printing, kept his slides and gave Andrew untrammelled access to his large wife Liz. She was a surrogate mother figure to Andrew, although she was the same generation as he, and there is no suggestion whatsoever that their relationship ever had romantic overtones. It was far too much the nurturer and the nurtured for that. They discussed everything together, from his romances and how they were going to his plans and hopes for the future.

Like many Mama's boys, Andrew was only truly comfortable with other men or with other women who offered him unconditional adoration. What he wanted was to find himself a wife who would accept him just as he was, and who would continue loving him no matter what he did. It was a tall order, not much more reasonable than his sister-in-law Diana's variation on the same theme, though it must be said in Andrew's favour that at least he was not unbalanced.

CHAPTER EIGHTEEN

A Star is Born

*T*he girl who would one day become the Duchess of York was born at 9.03 a.m. on 15 October 1959 to Ronald and Susie Ferguson. Their second daughter, she was christened Sarah Margaret and grew into a happy, endearing but wild child. According to her father, 'Sarah always had to do everything her own way,' but she was so considerate and eager to please that it seemed a pity to break her spirit with too much conformity.

Sarah Ferguson grew up in a comfortable upper-class home. The press often retail the fiction that she was not from a grand background, but this is not true. On her father's side she is descended from the Duke of Buccleuch and therefore from King Charles II as well as from several other ducal houses, and her mother Susie Wright was also from a privileged background. The family lived near Sunninghill in Berkshire at Lowood House, a ten-bedroomed Edwardian house set in fourteen acres. Although they were not rich, between them Ronald and Susie had enough money to bankroll a gracious lifestyle, with servants, nannies for their daughters Sarah and Jane and grooms for Ronald's polo ponies.

Ronald Ferguson was a career officer with the Life Guards and one of the finest polo players in the country. It was through polo that they became friendly with the Duke of Edinburgh and the Queen, through polo that they received invitations to shoot at Sandringham, through polo that Susie met Hector Barrantes, the man she would eventually leave her family for, and through polo that Sarah herself took her first steps along the road leading to royalty.

In 1969, the Fergusons sold Lowood House and moved into the farmhouse on the 876-acre Dummer Down Farm, which Ronald inherited from his father. With only eight bedrooms, it was smaller than their previous residence, but a fine Georgian house nevertheless. For the girls, its greatest appeal was that it had stabling for six horses. Both Jane and Sarah were keen equestriennes.

Although Ronald's star remained in the ascendant on the polo field, professionally he had reached his peak in the army. He was only a major, but he was left in no doubt by the staff college that a peacock like him had gone as far as he was going, so, rather than settle for a dead-end career, he resigned his commission and took a part-time job in public relations. This was a wise move, for it allowed him to use his organizational skills and social contacts to the full. Later on, he would move from Neilson McCarthy, where he was appointed a director to advise on polo three days a week, to the Guards Polo Club at Smith's Lawn, Windsor Great Park, by which time his marriage was crumbling.

In summer 1972, the death knell of the Ferguson marriage sounded when Ronald and Susie rented the Villa Petra on Corfu with a group of friends. With them was Hector Barrantes, whose pregnant wife Louisa had recently been killed, in a car that had crashed while his sister was driving it. El Gordo himself was injured badly in the accident, and the unhappily married Susie found herself being drawn to the grieving widower. One thing led to another, and by the time they all returned to England, Susie and Hector realized they had something between them that was worth pursuing.

Ronald Ferguson is a far more sensitive man than his public image indicates, and he took Susie's defection badly. Patience and tolerance might have seen off the competition and induced Susie to revert to the none too satisfactory status quo, but he reacted with anger and actually drove her into Hector's arms.

El Gordo, moreover, was not prepared to just be a lover. He wanted to share his life with Susie, though he was sufficiently honourable to refuse to do so until she was properly free. So for the two years that it took for Susie to extract herself from the marriage, move to London as a separated woman and obtain a divorce, the lovers remained apart but together. Only when the divorce came through in 1974 did she move to Iping near Midhurst in Sussex to live with the man who she says was 'the love of my life. With Hector, I knew real love.' In July 1975, when Sarah was fifteen, the lovers married at Chichester Register Office.

The life of a professional polo player is a peripatetic one. Susie and Hector made their base in Argentina, the country of his birth. Though they lived on a ranch at Trenque Lauquen, 300 miles south-west of Buenos Aires, they spent part of each year in Britain. Susie therefore remained in close touch with her daughter Sarah, though less so with Jane, who married Alex Makim the year after the divorce when she was eighteen, going to live on a farm in the outback of Australia.

Although the Ferguson divorce was not amicable, Ronald and Susie spared their children the trauma that Johnnie Spencer inflicted upon his. The result was that Sarah was far less damaged by the split. She loved her stepfather and developed an equally fond and friendly relationship with Susan Deptford, whom her father married in November 1976, the same year as Jane's marriage.

The ability to form good and happy relationships was a gift that Sarah would never lose. It caused problems for her, however, when she was made head girl of Hurst Lodge. According to Sarah, 'I was so uncontrollable they had to make me head girl so I would start behaving.'

But Jilly Adams, a schoolmate, saw the pain beneath the smile. 'She so desperately wanted people to like her and being head girl created problems. It was a responsible position, and she was often called on to bring other girls into line if they misbehaved. But as soon as she had done it, she would rush round and apologize for pulling rank.' Jilly Adams also thought that the young Sarah 'had such a massive insecurity problem that I used to despair for her sometimes. She was a real stunner even then, but she was convinced she was hideous. Fergie was always wailing, "Oh, just look at the state of me. I'm so fat and my bottom's so huge."'

That teenage insecurity would have a dreadful redolence when Sarah married Andrew, but in the meantime she continued winning friends and having a good time with her 'very sunny disposition: enormously cheerful, bubbly and fun-loving,' as her former headmistress Celia Merrick put it.

Rather like Diana, Sarah was more interested in shining in real life than in the Elysian fields of academe. Nevertheless, she did not occupy a dream world of her own or fail to live up to her academic responsibilities, and in 1976, just before Jane's wedding, she sat and passed O-levels in English Literature and Language, Art, Biology, Geography and Mathematics. She had no interest in furthering her education but wanted to travel before taking the secretarial course her father wisely insisted she do, so Ronald bought her a ticket to Argentina. Ever protective, the evening before the flight he contacted Gatwick and arranged for the seventeen-year-old Sarah to fly out, much to her chagrin, as an unaccompanied minor.

The six months Sarah spent living on the Barrantes ranch in Argentina matured her. She had already come to terms with the break-up of the family and the changes in her parents' personal lives. Now she was about to learn how enriching the results of a painful experience could be. 'Hector was a well-rounded person,' her mother stated. 'He was well read, had great common sense and an optimistic view of reality. They confided in each other a lot. When you're happy you've always got more to give, not only to your partner but to everyone. I told this to Sarah, and it is something she has always remembered.'

While broadening her mind Sarah lost some of the puppy fat that had caused her such anxieties as a schoolgirl. The outdoor life suited her, and it was a rudely healthy and happy Sarah who returned to Britain to start adult life.

There were adjustments to make, not the least of which was that Dummer Down Farm had a new chatelaine in the shape of her recently acquired stepmother Sue. The two women got along well, however, and there was never any conflict between Sarah and 'my wicked stepmother', as she jokingly dubbed Sue. The London flat had been sold, though, and Sarah was enrolled at Queen's Secretarial College in South Kensington, so she shared a flat with her cousin Ros Bowie.

Bored rigid with her course, Sarah plunged wholeheartedly into her social life. She had a wealth of friends, including her classmate, Lord Eden of Winton's daughter Charlotte, the Duke of Marlborough's nephew David Waterhouse (later Diana's bridge partner) and Laura Smith-Bingham, but what she really wanted was her own boyfriend. This being the seventies, when everyone had a good time and the consequences were nothing more lethal than a hangover, she experimented as much as everyone else with a series of lighthearted flirtations, which amounted to nothing more than adventures. Dashing young men such as Michael Corry-Reid, whose parents owned the Villa Petra, the launch-pad for Susie and Hector's romance, came, conquered and departed. For a while, it looked as if Sarah might become one of those girls who could not get a boyfriend, which was a demoralizing prospect at a time of life when an eternity is not measured in months or years but in days or weeks. She was saved, however, by the arrival on the scene of her friend Laura Smith-Bingham's brother.

Kim Smith-Bingham was two years older than Sarah. He was working in the City and had actually met Sarah in Argentina, where he worked as a ranch hand after leaving school. They did not strike up a particular closeness there, however. This only came as a result of his getting to know the exuberant Sarah through his sister. Over six feet tall and well-built, with thinning hair that promised of a plethora of testosterone, Kim started dating Sarah on a regular basis and was soon her first boyfriend.

It is worth looking at the type of person the young Sarah Ferguson was, for she would not change in essential ways. She had a warm heart, a passionate disposition and a strong sense of commitment. She was straight-forward and enthusiastic, generous spirited and easy-going, positive and optimistic. Beneath her dedication to fun and laughter there was a more serious side to her character. She was loyal, loving and kind, and when she gave her heart, she gave it totally. Not for the first time in her life, she was about to be disillusioned.

Sarah fell totally in love with Kim Smith-Bingham. Like many young men on the town, he sometimes rang, sometimes didn't. Sometimes he showed up, sometimes he didn't. Taking things very much to heart, the naturally ebullient Sarah began experiencing periods of gloom. Her father became so concerned by the misery that the romance was causing her that he arranged, in an effort to break Smith-Bingham's spell, to take her to Australia to see his elder daughter Jane at Wilga Warrina, the 8000-acre farm the Makims owned near the New South Wales border with Queensland.

Love, however, had Sarah firmly in its painful grip, and when she and Ronald returned to London, she returned to Kim Smith-Bingham as well. The romance continued in the same unsatisfactory fashion, though only too soon there was another problematic aspect to it. Smith-Bingham was not exactly setting the City alight, so he moved to Verbier in the Swiss Alps, where he worked in the ski business. From Sarah's point of view, the one advantage of the move was that she could perfect her skiing when she went to see him. Soon she was as good as many professionals, and while he worked in the day, she skied.

By this time, Sarah had gone to work in public relations for Durden-Smith Communications. Owned by television personality Judith Chalmers' husband Neil Durden-Smith, who was a friend of her father, Sarah was chosen for the job over two better qualified and more fashionably presented girls because of the sense of commitment and enthusiasm that Durden-Smith sensed she possessed. Never once did she give him cause to regret his decision, and to this day he sings her praises.

Working hard in London and playing hard in Verbier, Sarah's life was still not going where she wanted it to. The decade ended, and a new one came, and though she did not know it, a death was about to clear the way for a more fulfilling but equally frustrating relationship. In 1980 Paddy McNally's wealthy estranged wife Anne died of cancer, leaving him with two young sons, Sean and Rollo. A dedicated father, he had to readjust his life to incorporate the changes, but when he had done so, he continued playing in Verbier with all the dedication he had previously shown to pleasure.

Paddy McNally owned a large chalet named Les Gais Lutins with London property developer David Elias. Nicknamed the Castle by the fashionable British set that frequented it, it was the venue for many a party featuring a guest list that ranged from businessman John Bentley and Lloyd's underwriter Rupert Deen through property developer David Olivestone (for a while the boyfriend of Prince Charles's ex Anna Wallace) and industrialist scion Nigel Pollitzer to the present Lord Mancroft, who is now a recovered drug addict, the Marquis of Blandford, whose drug history needs no recounting, and Lord Cowdray's heir the Hon. Michael Pearson. They were a fast crowd, but they were also the in crowd, and Kim Smith-Bingham used to go up the hill to see them. Whenever she was in Verbier, Sarah invariably accompanied him.

Gradually, however, Sarah started going up the hill on her own. There was always something exciting happening at the Castle, and while Kim was at work she might as well share in the fun. Although she was twenty-two years younger than McNally, they had a rapport, and gradually she switched her commitment from Kim Smith-Bingham to his friend Paddy.

This relationship proved to be more satisfying than the other, but it too soon revealed itself to be unsatisfactory. Paddy did not want to remarry. Like all young women in love, Sarah tried to get him to change his mind by being a perfect companion. She was a superb hostess for his friends. She was so adept at commerce that she was invariably seated beside any businessman Paddy was associated with, so that she could direct the flow in a way that would enhance Paddy's interests. She got along well with his sons, who adore her to this day. There was no doubt she and Paddy had a loving and affectionate relationship, and though it was more than enough for him, without a wedding ring it was not enough for her.

For four years Sarah remained hopeful that Paddy would marry her. She left Durden-Smith Communications and started working in 1984 with an old racing friend of Paddy's, Richard Burton, as the acquisitions editor in London for his publishing house. This took her even further away from her goal of marriage, for Paddy travelled a lot in the course of his business, which was placing advertising hoardings on Formula One tracks worldwide.

Nevertheless, Sarah's job was satisfying, it gave her independence and responsibility, and she was good at it. This was some consolation for being in a relationship yet again with a man who would not commit himself to her, and while professional success added to her self-esteem, it did not solve the depressing problem underlying it. The result was that friends recount episodes during which they stumbled upon Sarah taking herself off to some corner of the Castle for a quiet weep, having first played the ideal hostess and attended to everyone's needs.

Diana came to the rescue. In June 1985 she put Sarah's name forward as a guest for the Windsor Castle houseparty during Royal Ascot Week. Ever romantic, she hoped that something would click between Sarah and her brother-in-law Andrew. Diana knew all about how demoralized and frustrated Sarah was. The two young women were the closest of friends. They originally met at the outset of Charles and Diana's romance, at the Sussex home of Sarah's mother and stepfather, following a polo match at Cowdray Park where Charles was playing. While the men talked horses and Susie acted as hostess, Diana and Sarah struck up a conversation that soon led to firm friendship.

Although Sarah and Diana genuinely liked one another, there were also worldly considerations militating in favour of the friendship. Diana was new to royal circles and was looking for friends within it. Sarah's father had been Charles's polo manager for several years and that made her, in Diana's eyes at least, a member of the royal inner circle. Moreover, she was the first cousin once removed of Diana's brother-in-law, Robert Fellowes, the Queen's ambitious assistant private secretary who looked set to rise to the top (and did). She was therefore, in worldly terms, a suitable friend for a prospective Princess of Wales. Nor were the worldly aspects of the friendship one-sided. From Sarah's point of view, a close friendship with the Princess of Wales gave her a tremendous amount of kudos. The fact that she truly liked Diana, whose charm and gentle manner have drawn scores of people within her orbit over the years, only made the more expedient aspects of the friendship that much easier to ignore.

Despite Diana's hope of striking a match between her close friend and her brother-in-law, Sarah was still very much involved with Paddy McNally, so much so that he dropped her off for her stay and delivered her into the hands of a waiting footman. Diana's perspicacity and intuitiveness, however, were as spot-on with Sarah and Andrew as they would prove to be in so much else in her life.

Over lunch at Windsor Castle prior to going to the races, Andrew and Sarah got along 'like a house on fire', as he says. Both of them liked to laugh, both of them were jocular and used to the ribbing that upper-class Brits go in for. So when Sarah took a sparing helping of profiteroles for dessert, Andrew encouraged her to forgo her diet with the promise that he would finish what she left. When he went back on his word, however, she punched him. At that moment, love struck Andrew, who stuck like gluc to Sarah for the rest of the day.

The process of switching loyalties was something Sarah had been through when she left Kim Smith-Bingham for Paddy McNally. Now the girl who no man ever wanted enough to commit himself to found herself repeating the old pattern yet again. This time, however, it was with the Queen's son, and his personality rescued her from the fate she dreaded, for Andrew displayed a tenacity that his brother Charles had never possessed with any woman, and that Sarah was unused to. If he telephoned Sarah and she was not there, he had a quick and personable word with her flatmate Carolyn Beckwith-Smith, in whose Lavender Gardens, Battersea flat she lived, before ringing off to try again.

For four months, Sarah remained in the transitional phase. That summer she took off to Ibiza with Paddy McNally to stay at Michael Pearson's house. He was cleaning up his act after a lifetime of sixties and seventies type fun and had just started a romance with a friend of Sarah's, the former MP John Cordle's daughter Marina. Sarah was on hand to share in her joys and the exotically scented cigarettes that were so much a feature of that way of life.

When Sarah returned to London, Andrew showed how stout-hearted he was when the hand of a fair maid was at stake. He was attentive, courted her with flowers and ardour and had her for amorous dinners à deux at his rooms at Buckingham Palace. By November, the romance had intensified to such an extent that Sarah 'swallowed hard' and summoned up the courage over lunch and dinner at the Capital Hotel, Knightsbridge, to tell McNally that she was moving on. The parting was amicable, he wished her all the best, and he attended her wedding.

Being a seaman, Andrew's time on shore was limited, but after 18 December, his ship the *Brazen* put into port at Devonport. He and Sarah spent every moment they could together. Mostly, they stayed in his rooms at Buckingham Palace, dining alone and feasting on each other the way ardent lovers do. Both of them are intensely sexual, and this side of the relationship was so electrifying that it left little room for anything else.

On the other hand, sex was not the only glue holding the romance together. Andrew possessed one virtue that neither Smith-Bingham or McNally, nor indeed any of the other men with whom Sarah had had flirtations, had. He was capable of commitment. For the first time in her life Sarah therefore knew what it was to be secure in a relationship. She did not have to jump through hoops, swallow her pride, tearfully wait by the telephone, or subject herself to any of the petty humiliations that women in love put up with when their men do not want them as much as they want the men. She and Andrew wanted each other equally, and she blossomed under the warmth of his love.

So sure were Andrew and Sarah about their feelings that they decided to 'go public' with the news of their romance before Christmas. Andrew took her to a concert given by his friend Elton John during which they held hands throughout in the hope that the press would add up two and two and come up with four. In the minds of the journalists, however, Sarah was not Andrew's type, for she was not a model or an actress or a beauty queen. So they dismissed the display of affection, and the news of their romance did not break until journalist James Whitaker published an erroneous story in the *Daily Mirror* stating that an 'attractive redhead is set to join Prince Andrew for Christmas at Windsor Castle'.

Of course, as everyone who is truly knowledgeable about the way the Royal Family functions knows, Christmas is a sacrosanct time. They never ask even in-laws, so the idea of having girlfriends along is preposterous. Sarah therefore spent Christmas at Dummer Down Farm with her family, though she did join the Royal Family at Sandringham for the New Year. Thereafter the news was out, with the inevitable question of when an engagement was going to be announced. This put a strain on Sarah, but, in a harbinger of what was to come during their marriage, not on Andrew. He is very much the old-school, rise-above-it sort of person like most of the royals and many of the aristocracy.

Towards the end of February, right after Andrew's twenty-sixth birthday, his ship berthed at Sunderland. He travelled to Floors Castle, the Borders stately home of the Duke and Duchess of Roxburghe, who were playing host for the weekend to the lovebirds. Sarah and Andrew were given adjoining bedrooms. Many of their friends thought a proposal was imminent, and it is reflective of Sarah's modesty and insecurity that she was the only person taken by surprise when Andrew went down on both his knees and asked her to marry him just before midnight. 'When you wake up tomorrow morning, you can tell me it's all a huge joke,' she said, not quite believing her luck. Andrew, however, did not want the out she gave him, and the following morning he renewed his offer of marriage.

Being a member of the Royal Family, Andrew could not, under the 1772 Royal Marriages Act, marry without first asking the Queen for her permission. Because of that, neither he nor Sarah dared say anything to Guy and Jane Roxburghe until he had got his mother's blessing, so the lovers departed from the picturesque castle hugging their secret to their breasts. The Queen, however, was on one of her many overseas tours, this time to Australia and New Zealand, so Andrew had to wait until she returned in mid-March before gaining her assent to a question she knew was coming before he even asked it. According to Andrew, 'She was overjoyed.'

The Queen approved of Sarah, whom she had known since her future daughter-in-law had been a little girl. Over the years, she had seen her repeatedly as a result of her many Sunday afternoon forays from Windsor Castle to Smith's Lawn, Windsor Great Park, to watch polo. Sarah was everything the Queen liked. Although enthusiastic, she was not highly strung, but even-tempered and easy-going. She was outgoing and mucked in unselfconsciously in company, instead of seething on the sidelines and resenting it when she was not the centre of attention, like Diana. Moreover, Sarah's interests coincided with the Queen's. She loved horses, rode well, liked dogs and even enjoyed playing charades.

On the Sunday of the weekend that Andrew spoke to the Queen, Sarah had lunch with her. It was the start of an easy and enjoyable relationship that both women relished. 'It's such a pleasure to have a daughter-in-law one can enjoy,' the Queen later observed to a friend.

Sarah's past had been preoccupying the British press, but once the engagement was announced, Ronald Ferguson dispensed with it by stating that any girl who had reached the age of twenty-six without at least one boyfriend had something wrong with her. So much for the much vaunted, and out-of-touch, requirement of virginity for royal brides.

In a rerun of the Wales engagement procedure, Sarah was housed in Buckingham Palace. Unlike Diana, who gave up her job on the day of the announcement (a flunkey from the Palace telephoned the Young England Kindergarten to say she would not be coming in any more), Sarah continued working until just before the wedding. She was working on *The Palace of Westminster*, a magnificent coffee-table look at the seat of Britain's democracy, and her dedication to her job and the announcement that she intended to continue it endeared her to the large mass of working men and women throughout the land. A star was born.

CHAPTER NINETEEN

Celebrity and Notoriety

F ergie's stardom could not have come at a more opportune moment from the point of view of Fleet Street. Diana had stopped playing ball with the journalists, whom she had courted assiduously during her engagement with polite smiles and discreet conversations, as soon as Charles slipped the wedding ring on her finger. While she still took care to look good and pose for the cameras, her days of actively co-operating with the press seemed to be over. Indeed, the Queen had even called the editors of the newspapers into Buckingham Palace shortly after the marriage to ask them to lay off Diana, and though they had not, making a darling out of an unco-operative princess had become an uphill struggle.

Even before her marriage to Prince Andrew, Sarah enjoyed a honeymoon with the ladies and gentlemen of the tabloids, who could not enthuse enough about her naturalness, her charm, her down-to-earth approach to royal life and, above all, her realness. At any given time, the Royal Family are a living soap opera. Invariably there are one or two stars, while the rest of the family play supporting roles. The British press has a long tradition of not sucking up to its rulers, and that, allied to sound commercial practice, dictates that only one of the royal superstars is ever built up in a positive light. In the fifties and sixties, for instance, they had Elizabeth the Good and Margaret the Bad, and in 1986 they happened upon Fergie the Real Person who quickly edged Shy Di into the dark as Diana the Birdbrain Spendthrift.

By the time Fergie departed from Clarence House, where she spent her last night as a single woman and walked up that aisle at Westminster Abbey on the arm of her father at 11.33 a.m. on Wednesday, 23 July 1986, she was the world's darling. Everyone seemed to be in love with the friendly, good-natured redhead who was the new Duchess of York, the Queen having elevated her second son to the peerage at ten o'clock on the morning of his wedding. Her Royal Highness was so refreshingly *unstuffy*, so obviously *nice*, so charmingly *natural*. Moreover, she was not a fashion plate, and she had no pretensions to being one. Only on her wedding day did she become a raving beauty, in Lindka Cierach's exquisite gown offsetting the figure she had reduced by twenty-six pounds.

At this point, Diana was happy to stand aside and let Sarah reign as supreme celebrity. Miserable in her personal life, fed up with the inconvenience of fame, Diana also knew the worm would turn against Sarah the way it had turned with her. She was therefore relieved to be out of the hot seat. At least for the moment.

While Diana was enjoying her sabbatical from the glare of publicity, Sarah and Andrew were basking in the pleasures of their sun-drenched honeymoon aboard the royal yacht *Britannia*. It cruised around the Azores, and, like Charles and Diana, the honeymooners stopped off for romantic picnics. Both Sarah and Andrew are intensely sexual, so they also spent a good part of their time in bed, but when they arose, there were already warning signs of what life with Andrew would be like. A true couch potato, the only form of non-sleeping activity he wanted to engage in aside from making love was watching videos on the television.

This was not a good sign. Sarah York has always been one of those people who are constantly on the go. During their courtship, Andrew could never stop commenting on how many different activities she managed to cram into a day. She would go to work, get through a full schedule of appointments, have lunch with a friend, go out to see various people involved with whatever project she was working on, return home, bathe and dress, attend three or four cocktail parties, go on to dinner, leave for Annabel's or one of the other smart members-only clubs afterwards, have a few dances and a drink, then go back home to sleep, only to repeat the entire process the following day. On weekends, she was up and about, riding or engaging in one of the many pursuits associated with country life. She literally never stood still for one second longer than she had to.

This basic incompatibility of temperament would prove to be a real problem during their marriage, but in the early days neither Andrew nor Sarah realized it. Like all the royals, he felt his marriage was for life, so now he was married, he planned to suit himself and continue in the way he had started. His attitude was that Sarah would just have to get used to it, and the ever obliging Sarah did try. She was grateful to Andrew for providing her with the only truly secure relationship she had had in her adult life, and if the price of that was that she had to tolerate an unacceptable level of inactivity, so be it.

Long after the honeymoon with Andrew ended, the honeymoon with the media continued. Andrew returned to sea and his naval interests and Sarah to the apartment at Buckingham Palace, from which she set out on her forays to the world at large. She gained everyone's admiration by continuing to be a working girl, without anyone but her closest friends realizing that she needed the money. Although Andrew was rich by everyday standards (the Queen had set up a trust fund for him at the time of Princess Anne's marriage to Mark Phillips, which was then worth over £2 million), they were poor in comparison with the high standards they were expected, as senior royals, to maintain.

Their office, staff and expenses gobbled up their Civil List allotment, while his private income went to maintain their lifestyle. That meant that Sarah had to have her own money to settle bills at Harry's Bar or Scott's if she went to lunch or dinner with girlfriends. Moreover, because he was in the navy, Andrew was seldom home. Sarah therefore could not call upon him for the odd hundred pounds to buy a present for a girlfriend the way most wives do, as he was simply not there to dole out petty cash. Work therefore fulfilled a dual function, filling Sarah's time while Andrew was away and bringing in spending money.

Adjusting to Andrew's absences was not easy. A solitary lifestyle does not come easily to people who are as passionate and insecure as Sarah York, but she has strength of character, determination and a gritty, let's-make-the-best-of-things attitude. Moreover, she had her plethora of friends, who included former flatmate Carolyn Beckwith-Smith, Lulu Blacker and the Princess of Wales. Older and wiser than Diana had been at the time of her step up in the world, Sarah did not make the mistake of distancing herself from her friends. They were therefore on hand to provide invaluable support, though they soon discovered that it often came at the end of a telephone wire. Like all royals, Sarah's diary was planned six months in advance, which left no room for a spontaneous lunch or dinner with friends, the way she was used to.

The restrictions of royal life took some getting used to, but at this stage Sarah was as eager to please and to fit in with the accepted way of doing things as she had been when she first worked at Durden-Smith Communications and Neil Durden-Smith ticked her off about having so many personal telephone calls. She enjoyed her public duties, which she carried out conscientiously, and was a great hit with everyone who met her.

Our paths first crossed in those early days, when she attended a ball at Syon House, the Duke of Northumberland's stately home outside London. I can still vividly remember her being so unused to wearing a tiara that every time she danced a fast dance, her hand swiped the central stone. Fearful that the setting would snap and the stone be lost, I pointed this out to her. For the rest of the evening, every time she saw me, she jokingly motioned to her tiara or mine. What struck me was how open she was, how without 'side' and how she quickly assessed your motive and behaved accordingly. There was nothing aloof about her, but she did possess dignity: a quality that Diana also shared.

Throughout the first year of marriage, Sarah's honeymoon with the press continued. Meanwhile, she and Andrew were trying to get their marital house in order, in both the literal and figurative meanings of the word. As a wedding present the Queen gave them a house on the site of the weekend retreat, which King George VI had given her and the Duke of Edinburgh, and which had been burnt to the ground.

Sunninghill Park was designed by Professor James Dunbar-Nasmith, head of architecture at Heriot-Watt University and Edinburgh College of Art. His firm had undertaken other royal assignments, notably a wing for the staff at Balmoral and a new kitchen for Queen Elizabeth the Queen Mother at Birkhall, so the popularly held belief that Sarah was responsible for his selection and the design of the house is farcical. Andrew took an active interest in the whole project, and though the house later came in for mockery as Southyork, it is actually a luxurious and elegant modern mansion, which accorded with his, not her, concept of what a dream house is.

While work on Sunninghill Park got under way, Andrew rented an inaccessible weekend house, which they seldom used. So when the lease lapsed, he came to an arrangement with King Hussein of Jordan. Thereafter, until Sunninghill Park was ready, Castlewood House in Egham on the outskirts of Windsor Great Park became the Yorks' main home.

Towards the end of 1987, Sarah became pregnant. She was still immensely popular, but the cracks in her image were becoming increasingly visible. A combination of factors was responsible. Firstly, she did not cultivate the press the way Diana had done in her early days. Secondly, her personality was too strong. It was easier to mock or pillory someone with a strong personality, rather than praise it and thereby seem to be in awe of it. The Princess Royal is another case in point.

To add insult to injury, the Duchess of York also appeared thoroughly to enjoy her work. On the basis of no news being good news, the view was taken that it would be unnewsworthy for a member of the Royal Family to be seen to enjoy her royal duties. The difficulties of bending Sarah's strong personality coincided with Diana rejoining the publicity race. It was one thing for the Princess of Wales to take a sabbatical from the number one spot, but now that it looked suspiciously as if she had been downgraded permanently into the number two position, her competitive instincts came to the fore. She therefore made a conscious attempt to rectify her omission by subtly cultivating the media once more. This was a simple task for Diana. In the course of her official duties, she came across the same photographers and journalists on a day-to-day basis. Where previously she had had no time for the quiet chat that ensured favourable publicity, she now found it. By practising the Lady Di tactics that had turned her into the world's darling, she gradually rescued her public image and restored herself to the pinnacle.

At the top of the Fleet Street tree of fame, there is space for only one crowned angel. Diana, moreover, was more suitable for the top spot than Fergie. She was less forthcoming and more restrained. She was also more glamorous, and by projecting little beyond a smile, left room for journalists to convey their own image of her to the world. This malleability of image as well as her undisputed gift for engendering adulation, was what, above all, assured her of the tremendous success she went on to achieve.

Once Diana started playing ball with the royal correspondents, it was only a matter of time before Sarah was edged off her perch. Diana the Good and Fergie the Bad were then born as a double-act, replacing Fergie the Natural Delight and Diana the Birdbrain Spendthrift, even though the latter casting was more accurate.

The birth of Fergie the Bad coincided with that of Princess Beatrice of York on Monday, 8 August 1988. Sarah had gained over three stone during her pregnancy and looked, in her own words, like 'an elephant. I felt fat and ugly.' High blood pressure combined with the weight gain to cause her obstetrician Anthony Kenney some concern, and everyone was relieved when mother and baby were both declared out of the woods. 'I never liked babies much before I had my own,' the straightforward Duchess admitted.

Like many women who have had chequered emotional pasts and have been subjected by men to the vicissitudes of uncertainty, Sarah was acutely conscious of retaining Andrew's attraction. He was on a six-month deployment with HMS *Edinburgh*, which was sailing from Portsmouth to Sydney in Australia in time for the bicentennial naval review in September. Though he was given compassionate leave to return to Britain from Singapore for the birth, Andrew had to go back shortly after it to rejoin the ship. Sarah, not yet as maternal as she would soon become, left the baby and flew out to Australia to join her husband, precipitating a deluge of condemnation in the press. The gist of it was that Sarah deserved to be despised for 'abandoning' her baby. When she pointed out that it was for a limited time and that Beatrice was being safety taken care of by her nanny, that only sparked off yet another round of abuse. Not one publication hopped to her defence with the point that the Queen and Queen Elizabeth before her had also left their babies to go away on tour.

To her regret, harsh treatment in the press was something with which Sarah was becoming only too familiar. Beatrice's birth coincided not only with the advent of Fergie the Bad but with Ronald Ferguson's fall from grace. That same summer he was caught patronizing the Wigmore Club, a massage parlour where many male members of the Establishment took their male members for the pleasure of hands well versed in the art of all over massage. Major Ron, as the tabloids called him, had become quite a media star in his own right by then, and they turned on him with sanctimonious glee. Missing the basic precept of morality, which dictates that one person should never have to pay the penalty for another's sins, the tabloids used the scandal about Ronald to sully Sarah's image, implying that any daughter who had a father like that was not fit to be a member of the Royal Family.

The whole Ferguson family was acutely embarrassed, Ronald 'for letting Sarah down,' as he himself says, 'but she was absolutely marvellous. Loyal. She gave me the encouragement I needed to see the thing through.' The Prince of Wales also reacted with commendable level-headedness, refusing to bow to media pressure and kick the Major when he was down by kicking him out of his position as Polo Manager.

As the dramas surrounding the Australian trip and the Wigmore Club died down, the tabloids sniffed around the Duchess of York and came up with yet another cause for disaffection. She was too fat. Even though she was on a diet and losing weight, they tore into her with unseemly relish. The Duchess of Pork, she became. Where previously her voluptuousness had been a positive reflection upon her innate 'ordinariness', now it was a flaw to be rebuked. The fact that she looks thinner in person than in photographs, that she has big bones, and that nature decreed that she can never be the svelte and slinky type, made no difference.

Sarah York is not a hysterical personality. Her initial reaction was therefore to ignore the unreasonable demands and ride out the storm. But she was not totally impervious to her manufactured press image, not that thick skinned. As she lost weight and developed maternal feelings for Beatrice, which surprised her in their depth and strength, she had no idea how totally the British tabloids were going to turn reality on its head.

She remained the same person she had been, doing the same job and taking the same breaks from it. Her skiing is a case in point. 'I love the mountains,' she says. 'Nothing refreshes me like skiing down them.' At first, her aptitude had been a cause for praise; now she became a workshy parasite who always wanted to be on holiday. Where previously she had been regarded as outgoing and natural in the execution of her official duties, now she opened up the papers to discover that she was being called undignified and embarrassing. To prove the point, each story would be accompanied by a photograph, which captured her grimacing, showing her legs, or contorting her body in a graceless position.

What the public might not have realized, but every celebrity knows, is that every time a public figure undertakes a public appearance, there are a fair proportion of unflattering photographs as well as more flattering ones. The Duchess of York did not undergo a metamorphosis from gracious to graceless in her personality or the way she appeared before people who actually saw her. The change came at the picture desks of the tabloids, with their choice of photographs.

What purveyors of news do not always appreciate is that celebrities are human beings, and there are no more exposed figures than members of reigning royal families. Irrespective of what has been written about them, they have got to get up and perform in front of the world's media every time they undertake an official duty. If they are subjected to personally offensive publicity the way Sarah was, they cannot run and hide. As long as they remain an official part of the Royal Family, they have to put themselves in the firing line, irrespective of the effect this has upon them.

To Sarah, the effect was terrible. All her life she had been sensitive about her weight. The criticism could not have been targeted at a more vulnerable spot, but, as she lost even more weight, the clamour became louder, not softer. In an attempt to get away from this, she began experimenting with diets, not all of which were to be recommended. One day she would starve herself, the next she would eat only fruit, the day after she would exercise as if she were being pursued by demons out of hell. Like everyone who diets, she reached the stage beyond which the weight refused to budge. This, of course, was because each body has a minimum weight barrier, beyond which the person strays at her peril. Nature was therefore telling her one thing, the press another.

To her cost, Sarah listened to her detractors, precipitating a spiral that would result in untold pain and misery not only for herself but also for those closest to her. She went to the Continent to see a doctor who specialized in a miraculous method of losing weight and returned to London with the prescribed tablets. Little did she know it, but the 'miracle' was achieved by suppressing her appetite and stimulating her central nervous system so that she could tap into the energy she no longer got from food. Before a fortnight was out, the miracle worker had hooked her on the agents that could so effectively speed up her system and suppress her appetite.

People who become addicted to appetite suppressants begin to experience perplexing mood swings. It changes their personalities and makes them subject to fits of irritability and depression. Irritability was not something the good-natured, optimistic Sarah had ever been prone to, so this came as a bolt out of the blue. After an outburst, she would often react the way she had done when she was head girl at Hurst Lodge and had to discipline a friend. On the other hand, she was no stranger to the cloud that topped silver linings. She had first displayed a tendency to take things to heart when she was with Kim Smith-Bingham, and he did not value her the way she wished, and, as the pressures upon her mounted, there were times when she succumbed to momentary spells of depression. These never lasted long, but they could be profound, and they made deeper and deeper inroads into her spiritual well-being when the pressures precipitating them mounted instead of lifting.

As the tablets continued poisoning Sarah's system and working their magic upon her figure, the reasons for her marital dissatisfaction sprang to the surface. Up to this point, she had coped magnificently with the many difficulties that all naval wives have to bear. Moreover, she had manifestly taken the flaws in Andrew's personality in her stride in a positive and constructive manner. He was utterly and totally dependent upon her, in the way that only a mother's favoured son can be with the mother substitute. This was not the easiest of situations for any woman to cope with, but where she had formerly shouldered the burden happily and retained her good cheer, now her shoulders began to sag beneath the weight. It did not help that he remained resolutely unresponsive to her needs.

As far as Andrew was concerned, life was fine. He had the woman he loved. She was vibrant and exciting. She mothered him. She was passionate in bed. She provided him with an interesting and amusing circle of friends. He was happy. What more did she want?

What Sarah wanted was someone who would acknowledge the way she felt and share not only the pleasure but also the pain that life brought. In other words, she wanted back some of the support and encouragement she gave Andrew.

Sarah York is one of life's triers. She was grievously wounded by the way the press were representing her. No matter what she did, it seemed to be wrong, and this not only hurt her but also offended her innate sense of fair play. Andrew, of course, had been raised in the public eye, and his way of dealing with unpleasant publicity was to ignore it. This was hard for someone like Sarah who did not possess the thick skin of a seasoned royal. Moreover, she did not have an ostrich mentality and could never resist the temptation to learn what was being written, not only about her but about her many friends and acquaintances as well.

As Sarah slimmed down, criticism shifted from what she looked like in clothes to her taste in them. The Royal Family have never been renowned for their chic, but you would never have known it from the barbs that winged in her direction. Quite forgetting that the Queen Mother has a style that can best be called inimitable, that the Queen makes a point of erring on the side of dourness, that Princess Margaret has long given up any attempt to be stylish and wears white platform sandals on just about every occasion, the press mocked Sarah's mode of attire. She did have one or two notable fashion disasters, but so too did Diana, though it must be admitted that Sarah's were more outlandish.

Once more, Sarah reacted by taking the criticism on board and adjusting her behaviour accordingly. She toned down her look, reserved the witty touches for the dinner table and became more conventionally well-dressed. So the criticism switched to the price of her clothes.

In the bat of an eyelash, Sarah was now Fergie the Freeloader who always cuts deals with designers instead of paying the full whack for what she wore. The fact that most celebrities do the same was purposely ignored by the fashion writers who are only too *au fait* with that knowledge. Before long, that theme had travelled from the fashion pages into the regular section of the newspapers. If Sarah went on a trip, she was condemned as a freeloader. If she went to lunch, she was accused of being a freeloader. If she took her girlfriends to dinner, she was reviled as a freeloader, even though she was the one who was writing the cheque.

Especially wounding to Sarah was the professional criticism that came her way. She published a children's book called *Budgie the Helicopter*, inspired during her pregnancy by her own experiences while training to be a helicopter pilot. She was condemned not only for plagiarism but for pocketing too large a proportion of the profits. Both accusations were unfair. The book from which she was said to have stolen the idea was called *Hector the Helicopter* and was published in 1964. She had never seen it, which is hardly surprising, as it was not in circulation. How she could therefore have copied it quite escapes the logic of a reasoned mind. Moreover, if every author had to come up with an idea that was totally original, there would be no new books.

Sarah was in publishing long before she met Andrew. She continued working not only because she enjoys being productive but also because she needed the money. That simple fact was not acknowledged in all media reports, and in fact she did give a portion of her income to charity. The royals, however, have a custom of not revealing the exact amount of any donation. This is something even ignoramuses should have known, but, if they did, the writers who attacked her chose to ignore their knowledge in pursuit of yet another stick with which to beat Fergie the Bad.

By this time, Sarah felt hounded for the simple reason that she was being hounded. She is a strong character and resourceful, but she is the first to admit that she was deeply distressed by the treatment being accorded her. Andrew, meanwhile, remained at sea. They were together so seldom that in an average year she did not see him for over 300 of the 365 days.

That lifestyle, of course, suited Andrew. He had lost none of his appreciation of masculine camaraderie. He was just as happy being at sea in the company of men as he was watching television at home. Indeed, he had the best of both worlds: a man's life among men at sea and a committed and vibrant wife on land to provide him with a rich social and family life. To add insult to injury, he had recently discovered the joys of golf. Whenever he was on shore leave, he headed straight for the golf course. If Sarah was not a grass widow, she was a golf widow, and it enraged her. 'You can't spend all your time at sea, then come home and never have time for me,' she once told him reasonably.

On the other hand, Andrew did not possess an abundance of empathy. He could not see that he was taking Sarah for granted, and that you actually had to do something other than be a Prince of the Realm to remain happily married. As she became more and more unhappy, they started having rows, which gradually grew in size. Andrew still had a temper that could erupt like a volcano and spew lava wherever it flowed. This only had the effect of increasing the strain between them, for after a particularly vitriolic row, Sarah could not simply shrug off the injury as if what happened yesterday had no effect upon the way she felt today.

By 1989, Sarah's life was in such bad shape that the Royal Family themselves were concerned. Fortunately for her, she got along well with the Queen, who has herself said, 'I have a soft spot for her.' This helped somewhat, for the other members of the family more or less fell into line. What criticism they might otherwise have voiced was restrained as a result. The Princess Royal and the Duke of Edinburgh especially should have been sympathetic, having themselves had image problems in the past, but neither one was particularly close to Sarah, with the result that they gave no support, though they gave no flak either. Indeed, Sarah's closest friend in the Royal Family was Diana, but Diana had purposely though discreetly put space between them after the Wigmore Club episode.

Yet Diana was doing even more than loosening the moorings on the boat of friendship now that its captain was experiencing a rough ride on choppy seas. She was actually disparaging Sarah behind her back, snidely referring to her, as she did on the Squidgy tape to James Gilbey, as 'the redhead' who was trying to cash in on her golden image. Had she done this within her personal circle alone, Diana might not have contributed to Sarah's problems.

In the midst of all this turmoil, Sarah discovered that she was pregnant again. The baby was not planned, but she welcomed it even though her marriage was in such bad shape. This time, however, she resolved not to gain weight and remained so slender throughout the pregnancy that she barely looked pregnant at seven months.

It was just as well that Sarah decided to keep looking good. Her life was about to change in a big way. And it was not because Andrew had learnt to curb his temper, to stop bullying her, to give up friendships and activities that kept him away from home, or to stop being anything but a royal receptacle for all she had to give him. History was about to repeat itself. Andrew was about to be relegated to the backburner the way Kim Smith-Bingham and Paddy McNally had been. Having given her marriage her all, and having failed to achieve a reciprocal relationship yet again, Sarah was ready to move on. The only trouble was, she did not know it yet.

CHAPTER TWENTY

Breaking Up and Down

On Thursday, 2 November 1989, the Duchess of York arrived in Houston, Texas for a five-day official visit. The Lone Star State was launching a tribute to 300 years of British Opera at the Houston Grand Opera. Her hostess, and one of the leading lights of the American social scene, was the beautiful Lynn Wyatt, wife of Oscar, mother of Steve and Doug, and friend of royalty. She numbered Prince Rainier of Monaco, the late Princess Grace, and more to the point, Andrew's aunt Princess Margaret among her personal circle. Sarah, who was popular in America, was looking forward to her stay at Allington, the famous Wyatt residence in River Oaks, which Margaret wittily stated was constructed in the style of Wyatt Regency. There, Sarah could enjoy the luxury of one of America's most lavish private residences while basking in the all too unfamiliar light of appreciation. She also had a most attentive swain to squire her around: Lynn's bachelor son Steve.

Steve Wyatt lived in London. He had moved there in 1985, going to work for one of his immensely wealthy father's companies, Delaney Petroleum. Oscar Wyatt was a close business associate of Iraqi president Saddam Hussein. He had been known as the King of Crude, as much for his oil interests as his tendency to resort to colourful language. 'Bullshit' was his favourite word, and though Steve did not emulate his father's language, he did take care to let everyone know precisely who he was. This seemed to arise out of a deep-seated anxiety, owing partly to his inability to scale Oscar's heights, and partly to a murky family secret, for Steve was not born Oscar's son. His natural father was Bobby Lipman, the ne'er-do-well scion of a rich New York real-estate family. After turning to alcohol, Lipman lost Lynn and his sons to Oscar, then his mind to drugs. In 1968, he murdered eighteen-year-old Claude Delphine Delbarre, a French student, in her Chelsea flat while on an LSD trip. Found guilty of manslaughter, he was sentenced to six years in prison. After his release, he disappeared from view. Steve claims he was killed by a tramcar in Vienna, others say he committed suicide, and still others say he has done the decent thing and dropped out of view, changing his identity.

Whatever Bobby Lipman's fate, his sons lived lives of material comfort. Lynn herself was a member of the Sakowitz family, which gave Texas one of its most famous department stores. Doug and Steve, however, were so interested in fringe spiritual movements that an incisive mind would have to ask if they had ever resolved the conflicts caused by their turbulent childhoods. Doug was a member of the Eternal Values cult founded by Frederick von Mierers, a con-man who charged Lynn $70,000 for a crystal ring to ward off evil spirits and who died of AIDS after being discredited as an anti-Semitic crook.

Steve, though less extreme, was also an aficionado of obscure cults, which believed in sleeping under pyramids and other equally bizarre notions. On the other hand, he did not allow his beliefs to overtake his reason. Instead, he used them to enhance an already formidable social charm. Although not good-looking in the conventional sense, he had a body rippling with muscles, a laid-back but earnest manner and access to one of the world's largest fortunes, including a fleet of limousines and private planes. Girls fell for him the way over-ripe apples drop off trees. He conducted a long romance with model Denice Lewis, to which his mother objected violently due to her humble origins, and though he was engaged to his Arizona college girlfriend, Dorice Valle Risso, on 15 April 1989 she called off the wedding at the last minute, so he remained unmarried.

The meeting between the discontented but energetic Duchess of York and the contented and highly charged Steve Wyatt was electrifying. His mother had specifically asked Steve over from London so he could take care of the Duchess, whom Lynn knew from Palm Beach and London. She had no idea how unhappy Sarah was, how starved she was for appreciation, or how responsive she would be to it. Nor did she imagine that Steve of all people would end up sharing Sarah's deepest secrets.

The British consulate, being mindful of Sarah's freeloading reputation, had been careful to pack her schedule in an attempt to silence criticism. Over the course of the next days, as she watched the students of the High School of Performing and Visual Arts in *Julius Caesar*; took in an anti-drug programme at school; called on the Mayor, Kathy Whitmire; donned a crimson suit for a tour of NASA's Lyndon B. Johnson Space Centre; watched a fund-raising polo-match; and attended a traditional Texas barbecue at the Wyatt ranch 200 miles away at Tasajillo, their ranch near the Mexican border in Duval County, Steve was never far away.

Like his mother, he enveloped Sarah in the warmth of traditional

195

Southern hospitality, and the Duchess of York who showed up for the high point of the visit, a performance of Gilbert and Sullivan's *The Mikado*, in a sleek, off-the-shoulder, yellow-rose-of-Texas lace dress by Belville Sassoon, was an altogether different Duchess of York from the one who had departed from Britain. She was radiant, aglow with the ministrations of kindness, looking truly beautiful.

From Texas, Sarah flew to New York to promote her Budgie book, which had been published recently. She also did some Christmas shopping, attended a reading class at the Children's Museum of Manhattan, gained the admiration of New York by putting Norman Mailer down in spectacular fashion when he embarrassed her at a dinner party organized by her agent Mort Janklow, then flew back to London for a rest and more adverse press publicity.

Steve Wyatt also flew back to London; Sarah suggested he get in touch upon his return. He did. The friendship they had forged in Texas travelled as well as they both did, and they began to see each other as friends. Up to this point, Sarah had never looked at another man but Andrew since making her commitment to him in autumn 1985. However, history was about to repeat itself. As with her affairs with Kim Smith-Bingham and Paddy McNally, Sarah ceased exercising tolerance and patience once she realized that the man to whom she had committed herself had an altogether less committed view of their relationship. To her, loyalty and fair play were two-way streets, and she was not prepared to collude with any man while he was victimizing her. It might not have been an altogether conventional approach to marriage, but it possessed a sound moral and ethical precept. Whether one agreed with it or not, one could not deny the integrity and code of honour that motivated it.

What Steve Wyatt gave Sarah York was support and appreciation. He validated her wounds instead of ignoring them the way Andrew did. She had actually reached a critical point in her life. She was crumbling spiritually, heading towards the point where either the pressure ceased or it would literally destroy her. The fight she was waging was more than a battle for her reputation. It was a war for her soul, and Steve Wyatt was one of the few people who had the sensitivity and the spirituality to appreciate this.

Moreover, Sarah was not the only member of her family who was fast approaching a crossroads. Her sister Jane Makim's marriage was over after a failed attempt at a reconciliation, and Alex Makim was threatening to deprive her of custody of the children. When the separation came, as it soon did, he did indeed manage to do so. The sisters had always been one another's best friends, and naturally enough Jane's fate was uppermost in Sarah's mind during this period.

The two threads that ran through this period were separation and opera, for on Friday 8 December Sarah flew up to Yorkshire in her capacity as patron of Opera North to attend the gala première of *Show Boat* at the Grand Theatre, Leeds. After the performance, she was unable to return to London because fog prevented her plane from taking off. She knew that Steve Wyatt, Andrew's best friend Charlie Young and his cousin Patrick, Earl of Lichfield, were staying nearby in a houseparty that included actor Nigel Havers and his wife Polly, ballet dancer Wayne Eagling, and Princess Anne's former fancy the Hon. Brian Alexander. So she and her lady-in-waiting, her old flatmate Carolyn Cotterell (formerly Beckwith-Smith) headed towards Constable Burton Hall, Charles and Maggie Wyvill's 3000-acre estate near Leyburn.

Because all the bedrooms were taken, Steve Wyatt had to double up with another man and Carolyn Cotterell and Sarah had to share a room. There was no question of the six-months' pregnant Duchess having an indiscreet assignation with a lover, and the following morning she happily posed for photographs with the shooting party in the only dress she had: her evening dress. She then said goodbye, tried to link up with Andrew at Sandringham but had to return to Constable Burton Hall for a second night when bad weather still prevented her plane from taking off.

When word of that weekend got out, and the photograph of Sarah and the rest of the shooting party was published, with her in her evening dress and the rest of them in their shooting clothes, she was made to look like a wanton hussy who had engineered an assignation with her lover.

That Christmas, Sarah and Andrew continued on their bleak downhill path. As if all that was happening was not enough to cope with, her mother telephoned her to say that the doctors in Buenos Aires had discovered that Hector Barrantes had cancer of the lymphatic system. This was devastating news for Susie, who adored Hector, but everyone rallied. Peter Brant, his American polo sponsor, made his private plane available to fly the Barrantes from Argentina to the Sloan–Kettering Clinic, the world's leading oncology centre, in New York. Sarah left Klosters, where she was on a skiing holiday with Beatrice, and flew via Gatwick Airport to America to comfort her distressed mother.

While Hector was being treated, Sarah kept Andrew posted about his stepfather-in-law's condition by telephone. She was also in daily contact with Steve Wyatt, who offered her a broad shoulder to cry on. When she returned home, she became a regular visitor to his rented flat at 34 Cadogan Square in fashionable Chelsea. Steve was now her closest friend, her prime encourager, her confidant. Andrew, of course, knew about the friendship and approved of it, though he did not appreciate how close Sarah and Steve had become. As far as he was concerned, she needed a 'walker' and who better than a rich and personable American whose mother was a friend of his aunt.

At 7.58 p.m. on 23 March 1990, Sarah was delivered of Princess Eugenie of York. Because the baby was in the breech position, a Caesarean section was performed. She and Andrew were both delighted about this second daughter, but Eugenie's presence made little difference to the state of their marriage. It continued spiralling downwards, and, in an attempt to shake off her troubles and lift her spirits, Sarah resorted to taking frequent trips of a few days' duration. One such took place six weeks after Eugenie's birth, when she took Beatrice, nanny Alison Wardley and two bodyguards from the Royal Protection Department to La Gazelle d'Or, the luxurious resort on the coast of Morocco. Steve Wyatt was the host, and the party was filled out by his ex-girlfriend, an actress named Pricilla Philips with whom Sarah had also become friendly. Andrew stayed at home at Castlewood House and took care of the baby.

Like any other group of friends on holiday, Sarah, Steve and Pricilla took photographs of each other. A batch of these would later turn up on the top shelf of a fitted unit in No. 34 Cadogan Square after Steve Wyatt had vacated the premises. But more of that later.

While Sarah was basking in the Moroccan sun, a tipster telephoned the Confidential diary on *Today* newspaper in London. Edited by Chris Hutchins, who has a reputation for investigative reporting, it was the one gossip column on which the story was sure to be used, for the other columns are known to protect certain individuals, and the tipster obviously intended the story to see the light of day. Sure enough, Chris Hutchins ran his quarry to ground and broke the news of Sarah's friendship with Steve Wyatt.

In his informative biography, *Sarah's Story: The Duchess Who Defied the House of Windsor*, written in conjunction with journalist Peter Thompson, Hutchins recounts how information continued pouring in from tipsters who were the antithesis of the norm. They were well-dressed, well-spoken and obviously well-placed. In his considered opinion, they had to be members of the Secret Service. He believes that their motive for rumbling Sarah was tied up with her association with Steve Wyatt. His father Oscar had been one of Saddam Hussein's closest business associates over a twenty-year period until UN sanctions severed their ability to trade. Before the war, he bought 250,000 barrels of crude oil per diem from the Iraqi government and was negotiating a deal that would give the Iraqi dictator a share in his American East Coast refineries.

Inadvertently, Sarah had stumbled into a real political quagmire. Iraq was about to invade Kuwait, the Al-Sabahs were about to flee their country, and Sarah was entertaining such friends of Steve and Oscar Wyatt as Dr Ramzi Salman, one of Saddam Hussein's closest associates and in charge of marketing the Iraqi state's oil, at a dinner party at Buckingham Palace.

Access is influence, and influence is power. The Secret Service therefore wanted to break up Sarah's friendship with Wyatt so that the Iraqis would lose the kudos her association was giving them. It was now well-known within political circles that Saddam Hussein's closest associates had direct access to Buckingham Palace through the Queen's daughter-in-law, and that Iraq would soon be perceived as being an opponent of Western policy.

So the calls to Chris Hutchins and the Confidential column continued.

Sarah flew to Nice with Steve, and the only reason why *Today* did not photograph her in a compromising scenario was that the caller made Nice sound like Greece. So the newspaper sent an investigative team on a wild-goose chase before they realized the error.

By summer, the family knew that Hector Barrantes had not been cured. Sarah flew back to New York to see her rapidly declining stepfather, who was now little more than a shadow of the powerful El Gordo. Steve Wyatt accompanied her with the approval of Andrew, who had also become a friend, albeit not quite so close.

The full measure of the acceptance accorded to Steve Wyatt in royal circles is best shown by what happened upon their return to Britain. The Queen entertained him to dinner at Windsor Castle, seating him beside her. She remained oblivious to the opposition her daughter-in-law's friendship was generating within the Secret Service, but this is hardly surprising, for the relationship between the royals and the Secret Service is akin to that between the Manchu Emperors and their court in Imperial China. They are often the last to know about what is being done in their name or in their interest.

Political intrigue was the furthest thing from Sarah's mind that summer of 1990. Hector Barrantes was not a rich man and once he was dead, Susie would not be able to maintain a comfortable lifestyle at El Pucara, their dream home. To his credit, Andrew came to the rescue. Although he could not afford to write a cheque, he did have the means to make a substantial sum of money. Utilizing his talent and his name, he therefore allowed the Marquesa de Varela, a friend of the Barrantes family, to arrange a photo-spread with *Hello!* magazine featuring himself, Sarah and the children. Andrew took the photographs, Gene Nocon did the printing and was credited with the photography, and Susie was given the sum of £200,000.

Late in July, while *Hello!* was still processing seventy of the photographs across forty-eight of its pages, Sarah learnt that Hector had weeks, if not days, to live. He had one last request. He wanted to see the stepdaughter he loved as if she were his own child. He also wanted to see Beatrice once more and to get his first and last glimpse of Eugenie. The trouble was, Hector was at El Pucara, and Argentina had not made its peace with Britain since the Falklands conflict. Sarah therefore had to approach the Queen and ask her for permission to take her two granddaughters to a country that was still officially hostile. Taking a compassionate view, the Queen assented to the visit, and Sarah, nanny Alison Wardley and a detective flew out to Buenos Aires. From there, they boarded a light aircraft, which touched down on a strip of grass on the ranch. The visit lasted over a week, and Hector rallied enough to drive around the ranch with his visitors and to watch Beatrice take her first riding lesson. A day and a half after their departure, El Gordo the magnificent was dead at the age of fifty-one.

• • •

Life had to go on for the living. For Sarah and Andrew, that meant more marital strife and more adverse publicity. It also meant a move into their new home. Sunninghill Park was finally ready. Though it is elegant inside, the exterior had come in for so much architectural criticism, all of it levelled against Sarah, who had had nothing to do with it, that she was already jaundiced about the place. Andrew, however, liked it, but refused to allow photographers in to defeat the rumours about its garishness. 'This is my home and I'm not having a load of press people traipsing around it,' he said, intent on preserving what was left of his privacy.

In October, Sarah and Andrew hosted a housewarming party for their friends. These included cousins such as Viscount Linley, showbiz folk like Pamela Stevenson and their close personal friends. By one of those curious twists of fate that have characterized so much of Sarah's life, the day of joy was also a day of sadness, for her stepfather's memorial service fell on it. Susie Barrantes, however, would not hear of altering either event. So, after paying their respects to Hector, they went home to prepare for a happy occasion. And they made Hector a part of the evening by asking Elton John to play ballads such as *Candle in the Wind* and *Song for Guy* in his memory.

The move to Sunninghill Park only deepened Sarah's dissatisfaction with her life, though Andrew took a more relaxed view of things. He was perfectly happy as long as he could watch television, play golf and sail away into the sunset for his naval exercises. On the other hand, she had now reached breaking-point. What caused this, aside from the state of her marriage and the hounding of the press, was the way the courtiers treated her. Chief among these was Sarah's own cousin, Sir Robert Fellowes, who used to barge into her room without even knocking, wave the latest batch of newspapers under her nose and make snide comments such as, 'You've been at it again,' or 'I don't suppose you've seen these,' or 'Congratulations, Ma'am, on an excellent job well done.'

For someone who is intelligent, Robert Fellowes's attitude was remarkably emotional. He refused to see that Sarah might simply be the latest in the long line of royal victims of sensationalism. It was as if he were taking advantage of their blood ties to make things worse instead of taking an objective view that would help to lift her off the ground. These visits, which were too frequent for Sarah's liking, distressed and humiliated her, but she was powerless to stop them. And Andrew refused to get involved.

Nor was Robert Fellowes the only courtier who had Sarah in his palatial grip. She and Andrew shared the same private secretary. Lieutenant Colonel Sean O'Dwyer was the first, but she had such difficulty working with him that she asked for him to be replaced. He therefore went to work exclusively for Prince Edward when Captain Neil Blair was appointed. He turned out to be no easier, and I myself crossed swords with him when I organized a charity ball at which the Duchess of York was guest of honour.

This was in April 1991, at the height of her press problems, and Blair tried to pull her out of attending a week before the ball was due to be held on the grounds that she might receive adverse publicity because the cabaret was the famous transvestite revue from Soho's Madame Jo Jo. When I pointed out to him that Diana's brother Charles, who was then Viscount Althorp, had had the same revue at his twenty-first birthday party, and that the Prince and Princess of Wales had been there and had enjoyed it, he said that that had been a private party, not an official occasion. So I pointed out that every member of the Royal Family from the Queen downwards had seen Danny La Rue and Dame Edna Everage in some official capacity, that drag was accepted as a traditional form of British entertainment, and that members of the Kuwaiti Royal Family, who were also attending, would be offended if the Duchess cancelled. I also pointed out that one of the charities benefiting was the Soldiers', Sailors' & Airmen's Families Association (SSAFA), which needed money because of the Gulf War, and that Sarah's attendance would only bring her favourable publicity.

Though Blair agreed that everything I said was valid, and though we agreed to proceed, I then discovered that he was trying to get Admiral Sir Peter Herbert, the head of SSAFA, to cancel. That would have afforded him the excuse of saying to Sarah, 'If Sir Peter doesn't think it fit to go, neither can you.'

Blair, however, did not reckon on my determination, nor on the Duchess's desire to honour her commitment to us. Through a mutual friend, I tipped her off about what her private secretary was trying to do, and we managed to outmanoeuvre him. But it was a thoroughly unpleasant and needlessly stressful experience, and one which would have seriously back-fired at her expense had he got his way. As it was, she attended, was a huge hit with everyone, received positive publicity and agreed with me that her private secretary was making her life, and those with whom she came into contact, hell.

'I don't know how you can stand dealing with him day after day,' I told her. 'You must have nerves of steel. If it were me, I'd have a nervous breakdown after a month.' Little did I know at the time, but she was being driven perilously close to that very point. However, she was stuck with Blair, because the royal system would not allow her to replace yet another private secretary.

As matters hurtled towards a denouement, gossip about Sarah's friend-ship with Steve Wyatt flew around society salons to such an extent that the Queen finally heard about it. Sarah was duly instructed to 'chill Steve out', according to a friend of Susie Barrantes to whom she spoke. She was not even allowed to telephone Steve to let him know. He discovered what social Siberia felt like only when Sarah failed to turn up to a dinner party he had arranged for friends of theirs. 'It's very embarrassing,' his mother Lynn said, after Sarah had managed to get in touch. 'Prince Andrew even called Steve to tell him how sorry he was about it all.' Faced with the prospect of shivering in ostracism in London or returning home, Steve gave notice on flat F at 34 Cadogan Square, said his goodbyes, packed his bags and left for the sunshine of the US of A.

At the height of his friendship with Sarah, Steve had introduced her to his good friend and connection by marriage and divorce, Johnny Bryan. Tony Bryan, Johnny's British father, had four wives, the second of whom was Pamela Zauderer Sakowitz, ex-wife of Lynn Wyatt's only brother Robert T. Sakowitz. The boys became close friends at St John's School in River Oaks. They had much in common, aside from holiday homes, which the Wyatts and the Bryans owned in Vail, Colorado. They enjoyed skiing and other athletic pursuits, played the field together and played it some more. After leaving school, they remained dedicated followers of the lotus-eating life. That arbiter of American chic, *Town & Country*, declared, 'They are eligibles. They are hard to catch, but worth the effort.' The girls who tried were doomed to disappointment, however, for both men remained assiduously single.

In 1987 Johnny left New York, where he had met just about everyone whom he could through a member of one of the old, established families, Whitney Tower, and joined Steve in London. The Big Bang was the catchphrase of the moment, and the sharp Johnny and his father Tony set about using the opportunities created. Tony Bryan was a successful businessman whose directorial history included stints on the board of Federal Express and Chrysler. He and Johnny bought Oceonics Group plc, a high tech company, in 1988. Within eighteen months they had made millions, though some of these were subsequently lost when they formed Oceonics Deutschland, which lost £7.5 million in 1990.

Despite that setback, Johnny Bryan, whose nickname was the Nose, was the son of a rich and successful businessman with his own track record of success. He was charming, extremely energetic and adept at chatting up the girls. Tall and well built, he was not exactly handsome and was almost completely bald, but he succeeded where other, better looking men failed, by perfecting the art of the well-delivered line and developing a reputation for generosity. When she met him, the journalist Christa D'Souza noticed that he bounced about the room, 'radiating confidence and goodwill,' giving 'a brilliant impression of a very powerful person'. He was also adept at the gentle art of name-dropping and peppered his conversation 'with the name of Fergie'. His technique worked well enough for him to squire around a host of Britain's most eligible single women, including Viscount Rothermere's daughter Geraldine, Lady Ogilvy, Earl Cawdor's daughter Lady Liza Campbell, Lord St Just's daughter the Hon. Natasha Grenfell (whose sister Katya was the girlfriend of Philip Dunne when the Princess of Wales began confiding in him) and Lady Antonia Fraser's daughter Flora. This was not bad going for someone who promised the world and only occasionally delivered anything, but in a world where people do not need that extra dress or the promised handbag, the gesture is often confused with the deed, and one's reputation flourishes accordingly.

Certainly, Johnny had the knack of developing the right connections. He rented a cottage near Painswick on the Gloucestershire estate of Detmar Blow, grandson of the famous architect and nephew by marriage of Prince Philip's great-niece, Princess Katarina of Yugoslavia. He employed Detmar's sister-in-law Julia Delves Broughton, of the Delves Broughtons of *White Mischief* fame, as his personal assistant, rented a flat in Chelsea near Foxtrot Oscar, a famous Sloane hang-out, and leased a snazzy-looking Vauxhall car. Suitably surrounded by the right people and the right trappings, the fast-talking Johnny solidified his perch on society's ladder when Steve introduced him to Sarah, and he was invited to attend the housewarming party at Sunninghill Park in October 1990.

After Steve's departure from London in 1991, Johnny stayed on. He was not yet a close friend of the Duchess, but he was a good social acquaintance of both Andrew and her. They were much impressed by the music he made when he blew the trumpet about his financial ability, so Sarah asked him to represent her in dealing with film and television companies. She was hopeful of turning her Budgie books into a huge commercial success, and in the event Johnny Bryan would help to clinch a deal that would have eventually brought her in a reputed £5 million had scandal not scuppered her money-making prospects.

Impressed as Andrew and Sarah were by their loquacious and hyper-energetic friend, they were both too wrapped up in their own personal problems to give anything more than gratitude. Diana was also unhappy, having faced the fact that Charles would never forgive her for the secrets she had shared with Barry Mannakee. The two sisters-in-law, once such close friends, more recently less, now became co-conspirators. Diana suggested they leave together, and Sarah, trusting by nature (a trait inherited from both her father and her mother), never questioned her sincerity. Diana, however, had no intention of leaving Charles when Sarah left Andrew.

Christmas 1991 was the last that Sarah and Diana would spend in the bosom of the Royal Family. Much of the discussion within the family then resolved around Andrew and Sarah's marital problems. That in itself should have given Sarah something to be suspicious of, for if Diana planned to honour the pact they had made, why wasn't her departure also under active consideration? It wasn't, however, and in January the Queen told Andrew and Sarah that she would agree to a separation if they could not resolve their differences.

At this juncture, it is important to remember that Sarah's greatest objection to remaining in the marriage had very little to do with her unsatisfactory personal relationship with Andrew. She was mature and honourable enough to appreciate that her commitment upon marrying Andrew entailed tolerating a less than happy married life, if that is what followed, as long as the interests of the monarchy required it. What she was not prepared to accept, however, was the absence of support from any quarter, as well as the carping of the courtiers while she was being subjected on a daily basis to an adverse press. Being publicly humiliated was bad enough. But being treated with contempt by the very servants of the crown whose job it was to protect her was too much. Sarah's battleground, however, was the one venue on which the deeply traditional Queen was being kept in the dark, for no one had the nerve to spell out the true state of affairs to Her Majesty.

After seeing in the New Year at Sandringham, Sarah, Diana and their husbands prepared to go their respective ways. Meanwhile, the *Daily Mail* was getting ready to issue a nasty shock. In November 1991, a window cleaner named Maurice Maple had turned his passkey in the oak door of Steve Wyatt's old flat at 34 Cadogan Square as he prepared to brighten up the flat for its latest tenant, who was due to move in shortly. While cleaning the guest bedroom's window, some packets on the top of the shelves caught his eye.

'You couldn't see what was on top from ground level, but from the top of the ladder I could see plastic packets,' he said. Moving his ladder so that he had access to the top of the nine-foot unit, he scooped up the packets, thinking they were pornographic photographs, which someone had hidden there. He was stunned to recognize the Duchess of York and Princess Beatrice in holiday snaps.

Intent on making himself a 'few bob', Maple approached the *Daily Mail* through an intermediary. His contact was the paper's chief crime reporter, Peter Burden, who waited an extraordinary two months before coming to the decision that the best course of action was to turn the photographs over to their rightful owners. On 7 January 1992, Burden accompanied Maple to New Scotland Yard. The photographs were examined by the head of the Royal Protection Department, Deputy Assistant Commissioner Charles Rideout, who handed them over to the Yorks' equerry, Captain Alexander Baillie-Hamilton. The *Daily Mail* then broke the story, running water-colours of the photographs in a display of rectitude that seemed hypocritical in the extreme.

The rest of Fleet Street took up the story, leaving readers with the impression that the relationship between Wyatt and Sarah was anything but innocent. Her biographer Chris Hutchins, who was the editor of the Confidential column when it was the recipient of repeated 'gentlemanly' leaks, remains convinced that she was set up by the Secret Services. Steve Wyatt is adamant in his contention that he never left the photographs in the flat. Indeed, he goes even further and says that he never had a set of the photographs. This is credible, for everyone in royal circles knows that photographs involving memberrs of the Royal Family are always processed separately by the family's own processors. The negatives are retained by the royals and prints distributed at the behest of the royal concerned.

Whether Steve Wyatt hid the photogrraphs and then left them behind, or whether the Secret Service let themselves into the flat, hid them, then waited for the Duchess to be discredited, will never now be known as a certainty. At the time, however, Diana was still lying low about her desire for a separation from Charles, and the family and courtiers, believing that she was there to stay, were trying to ensure her a good press.

The next story about the Yorks' marriage was deliberately planted. The source was Diana, the time March 1992, the journalist Andrew Morton and the paper the same *Daily Mail* that had recently exposed the existence of the holiday photographs. The story asserted that the Yorks were about to separate, and it had a dramatic impact. Not only did it drown out the stories about Diana's marriage and private life, which had featured on the front pages of the world's tabloids for the previous two weeks, but it also forced the Palace's and Sarah's hands. Sarah had not actually made a decision about leaving, but once the story was out, and the Palace was put in the position of having to deny something they might then have to retract in a few weeks or months, the pressure was on for her to make up her mind. Still believing that Diana had genuinely intended to join her, and that the only reason she was not now doing so was that circumstances had not forced her, Diana, to act precipitately, Sarah agreed to the Palace making a hurried announcement of the separation. So premature was it, however, and so ill-prepared was she, that she and Andrew continued to sleep together even afterwards.

Andrew took the separation as badly as Sarah did. As she wanted it and he did not, that at least made it more bearable for her. However, she now found herself in an even more invidious position than the one from which she was trying to escape, for the courtiers sent out the word to the press to slit her throat. So outraged was one journalist, however, that he blew the whistle on the instruction, and Charles Anson, one of the Queen's press secretaries, had to apologize to Sarah. In a display of manliness lurking beneath his potato skin, Andrew hopped to his wife's defence, and her staff and dignity were promptly restored. As the separation began in earnest, Sarah looked around for a house to move to. Expat Home Minders of Ascot found Romenda Lodge in the heart of showbiz land on the Wentworth Golf Course near Sunninghill Park for her, and while the neighbours such as golfer Sandy Lyle, comedian Russ Abbott and Prince Philip's good friends Bryan Forbes and Nanette Newman were less than ecstatic about having their privacy invaded by hordes of newsmen, Sarah was pleased with the house. Nina Campbell filled it with two van loads of reproduction antique furniture from Roomservice Designs of Chelsea, after which Johnny Bryan hired the modernist interior designer

Tchaik Chassay to snazz the place up.

Johnny Bryan was figuring increasingly in Sarah's life. He was acting as the honest broker between Andrew and herself in the financial arrangements that become necessary when any couple separate. Andrew's behaviour was exemplary. Realizing that he had lost the light of his life because of his bullying, his naval way of life and his thoughtless ignoring of her, he now resolved to do everything he could to make things easier for her. Where other men would have quibbled, he displayed largess. Sarah deserved the best. She was worried about her £300,000 overdraft. Let him work with Bryan and herself to have it cleared. She wanted a settlement that assured her security. Let them try to get her the maximum, whatever that might prove to be. In defeat he was displaying all the generosity of a victor, and it endeared him to Sarah as nothing else had. 'He is my best friend,' she started saying to friends. 'I love him dearly.'

Nevertheless, Sarah and Andrew were separated, and the whole drama had been a tremendous strain. Hoping to unwind, to cut down on her intake of alcohol and the diet tablets, which still played too large a part in her life, especially at stressful times, she took off for Phuket with Johnny Bryan, the girls, their nanny and the detectives. At first she was blissfully anonymous, but when some European tourists spotted them and advised the press, she found herself involved in yet another paper chase. Inevitably, the press speculated about the nature of her relationship with Johnny Bryan, but, short of catching them in a compromising situation, no one could prove anything.

Soon there was even talk of Andrew and Sarah getting back together, though she was less keen on the idea than he was. In the Palace, some of the courtiers were even less keen than Sarah on the idea of a reconciliation. She had made some formidable enemies. They now decided to offer her up as a warning to Diana, who was once more pressing for the separation she had been so reluctant to pursue only a few short months before.

The idea of Sarah's enemies at court was to discredit her so thoroughly that she could never be readmitted into the Royal Family as a fully fledged member. Diana would get the message that if she persisted in travelling down Sarah's path, she would go her way in more ways than one. So they set Sarah up when she took a week's holiday at Le Mas de Pignerolle, a pink villa in the densely wooded hills above St Tropez on France's Côte d'Azure.

Normally, whenever a member of the Royal Family is visiting France, the gendarmerie are advised so that they can protect the outer perimeter of whichever property the royal is staying in. Not only is this practice standard, it has also been crucial since all members of the Royal Family became targets for the IRA.

On this occasion, however, the British authorities failed to alert the French about the Duchess's arrival, or to request policing for her and Princesses Beatrice and Eugenie of York. This was no oversight. It was done deliberately. The plan was to tip off a photographer that Sarah was in residence, then give him access to the villa so that he could take compromising photographs of her. This was duly done. Over a period of days, ace paparazzo Daniel Angeli, renowned as the hitman's hitman, was able to secrete himself without any need for anxiety between the trees near the swimming pool and shoot Sarah, Johnny Bryan, the children and the detectives from Scotland Yard to his heart's content.

Without realizing that she had been compromised, Sarah returned to London and headed for Balmoral with the children. She and Andrew were having yet another of their cosy *en famille* holidays when she learnt from Johnny Bryan that they had been snapped in delicate positions and that the *Daily Mirror* planned to publish.

Sarah promptly went to pieces. Bryan assured her he would try to stop publication by applying for an injunction, but Mr Justice Latham refused his application. The following morning, the first of the pictures were splashed across the front and inside pages of the *Mirror*, and Sarah had the excruciating experience of having to face the whole family. Andrew once more behaved in an exemplary manner, taking Sarah's side and asserting that as she had been 'set up' no one should condemn her. Moreover, she was a separated woman, and if she wished to flirt with a man, she was only doing what all separated women are entitled to. And, of course, she was only doing what many married women, Diana included, were doing on the quiet. Despite this, the Queen and the rest of the family were acutely embarrassed, and the following morning Sarah departed from the Castle under a cloud.

Significantly, Diana did get the message, as this and other blows such as the release of the least damaging parts of the Squidgy tape flooded into the public arena. She dropped her demand for a separation – at least until October.

Devastated by what had happened, Sarah returned to Romenda Lodge and took to her bed. Finally, the strain and the pressure reached her. She underwent a total physical and nervous breakdown. Unable to function, she stayed in bed crying and cut herself off from all but her closest friends. The only people who had uninterrupted access to her were Johnny Bryan and Andrew. Sarah was in such bad shape she did not even bother to put on make-up, and on the few occasions she was seen in public, she looked like the living dead. About the only thing she managed to do, aside from the school run, was to visit the sufferers of motor-neurone disease and her other charities. The warmth and love and acceptance she received from them sustained her. It was something they were all happy to do for her, for she has always been a great sport where her charities are concerned, and though she gave them the option to drop her, they all refused to do so.

In autumn, just as Sarah was making the first tentative steps towards piecing herself back together again, she took steps to ensure that her privacy would always be protected. Unsubstantiated rumours were floating around Fleet Street that Johnny Bryan was trying to sell the story of their friendship with her, and while she did not believe them, she suggested to him that he show good faith by undertaking never to reveal any information about her, her family or their friendship, which, of course, he gladly did.

Finally, Sarah was taking a long look at her life. While some aspects of it were good – Andrew, her parents, her stepmother and her sister had all provided vigorous support – she saw that others needed attention. She had hit what is popularly known as rock bottom, and she realized she would have to turn to professionals for help or be destroyed. So she went into therapy, discovered that she had to wean herself away from the dietary tablets that caused her mood swings and went to a self-help group.

'Hello, my name is Sarah,' she says at each meeting and states what her problem is. She has also given up drink, for the steps by which she now lives her life preclude the use of any substance that has a potential to become addictive. She has taken to the programme the way a duck takes to water for Sarah York is, above all else, a spirited and essentially good human being who has only ever sought to bring as much sunshine into her own and everyone else's life as she possibly can.

Andrew, who has always been a teetotaller, is especially pleased at the path she has taken. He still hopes to be reconciled with Sarah. And she is more open to the idea than at any time since the separation, for Andrew has shown himself to be her truest and most loyal friend. In separation and in adversity, he has given her the support he never did while they lived together as man and wife. It seems likely that the marriage will end in divorce, though with the Yorks anything is possible.

CHAPTER TWENTY-ONE

Prince Philip in Skirts

Straightforward though the marriage of the Yorks was, it was as convoluted as a corkscrew compared with the marriages of the Princess Royal to Mark Phillips and Tim Laurence. This is hardly surprising, for Anne herself is more direct than even Sarah, Mark is more direct than even the very direct Andrew, and that in itself is one of the reasons why the marriage ultimately failed. It also explains why Anne chose as her next partner someone who was in many ways the antithesis of her first husband.

The key to the princess is that she is Prince Philip in skirts. Born on 15 August 1950 at Clarence House, Anne Elizabeth Alice Louise Mountbatten, as she then legally was, was a pretty, Nordic-looking baby with grey blue eyes. While Charles was dark like his mother, she was as fair as her father. Nor was her colouring the only thing she inherited from him. Turned over to nanny Helen Lightbody and nursery assistant Mabel Anderson, who already had charge of her elder brother, as soon as she could speak Anne displayed a temperament in marked contrast to Charles.

As the two children were brought up together very much as a unit, the fact that one was so much like his mother and the other so like her father was often commented upon. The almost claustrophobic atmosphere of their early years, secluded behind Palace walls and allowed to play only occasionally with other children, intensified their innate characteristics when dilution, resulting in the development of counteracting traits, might have been in their best interests. The result was that the naturally assertive and fearless Anne developed as an almost perfect foil to the more reticent and sensitive Charles, and by the time they were sent to school it was too late to alter the die. Their formative years had passed, and it was cast.

Because she was a girl, Anne was never subjected to the pressure that Charles experienced almost from the day of his birth. Philip especially was intent on turning out a tough son in his own image. While the boy adored his father and emulated him, he was never able to please him, which only had the effect of turning Charles even more in upon himself. Anne, on the other hand, responded positively to her father's robust approach. Whenever Philip snapped at her, she did not wilt. She either bucked up or stood up to him, both of which earned his respect and further enhanced the natural affinity between them. Of course, she was also her Daddy's little girl, and, like all little girls, this meant that she enjoyed a status with him that no brother could ever share.

Being so temperamentally different, but reared together in such close proximity, Charles and Anne's early relationship was fraught and fiery. They bickered constantly, fought frequently and annoyed one another just by existing. To Charles, Anne's pushiness and pluck were anathema, while she resented always having to be number two in the pecking order.

Even at so early an age, the question of rank was a factor. Charles was one day going to be King, while Anne would only ever be a back-up member of the team and most likely would go down from the number two spot to three, four or even five, depending on whether the Queen had any more sons – which, in the event, she did.

As both Charles and Anne were brought up with the spotlight shining brightly upon them, in a way that Andrew and Edward were not, they were both aware from an early age of their celebrity, though paradoxically, not of the meaning of their rank. This celebrity, to Charles, was almost a matter of embarrassment, but to Anne, it was a delight to be relished. It also remained one, so that when she was older, and the guards had to snap to attention each time she walked back and forth, like her aunt Margaret she would do as frequently as she could, just so she could have her importance reaffirmed. Charles, on the other hand, always contrived, in an innate display of modesty, to avoid walking past the guards if he could.

As children, Anne and Charles were the most celebrated kids in the world. They could not go anywhere without being photographed. This blighted Charles's school-days at Hill House and Cheam, but Anne did not have the same problem because she was educated at the Palace. She had two school mates, Susan Babington-Smith, whose grandfather had been an equerry to King George V, and Caroline Hamilton, whose grandfather was the Dean of Windsor. They formed a happy and very privileged triumvirate.

Taught by the governess, Catherine Peebles, who had taught Princess Alexandra and Prince Michael of Kent before, the girls were given an education that approximated to a normal one in terms of the subjects studied, but which surpassed the norm in every other respect. The adult Sukie Babington-Smith recalls how very privileged they were in having a great many field trips, all with the best of everything. Whether they were visiting Wimbledon to see the tennis, having their weekly music and dance lessons at the Palace, ice-skating at Richmond, or being shown around one of the museums, they went first class all the way. Anne even had Dan Maskell as her tennis coach. Although they took such a high standard for granted, the education did have the desired result, and the girls it produced were informed, interested, interesting and confident.

Confidence was not Anne's problem. In his excellent biography of Cecil Beaton, Hugo Vickers recounts how the famous photographer, called upon to photograph the Royal Family after Prince Andrew's birth in 1960, was compelled to write in his diary: 'I felt as if I were being chased in a nightmare, when one's legs sink into the mire.' When Nanny Lightbody brought in the nine-year-old Anne ahead of her parents, and Beaton ventured the opinion that it would be all right to start the session, she replied haughtily, 'Well, I don't think it will be.' Later, when he took her to a window to photograph her there, 'The wretched girl shrugged her shoulders and pulled a face. I said, 'You hate it, I know. But hate it by the window, hate it looking this way, hate it looking that way, hate it in profile. Now detest it looking straight at the camera.'

When she was thirteen, the self-assured princess whom Palace staff said was 'above herself' was packed off to Benenden School in Kent. It was chosen because it was near enough to London to be accessible for visits from the Queen and the Duke of Edinburgh, but far enough from the road, like Gordounstoun, for the inquisitive press to be denied the photographs they had snatched at Cheam.

School was something of a shock for Anne, not because she was unused to discipline – at the Palace her days had been mapped out from birth – but because it afforded her the freedom she had never had. Being one of 300 girls, she discovered how delightful ordinariness could be. Even though her version of it was unique, and she stood out no matter how hard everyone tried to pretend she did not, she had never blended in to quite such an extent before. This struck a chord deep within Anne, far deeper than it would in her brothers, and for the remainder of her life she would pursue the comfort that being an ordinary human being brought. When she got older and was launched upon the national and international stage as a performing royal, this became the source of tremendous friction between Anne and the press, for she made a sharp differentiation between Anne the Princess when she was on duty, and Anne the Human Being when she was off. The press, on the other hand, did not, and an increasingly fractious princess ended up telling them on many occasions to 'Fuck off.'

Throughout the four years of Anne's stay at Benenden, the press respected her privacy, partly because of her inaccessibility, and partly because there was nothing of interest to recount. True to her goal, she was ordinary in every way but one, her rank aside. Firmly in the middle of the class academically, she only shone when she was riding her horse High Jinks, which her parents had given her, and which was stabled at Benenden. Whether competitively or for pleasure, the art of equestrianism was her great love. In this, though in nothing else, she wished to stand out, so Cherry Kendall, the well-known three-day eventer who had ridden to glory at Badminton, was brought in to coach her. Excelling at the sport, Anne decided that she wanted to make as much of a career of riding as her rank allowed.

When Anne left Benenden at the age of seventeen, she was not in the position of the ordinary girl, whether upper, middle or working class. She had no choice in her career. Irrespective of what her own inclinations were, she had to live up to her responsibilities as a royal princess, to fulfil a full schedule of official duties, to become a performing member of the Royal Family. That was her career. The choice had been made by an accident of birth. Knowing this, she did not buck the system and make herself miserable in the process. She simply tried to work her way around the limitations.

Because the course of her professional life had been taken out of her hands, Anne decided not to waste time going to university. 'So many of one's friends went for the sake of going. I saw no point in going unless I was going for something specific,' she says. So, in 1968, at the peak of the sexual revolution, when the World was Young, and London was the grooviest place on earth to be, Anne left school and enrolled for a six-week autumnal course in French at the Berlitz School in Oxford Street. Then she retreated to the *Britannia*, for a cruise of the Western Isles where she celebrated her eighteenth birthday. Afterwards, she took possession of a Rover 2000 from her parents, was awarded £6,000 per annum from the Civil List and prepared for her professional début as a fully fledged member of the Royal Family.

No matter how self-confident they are, all eighteen year olds face the world with butterflies in their stomachs. Anne's misgivings increased tenfold before she was even launched upon the stage. One woman's magazine asserted, 'She's eighteen, and nobody thinks she's a pretty girl. If I were her mother, the first thing I would do is slim her down.' Another opined that she was 'frumpy, dumpy and grumpy'. Taking the criticism very much to heart, Anne went on a diet, bought a new wardrobe of trendy clothes in bright colours and hoped her efforts would be rewarded with approval. In March 1969, she made her début in a traditional ceremony, presenting leeks on St David's Day to the Welsh Guards. She wore a stylish cap, a jaunty mini and looked fetching. Any hopes she had of universal acclaim were doused when she read the following morning's papers and discovered that she was being criticized for, among other things, wearing short skirts that revealed knobbly knees.

Anne has good legs and a good figure. She is also infinitely better looking in person than in any photograph. When she was younger and blonder, she was actually very attractive full face. Only in profile did the weakness of her chin detract. However, the journalists had obviously made up their minds that Anne did not accord with their image of what a fairy princess was, and from the word go they had it in for her. From that first solo official duty in March 1969, until the mid-1980s, when she was extolled for her work for the Save the Children Fund, the tabloids hounded her mercilessly.

At first, Anne reacted the way Fergie did, by taking the criticism on board and rectifying whatever it was that failed to please. No amount of rectification, however, resulted in the balance redressing itself in her favour, and rather than turn her sense of injustice inwards, as Sarah would do with such self-destructive results, Anne turned it outwards, to the source of her torment.

Nor has Anne ever forgotten the lessons or the pain. Even after a decade of publicity, which extols her virtues professionally, Anne remains at daggers drawn with her old enemies. She has been too badly burnt to ever allow them anything but grudging co-operation. Of all the royals, she is the only one who will never break her pace to give photographers time for snaps, even when she is on duty, and even when she knows that the publicity she receives will be favourable.

Like her father, Anne has an innate sense of justice. Where the press is concerned, this means that she shows the men and women of the Fourth Estate as little compassion as they have shown her. This applies even when their lives are in danger and is best illustrated by an incident that took place in 1984, when she was in India for a tour associated with the Save the Children Fund. Indira Gandhi was assassinated, and the press corps was advised to leave. However, some of the journalists had no transportation out of the village where they were. Anne ignored their plight, even as her lady-in-waiting pleaded for them not to be left stranded. Her attitude was, and remains, implacable, not only against her press tormentors but also in every other area of her life, for Anne is nothing if not strong-minded, almost to the point of intransigence.

The Save the Children Fund was pivotal in turning round Anne's publicity and has been the single most important part of her professional life. Appointed President at the early age of twenty in 1970, she followed in the footsteps of one of the world's most formidable charity-workers: her great-aunt Edwina, Countess Mountbatten of Burma, who worked herself into an early grave in 1960 with her commitments to that fund and to St John Ambulance. From the outset, Anne was no honorific president. She took an active part in raising funds and attracting much-needed publicity for the charity, touring not only Britain on its behalf but also much of the world. Her first tour was to Kenya in 1971, when she appeared on the popular BBC television programme *Blue Peter* with Valerie Singleton. This inevitably caused controversy, with the princess being the primary focus of attention instead of the charity, but Anne did not mind brickbats as long as they were fair and served the purpose of publicizing a cause other than herself.

In the years to come, Anne stretched the boundaries of acceptable limits for royal presidents of charities by touring much of the world on behalf of the Save the Children Fund. Nor did she limit herself to soft spots or chic countries. She went to Beirut at the height of the Lebanese civil war, toured Somalia and Ethiopia before Bob Geldof, thereby helping to bring the scale of the tragedy taking place there to the attention of the world. She now knows the Indian sub-continent intimately through her repeated tours of India, Bangladesh and Pakistan. She has travelled to more countries in Africa than just about any other white woman. Whether she is in Uganda or Mozambique, Burkina Faso or Morocco, Gambia or Tanzania, Zambia or Sudan, Zimbabwe or Somalia, she travels light. Not for her the silk dresses and straw hats of a fashion-conscious princess.

Unless she is representing Britain, which she does not do in her capacity as President of the Save the Children Fund, she pulls on jeans, a cotton shirt, ties her hair back with a scarf or headband and bounces over dirt roads in uncomfortable jeeps, finding out facts, bringing aid, speaking to the workers at inaccessible as well as accessible outposts, discovering what needs to be done, then finding a way of using her position so that it does get done. From her father she inherited tenacity of purpose as well as compassion for suffering, for Anne remembers her grandmother Alice, Princess Andrew of Greece, well and knows what it is like to love someone whose disability cuts them off from many of the benefits of life, which we all take for granted.

In the early days of her career as a princess, while Anne was embarked upon the good work that would eventually bring her such praise, she set about forging the career for herself that she would have developed full-time had she not been born who she was. A natural equestrienne who had inherited a love of horses from her mother and of riding from her father, Anne decided to take up eventing and to try to bring herself up to world-class standard. Her choice of category was shrewd, because three-day eventing is one of the few equestrian sports that does not require full-time commitment. Anne could therefore snatch a few hours here and squeeze in a few there between official duties.

If Anne's status as a royal prevented her from a full-time commitment outside her official duties, it had the benefit of according her access to the very best trainer available. She therefore chose Alison Oliver, who set to work with her and the three top-flight horses that Anne bought: Doublet, Royal Ocean and Purple Star. Her ambition was to qualify for the 1972 Olympics, and, with that in mind, she spent every free minute she had pursuing her goal. Her early entrances in the various horse trials were a necessary part of qualifying for a place on the Olympic team. At the Badminton Horse Trials of 1971, she led the field against such eminent riders as Richard Meade, Lucinda Prior-Palmer and Mark Phillips, who came second, though he emerged the winner at the end of the third day, with Anne placing a respectable fifth out of forty-seven. That qualified her for the Burghley Horse Trials, which she won, becoming the 1971 European Champion, to the delight of all her supporters, even if it meant that the photographers hovered 'at every fence hoping I'd fall off'.

Anne's victory at Burghley was the first of her successes in altering public perception of her as the ugly duckling who waddles through her duties and can get nothing right. Her achievement was recognized as remarkable and praiseworthy, when Fleet Street gave her its Sportswriters Award. The BBC voted her Sports Personality of the Year. And the *Daily Express* selected her as their Sportswoman for 1971.

Through her sporting activities, Anne made the friends who have remained close to her to this day. She does not have a wide circle, preferring to limit herself to a few close personal friends. One such friend she made during her reign as Sportswoman of the Year in 1971 was Jackie Stewart. The racing driver had been selected as the *Daily Express* Sportsman of the Year. At the various presentation and award ceremonies, they struck up a friendship, which has lasted to the present. He and his wife Helen soon became an integral part of her inner circle, to such an extent that they are one of the few couples with whom Anne has stayed, at their hillside house above Lake Geneva in Switzerland.

Anne enjoyed her reign as Sportswoman of 1971, not only because she was receiving favourable publicity but also because she was meeting interesting people in a field that mattered to her. She set about living life to the hilt. She was extraordinarily busy, what with her official duties and her equestrian obligations, but, being fortunate in having inexhaustible energy, she lived a full and active social life as well.

Like most girls of her age, Anne was interested in finding herself a boyfriend. She was not her father's daughter for nothing. She had a relish for the opposite sex that was positively Schleswig-Holstein-Sondenburg-Glucksburg, and surely understood the passions that motivated her grandfather Prince Andrew of Greece until his marriage was rent asunder with his appreciation of animate form. Princesses, however, are fortunate. Unlike working- or middle-class girls, they are constantly bombarded with young men in various sizes and shapes. Royals are constantly staying with or entertaining each other, so Anne was meeting not only young princes but also their attendants.

There were also scions of the aristocracy such as Lord Irwin, the Earl of Halifax's heir, and Lord Rupert Nevill's son Guy. Then there were the young officers of the Household Cavalry and Guards regiments who guard the Royal Family and play such an integral part in the ceremonial surrounding the sovereign. Some of these were good-looking as well as well-bred, as Anne discovered when she met a handsome captain in the Household Cavalry who had ridden his horse, The Fossa, to fourth place in the Grand National. His name was Andrew Parker Bowles, he was a cousin of the Duke of Marlborough and Earl Cadogan, and he and Anne quickly struck up such a close and affectionate relationship that he was her escort at Royal Ascot in 1970.

Andrew Parker Bowles's relationship with Anne, however, was destined to remain nothing but a pleasing interlude in both their lives. He was a Roman Catholic; she was forbidden by the Act of Settlement from marrying one. So, after an agreeable dalliance, he went his way and she went hers.

Andrew Parker Bowles was eleven years older than Anne. So was her other early boyfriend, the Hon. Brian Alexander. Son of Field Marshal Earl Alexander of Tunis and a great friend of Queen Beatrix of the Netherlands, Brian Alexander was blessed with striking good looks, stature and charm. He was well used to socializing with royalty through his association with Beatrix and was, moreover, a close friend of Anne's cousin Patrick Lichfield. He was also a racing driver, although his category was Club sports cars, as opposed to Jackie Stewart's Formula One. That romance, however, amounted to nothing, as did Anne's relationship with another member of that circle, Piers Weld-Forester.

Waiting in the wings, however, was a horseman who would ride into Anne's life and sweep her off her feet on to the stage of *Hair*. His name was Sandy Harpur, and, unlike Patrick Lichfield's friends or Andrew Parker Bowles, he belonged to Anne's age group. More significantly, they shared the same passion: horses. They also shared as normal a relationship as any unmarried British princess and a British subject can have. They went to dinner together. They visited friends. They rode. They even attended the above-mentioned hit musical twice. And, in yet another display of her intention to be ordinary when she was not forced by circumstances into being extraordinary, Anne joined other members of the audience on stage. That, and the fact that she was wearing a trouser suit, excited tremendous comment in the tabloids, as did their presence at the most avant-garde discothèque of the day, La Valbonne. There were predictions of the relationship ending in marriage, though such a large commitment was the furthest thing from Anne's mind.

Furthermore, Anne was not leading a normal life. She was constantly going off on trips with her parents. Between her début as a single princess in 1969 and her marriage in 1973, she accompanied the Queen and the Duke of Edinburgh to Austria, Norway, Fiji, Tonga, New Zealand, Australia, Canada (twice), the United States of America, Turkey, Thailand, Singapore, Malaysia, Brunei and Yugoslavia. She also went with her father to Iran, for the 2500th anniversary of the monarchy, travelled with Charles to Kenya and flew on her own to Germany three times as well as Hong Kong. It was difficult to sustain a relationship under those circumstances, especially at such an early age, and Sandy Harpur eventually made off and married the actress Suzy Kendall.

216

Being manless when you have as much integrity and passion as Anne is difficult. Fortunately for her, she did not have to suffer the ravages of a thirst unquenched for long. Waiting with a cup overflowing was a handsome young athlete whom the Palace staff quickly nicknamed 'the Stud'. His name was Mark Phillips. A lieutenant in The Queen's Dragoon Guards, he was not only one of the foremost horsemen in the world but also someone of such bland and respectable background that no one could either complain or exult about him.

Mark Phillips was from a long line of soldiers, bankers and mining engineers. His father was Peter William Garside Phillips, MC, a soldier who had gone into the army right from school, fought a commendable war, then been left high and dry when the government nationalized the mines and removed his chance to enter the family business, which was mining.

Gentlemen of so resolutely middle-class a background had few career options open to them in that day, so Peter Phillips went to agricultural college before settling down to a life as a farmer in Gloucestershire. For nine years he struggled against what he terms 'under-capitalization' before farming became untenable when another government cut a swathe through his career yet again, this time quite literally by 'putting a motorway through the best part of my farm'. With no option left but to go into business, he joined Walls, the famous ice-cream company, in 1957 as an area manager, rising to become purchasing director. There he remained until his retirement, shining brightly only in his ordinariness and his competence.

Mark Phillips's mother was the one whose background almost threatened to break the spell of ordinariness that enthralled Anne so much. Mrs Peter Phillips was born into the well-known banking family of Tiarks. Her father, Brigadier John Tiarks, was a career officer who had once been an aide-de-camp to King George VI. She was an attractive woman from whom her son inherited his looks, but, her face and lineage aside, she, too, opted for a life of resolute ordinariness as your typical, upper-class country woman.

The Phillips family home was at Great Somerford in Wiltshire. It was small as big houses go, but it was nevertheless a comfortable and substantial residence. Like most boys of his class, Mark left home at the tender age of eight to attend preparatory school at Stouts Hill, after which he went to public school at Marlborough College. Like his future wife, he was a brilliant athlete but no academic, and he graduated with five O-levels and only one A-level. This presented him with a problem if his ambition of being a career officer in the army were to be achieved, for he did not have sufficient A-levels to gain admission to the staff college at Sandhurst. So he signed on as a private who was potential officer material, spending six months in the ranks before being accepted for officer training.

Aside from the army and riding, Mark had one other interest. He was crazy about girls. He was a popular young buck at a time when being young and popular meant having a better time than anyone had had since the sybaritic, sensual, bacchanalian good times of Renaissance Italy and Ancient Rome. His nickname, 'the Stud', was no put-down or envious crack, rather a witty acknowledgement of his aptitude for providing pleasure.

While his skill at riding human mares cemented his romance with the passionate Anne, what earned her respect was his ability at controlling equestrian mares. A born horseman who literally could ride before he would walk, Mark was given his first pony when he was a year and a half old by his mother, who was herself a gifted equestrienne who had once been a master of one of the local hunts. By the age of eighteen he was competing at the leading horse trials such as Burghley, where he came fourth, and at twenty he was a member of the British Olympic team at the Games in Mexico City.

As far as Anne was concerned, Mark was perfect for her. Not only did they have the same interests and tastes, but they also had compatible personalities, for the volatile and wilful princess liked the fact that she had found a man who was so quietly confident and strong-minded that she had to bend her will to his. This was a trait that she had acquired straight from her mother, for Lilibet had always played the traditionally feminine role in relation to Philip's rampant and overt masculinity, and even after the romance left their relationship, they continued relating to one another very much as the little woman and the macho man. Anne was therefore perpetuating a family pattern of behaviour, though within a few years, as she blossomed into mature womanhood, her natural instincts would rise to the surface and Prince Philip in Skirts would gain ascendancy over Anne the Woman Emulating her Mother. Then the problems in the Phillips marriage would start with a real vengeance.

The early part of Anne and Mark's affair was conducted in absolute secrecy. Like her brother Charles, Anne has always had the knack of choosing loyal and discreet friends who would sooner lose a limb than loosen their tongues. They all came in handy, arranging discreet dinner parties and weekends for the young lovers who just 'happened' by some 'twist of fate' or 'coincidence' to have been asked at the same time, albeit quite, quite separately, of course. These same friends would also meet up with Anne at unfashionable restaurants, at which Mark invariably arrived and from which he departed separately. The only place where Anne and Mark could afford to lower their guard was at Alison Oliver's stables. Both had an equal excuse for being there, Anne because Alison Oliver was her trainer, and Mark because her stables were where Columbus, the horse the Queen had given him the use of, was kept. Otherwise, they maintained a charade of non-togetherness, which enabled them to conduct a relationship that was as normal as any two ordinary people, albeit well-placed, could have.

The happy anonymity came to an end in November 1972, when the press spotted Anne out fox-hunting with Mark. She was staying with him at his parents' house, which convinced the Fourth Estate that an engagement was imminent. Anne has always been adamant that the subject of marriage had never come up. Moreover she asserts that she herself had no particular desire to be married at so early an age. Mark also says that he was 'a confirmed bachelor' with no intention of losing his freedom at that stage.

However, the more the press were insistent on a forthcoming betrothal were, the more insistent Anne and Mark became in their denials. So fierce did things become that Anne and Mark found their concentration affected, and hence their performance, at competitions. Both took to complaining and denying with equal vociferousness, and continued doing so until shortly before the announcement of the engagement itself.

On 29 May 1973, Buckingham Palace announced the engagement. This caused a furious eruption over the question of earlier denials. Mark Phillips answered their detractors: 'People don't believe us when we say that in March we had no intention of getting engaged. In fact, it is absolutely true, and it was only after Badminton [in April] when the pressures of competing were less, and we weren't so busy and had time to look and think about the future, that it seemed like a good idea.'

As far as Anne and Mark were concerned, they looked forward confidently to a satisfying future together. Being both achievers, but passionate ones, their emphasis was as much on what they would achieve individually and jointly as what they would enjoy together.

CHAPTER TWENTY-TWO

Fire and Ice

On Wednesday, 14 November 1973 Princess Anne married Mark Phillips at Westminster Abbey. As she walked up the aisle on the arm of her father to meet her handsome bridegroom in his fetching scarlet tunic and fitted blue trousers, with his brightly shining black boots and silver spurs, the lightly veiled bride looked ravishing in an ivory silk Susan Small gown intricately embroidered with pearls.

The British nation was being treated to a glorious spectacle at a time when everyone needed a distraction from travail. The Heath government was on a collision course with the miners, Britain was about to endure the hardship of a three-day week, daily power cuts, candles instead of electricity, sweaters as a substitute for central heating. And the IRA had begun a bombing campaign earlier that year that was about to peak in several bloody massacres of the civilian population.

The newly-weds, however, disappeared on a Caribbean cruise on the *Britannia*. Unlike Charles and Diana or Andrew and Sarah, Anne and Mark barely left the boat. They spent the whole time cooing like lovebirds in their own, luxurious nest. This was solitude in the midst of 256 crew and 21 officers, some of whom Anne and Mark dined with, as the Royal Family do, in the evenings. But the days were their own, as were the nights, and they spent as much time as any two human beings can in the privacy of their stateroom, doing what all newly-weds do. However, they had to do it on twin beds lashed together, for no one had thought to replace the functional with a romantic double bed, and Anne was careful to make this point to Charles when the time for his honeymoon rolled around, so that a proper bed could be procured.

The honeymoon cruise was a precursor to a royal tour, and after a fortnight, *Britannia* steamed into harbour to begin the first of their visits to countries that included Antigua, Montserrat, Jamaica, Colombia and Ecuador. Now that Mark had married into the Royal Family, he was going to have to earn his keep by becoming the supporting half of a double act. No actor, he was daunted by the necessity to make plausible chit-chat to people he had never seen before and would never see again. He wisely decided to stay in the background as much as possible and also resolved that he would hereafter only partake of royal engagements as and when it was crucial that he had to. The alternative, to endure a lifetime in a predicament that made him uneasy, was too awful to contemplate. Anne, of course, understood. She herself was a dutiful star who would have shied away from the limelight had she been able to follow her natural inclinations, so his reluctance was a bond, not a problem.

After the tour, Anne and Mark returned to Britain to move into their first marital home. This was Oak Grove House, a comfortable, five-bedroomed Georgian house, which was normally occupied by whichever colonel was Sandhurst's Director of Studies. Mark, of course, was a mere lieutenant, but Anne already had superior military rank due to her honorific positions with various regiments. Moreover, it would have been unthinkable for Her Majesty's army to denigrate the Queen's daughter by refusing to acknowledge her social as well as honorary military rank, so the house was made available to them, but at the same rent that a colonel would have to pay. As this was only £8 per week, however, it was actually not going to break Lieutenant and Mrs Mark Phillips.

From the very outset of her marriage, Anne resolved to set as ordinary a tone as she possibly could in their life together. Mark was no snob, nor was he a leech. He therefore did not wish to benefit in any way from having a wife who was also a Princess of the Blood. That extended to accepting a peerage for himself. He refused one and continued to refuse one despite press speculation and the Queen and the Duke of Edinburgh's desires. Anne was resolutely behind Mark's choice, even though it would mean that any children they might have would be the first misters and misses whose grandmother was a sovereign. Innovative by character like her father, Anne had no fear of breaking new ground, especially if it brought her that much closer to her objective of being just another human being.

As they forged a life together, Anne and Mark were making the friends they would keep thereafter. Anne had reached the stage in life where she wanted to form relationships that would be lasting. This was in contrast to her upbringing as a child, when she had been discouraged from maintaining friendships once expediency severed the link. For instance, Sukie Babington-Smith and Caroline Hamilton never saw anything of her once she left the Palace school for Benenden, and her friends from that school did not travel with her into adult life either. Now that she was married and free to evolve as she saw fit, however, Anne cast aside the royal way of never having friends outside the family.

Sport, more usually in an equestrian form, was the common denominator in all her friendships. Some, such as with the actor Anthony Andrews and his heiress wife Georgina Simpson, became friends of both Mark and her, and they would remain so even after the marriage fell apart and ended in divorce. Other friends, such as Jackie Stewart and his wife Helen, were primarily Anne's friends but went on to become both their friends. Major Malcolm Wallace of the British Equestrian Association and his wife Caroline were another couple to whom Anne and Mark became close, asking them around for casual lunches and dinners in jeans. Anne's old beau Andrew Parker Bowles had married by this time, to her brother Charles's flame Camilla Shand, and the riding-mad couple also became regular guests at or hosts to Mr and Mrs Mark Phillips.

There were, of course, people who were really Anne's friends alone. These included her lady-in-waiting, the former Lady Leonora Grosvenor, sister of the Duke of Westminster, who went on to marry and divorce Anne's cousin Patrick, Earl of Lichfield, and stood as godmother to her daughter Zara when the child was born. Mark also had friends who were particularly his. These included film director Roman Polanski, which raised a few eyebrows in court circles.

As Anne and Mark settled down to married life, they developed a rhythm that suited them. Most of their free time was taken up with riding, for both were still committed equestrians with ambitions to win competitions and represent Britain at the next Olympic Games. Between that, and working, they seldom had time for anything else but seeing friends and relations.

Anne, however, did not see a great deal of her family except when they were together for family holidays or on occasions connected to official duties. Her relationship with the Queen had never been especially close and had, throughout her childhood and teenage, been 'difficult'. This was due more to a natural conflict of personalities than to any fault on either part. Lilibet's instinctive gentleness and conservatism jarred with Anne's more robust and innovative personality, and the more the Queen tried to encourage her daughter to modulate her behaviour, the more rebellious Anne became.

Only when Anne joined the royal scene as a performer did she begin to appreciate the wisdom of her mother's stance, as she herself admits, though even then she found it difficult to emulate. Grudgingly at first, then more willingly, Anne grew to respect the mother she had discounted, but while time made the relationship easier, it could not endow such widely differing personalities with enough common ground to impart a natural affinity or the gift of closeness. The same was true of Anne's relationship with Queen Elizabeth the Queen Mother and with Prince Charles. She got along better with her younger brothers, even though the large age gap had its effect, and the result was that Anne saw more of her friends socially than she did of her family.

The only person with whom she had a genuine affinity, and with whom she enjoyed a degree of intimacy, was her father, but he of all the Royal Family was the one whose lifestyle ensured that they would seldom see one another, for he spent a good third of each year out of the country travelling on his own, another large portion travelling with the Queen, and for the rest of the time he was so occupied with his official duties or private activities that meeting up with him was a logistic nightmare. Indeed, the junior Phillipses seemed to see the senior Phillipses more frequently for purely family reasons than they did Anne's more illustrious relations.

Four months after the wedding, on 20 March 1974, Anne and Mark attended a gala preview in aid of the Riding for the Disabled Association, her main charity after the Save the Children Fund. Already they had decided that Mark would only accompany her to the most necessary of events, because he felt uneasy in the royal milieu, and, in any event, how many husbands go along to hold their wives' hands while they are at work?

They were nearly back at Buckingham Palace when they were ambushed on the Mall by a gunman in a white Ford Escort. Ian Ball had an audacious plan to kidnap Anne and hold her for a ransom of £3 million. Having spent months planning the scheme meticulously, on the evening itself he panicked, changed his mind about the course he was going to take, and he very nearly killed someone as things spiralled out of control. Armed with a .22, he used his car to block her limousine, ran to her door and tried to drag Anne out of the back seat while Mark Phillips thwarted his attempt by pulling her back inside by her other arm. Her private detective Inspector James Heaton came to the rescue, only to be shot twice in the first instance, then shot again later.

Anne, meanwhile, was thinking, 'It was very unreal. I was amazed that things were still going on outside as usual, cars and taxis passing us as though nothing was happening. I didn't have time to be frightened. I just got angry with him.' Three other people who came to her rescue were shot before the police arrived on the scene in sufficient force to apprehend Ball, who was later tried and sentenced to be detained at Her Majesty's Pleasure, at the Rampton Hospital for the criminally insane in Nottinghamshire.

World-class equestrians have to have nerves of steel, and Anne and Mark displayed their mettle during the kidnap attempt as well as immediately afterwards by driving home, she in the Scimitar sports car her parents had given her for her twenty-first birthday, he in the Rover 2000. Anne's resolute refusal to ever flap about anything was quite obviously no pose, though they both had police escorts.

Oak Grove House at Sandhurst remained the base from which Anne and Mark made their forays into the world at large for the first two years of their marriage. During that time, they established a pattern in other ways apart from the social and professional.

One of the most important effects of the way they functioned as a couple was the relationship they had with the courtiers who run the Royal Family, its palaces and its way of life. Unlike Charles, Diana and Sarah, all of whom would end up having protracted battles with the courtiers surrounding them, or Philip, who had been fought to a standstill, Anne and Mark both had the gift of doing what they pleased without making palatial waves. Of course the courtiers would have preferred it if Mark had been keener to be Anne's sidekick. However, Mark was an army man, dedicated to getting on in his career as well as in his chosen sport of riding. Many of the courtiers also had army backgrounds. They rode. They understood Mark Phillips. He did not threaten them. And, by keeping himself scarce, and refusing even to meet them on their turf much less play or challenge them at their game, he spared himself the difficulties that might have arisen had someone as strong-willed as he was been on the scene more. And Anne did not present a challenge to the courtiers either. She was so conscientious and traditional in her approach to her job that they did not mind her breaking new ground with the Save the Children Fund.

During this phase of their married life, Anne and Mark were bound by one major objective: to qualify for the Olympics at Montreal in 1976. The first obstacle to the realization of that ambition came in January 1976, when Princess Margaret took off for her holiday home on the West Indian island of Mustique with Roddy Llewellyn. The *News of the World* splashed a photograph of the married princess and her charming and attractive toy-boy over its front page, embroiling Margaret and her husband in an international scandal.

This was the straw that broke the Earl of Snowdon's back. He had long wanted out of the marriage so that he could marry his inamorata, Lucy Lindsay-Hogg. He now demanded a divorce, preparatory to which the Queen assented to an official separation. Margaret then faced the prospect of having to relinquish her official duties, and only the Queen's refusal to succumb to Establishment pressure spared her sister from public ignominy. Margaret's public role, however, was cut back as far as it could be, with the result that Anne found her workload increase dramatically at the very moment she needed it lessened.

The next brickbat to hit Anne did so three months before the team was selected in July. At the Durweston Horse Trials in Dorset she was knocked unconscious and suffered a hairline fracture of a vertebra during a particularly bad fall when her horse rolled on top of her. The doctors advised her to expect several months of pain, after which it would be a similar length of time again before she could remount a horse. They reckoned without Anne's determination. Submitting to intensive physiotherapy, she rode through the pain and was one of the five riders selected to represent Britain. Mark was another.

In the event, neither Anne nor Mark won a medal, but 1976 was not a dead loss in every way, for that was the year in which Anne and Mark got a house of their own. Gatcombe Park was owned by Lord Butler of Saffron Walden, the best Conservative prime minister Britain never had and the obliging Master of Trinity College, Cambridge, who aided and abetted

Anne's elder brother in the conduct of his first romance with Lucia Santa Cruz when he was a student at that university. The house itself was comfortable rather than palatial. It had a drawing-room, sitting-room, library, ten bedrooms, insufficient bathrooms (typical of old British houses), a good-sized kitchen and sufficient quarters to house the household staff and Anne's detective.

The Butlers had seldom used it, with the result that it needed several thousand pounds being spent on it to bring the interior up to an acceptable modern standard. Nevertheless, it had charm; it nestled in the heart of a spot of outstanding natural beauty; it was on a 733-acre farm with 483 acres of arable land and 250 of woodland; and it possessed a full complement of farm outbuildings as well as four cottages and a decorative 12-acre lake. All in all, it was paradise, and Anne loved it upon sight.

Procuring a property of Gatcombe's worth was beyond Mark Phillips, who had to make do with an army salary of less than £5000 per annum. Anne, however, was not going to allow Mark's sensitivities to look a gift horse in the mouth, so she happily accepted the Queen's offer to buy the house for them. It cost £500,000, but, in yet another display of independence, Mark decided that they must raise the money for the renovations with a mortgage, which he would repay. The Queen thought the proposition unnecessary; Anne thought it admirable; and the Phillipses could now lay claim to yet another aspect of ordinariness. They possessed a mortgage for £35,000, which Mark had to work to repay. In yet another display of ordinariness, albeit upper-class ordinariness, Anne and Mark contracted her cousin by marriage, Lady Pamela Mountbatten's husband interior designer David Hicks, to oversee the renovations and do up the place. His budget, however, was rather lower than he was used to. It was the precise sum of the mortgage: £35,000.

Although Mark's original intention upon marrying Anne had been to continue the course of his life, allowing her rank to encroach as little as possible, he now realized how this goal simply was not viable. Anne's position had affected his career and would continue to do so, thwarting him from achieving the heights he might otherwise have scaled.

Already he could not be considered for an overseas posting or for a tour of duty in Northern Ireland, without which he could never rise beyond a certain rank. He sometimes had to miss army obligations to fulfil official duties beside Anne, and while the army understood, they did not like the situation. Already he had been sidetracked into a post he would not otherwise have relished, as an instructor at Sandhurst. The alternatives to that were limited to a choice between one boring sinecure or another behind a desk in London. To someone as energetic and assertive as Mark, the prospect of spending the rest of his life in a position of impotent dullness filled him with dread. Moreover, he had no desire to have anyone but himself support his wife. That meant that he had to leave the army and go into business.

Mark Phillips is a good businessman. He saw the money-making possibilities of the farm as well as of his riding. He therefore set to work with the abundance of energy and tenacity he possesses, to turn both Gatcombe and himself into viable, profitable enterprises. From his father, who farmed 300 acres, he got some tips, but the rest he picked up from a variety of sources, including books, friends and neighbours.

Intensiveness and intensity were as much his styles as Anne's, and by being true to his nature he was soon immersed in intensive-farming methods. Then in 1977 he had a casual conversation with a neighbour, which resulted in the expansion of the enterprise beyond his wildest dreams. He wanted to buy a few fields adjoining Gatcombe, but, to his surprise, Captain Vaisey Davis offered to sell him the complete 533 acres of Aston Farm. A 1266-acre estate has far more potential for turning a healthy profit than two separate farms, and, with that in mind, he approached a variety of financial institutions with the proposal that they buy the farm and lease it back to him at a profit. When the Queen heard of this through Princess Anne, she became the purchaser and lessor. Mark was now in farming in a substantial way.

Farming, however, was not the only string to Mark's bow. Intent on turning his riding to pecuniary advantage, he struck a deal with British Leyland, the almost bankrupt vehicle manufacturers. At a cost of £60,000, they were to underwrite, over a three-year period, five horses, which he would ride in competitions under the name, the Range Rover Team. The deal undoubtedly benefited Range Rover as much as it did Mark Phillips. In fact, from British Leyland's point of view, it was a coup at the price, for Mark Phillips would keep the name of Range Rover before the public gaze and, more importantly, in front of the very people who had the means and the need to purchase a country vehicle. On the other hand, the politicians did not see the deal that way. There was a chorus of disapproval in parliament, capped by anti-monarchist MP Willie Hamilton, who cried, 'Some people say Mark and Anne haven't much money. They are rolling in it. They are grubbing around for anything to keep them going. They are parasites.'

That furore aside, 1977 was a momentous year in Anne and Mark's life as well as for the Royal Family generally. It was the twenty-fifth anniversary of the Queen's accession to the throne. Everyone in the Royal Family was caught up in an explosion of popular acclaim, centring on the affection in which the British people hold their sovereign. Already busy schedules were crammed even fuller in an attempt to meet some of the many requests flooding into Buckingham Palace for a royal visit. Charles was spearheading the Silver Jubilee Committee, the Queen and Philip were showing themselves to the Commonwealth as well as the British nation, and Anne, who was already inundated with commitments, had to shoulder an even greater number of obligations than usual. Then, to crown it all, she discovered she was pregnant.

The baby was due on 14 November 1977. That was a double anniversary: its parents' fourth wedding and Uncle Charles's twenty-ninth birthday. However, he did not oblige by making a double into a treble and arrived one day later, at 10.46 a.m.

Master Peter Phillips was unique in more ways than one. He was the first grandchild of a British monarch to be born without a title and to be born in a hospital. Previous to his birth, only one member of the Royal Family had been born away from home: the Duchess of Gloucester's young daughter. The Gloucesters were as resolutely ordinary as the Phillipses, but even they were unable to aspire to such outstanding heights of ordinariness as producing a baby whose rank was identical to tens of millions of his grandmother's subjects.

When Anne took her baby back home to Gatcombe Park, which David Hicks had only recently made ready for occupation after its extensive but tightly budgeted refurbishment, she resolved, in conjunction with Mark, that her son would never become caught up in the royal hoop-la. He was not royal. He would never be royal, unless some catastrophe wiped out the many members of the Royal Family who stood between him and the throne. And, as that was not likely, Mr and Mrs Phillips planned to bring him up to be just another ordinary, upper-class young man, like the many tens of thousands of his peers who plump out the stuffing of the Establishment. That therefore meant that he must never be exposed to the relentless publicity that turned every royal into a star, and every royal life into an obstacle course.

Peter's birth reopened the debate about whether Mark should accept a title. He was adamant that he did not want one. He was openly disparaging of Tony Armstrong-Jones for accepting the Earldom of Snowdon, accusing his uncle by marriage of snobbishness. As far as Mark was concerned, he was perfectly good enough just as he was, and if that did not suit the Royal Family and the acolytes who surround them, reflecting in their glory, that was just too bad. Needless to say, any princess who opts for ordinariness and has integrity, as Anne does, was not going to take any side that would take her son out of the milieu of ordinariness and pitch him into that of extraordinary privilege. She was therefore solidly behind Mark, much to the chagrin of the deeply traditional Queen. Nor did Anne have the support of her father on this issue, for Philip is a dyed-in-the-wool royalist who takes pride in his royal blood and did not understand why Anne and Mark were making an issue out of something that should have been taken for granted. But when he realized that no one could make any headway with Anne or Mark, he and Lilibet wisely decided to let the matter rest until Peter was an adult. At that point he could be given a hereditary peerage.

By Anne's own admission, she is not particularly maternal. Peter was therefore turned over to the care of a nanny while his mother got on with her life. She was still deeply committed to riding and was taking on an ever increasing workload of official engagements. But these activities were beginning to take a toll on her personal life. She and Mark, having pledged at the beginning of their marriage that they would respect one another's independence, were beginning to discover that couples who are too independent fracture their union rather than foster it. Furthermore, Anne was undergoing a profound change as she matured and grew into herself. She was changing the way in which she related on a sexual level to men. She was crawling out from under the rock of feminine submissiveness into assertiveness and dominance, casting off the childhood influences that had impelled her to take the vow of obedience upon matrimony, and while this move brought her the satisfaction of being true to her real character, it was creating problems within the marriage.

Mark was a traditional male who expected to be master in his own house. He was not prepared to tolerate constant opposition from any woman. Whether she was a princess or not made no difference to him. A woman, even an independent woman, must defer to her man. Not all the time, for that would be boring, but enough of the time for the man to retain his masculinity and position as head of the family. The development of Anne's personality, however, had reached the point where such conduct was impossible for her. Prince Philip in Skirts was stepping into Queen Elizabeth the Queen Mother's shoes. She was on her way to being the real leader in her personal life, and who didn't like it, could lump it. The Stud included.

Marriages seldom unravel cleanly and decisively. The disintegration usually takes place in spurts. Rapid progression is followed by a lengthy pause, during which both parties catch their breath, try to figure out what is happening and waver between accepting the reality and denying it. Anne and Mark were no exception to that rule. In a curious example of irony, the marriage was even ending parallel to how it came together, for they had been the last to realize that they would get married, and now they were also the last to realize that the marriage was ending. Just as how the press had been reporting an engagement before the parties to it had decided upon one, now, too, it was full of the strains accompanying its disintegration. Anne and Mark were rowing too constantly and too publicly, being too pointedly callous to one another, for their detractors to miss what was happening. They, however, continued to do so for two more years, until they had one row too many and the heart of the marriage died from a combination of too much fire and too much ice.

Mark Phillips, of course, was in a better position to cope with a union whose life had expired than Anne. He was a handsome young man who travelled about the place and could therefore indulge in light-hearted flirtations with women who would not confuse admiration with permanence. Anne, on the other hand, was trailed everywhere by her private detective. She was usually in public, and, unless she involved her friends — most of whom were also Mark's – she would have grave difficulty in finding someone who could provide her with the comfort and succour that any normal young woman needs. Guarding one's reputation is as instinctive to born royals as breathing. In Anne's case, this was even more so, for she cherishes her privacy in an exceptional manner. The idea of involving herself or her friends in anything that would result in her being the cynosure of all eyes was therefore anathema. Then fate smiled upon her.

Towards the end of 1979, a burly, blonde policeman named Peter Cross was assigned to Anne's staff. Although he was married and the father of two young children, the attractive detective was a man who found women as irresistible as they found him. Anne 'adores men', as a spokesman at Buckingham Palace ill-advisedly stated last year, so it was inevitable that the electric currents would flow between the lonely, impassioned princess and her masculine protector, some three years her senior. According to Peter Cross, he and Anne quickly struck up a secret relationship, which began late one night after he had accompanied her on an official engagement. They were in the kitchen at Gatcombe Park having a drink and talking about the events of the day when she rested her hand on his knee. Astonished at first, he quickly recovered his composure and acquitted himself like one of nature's gentlemen. Thereafter, he was her firm confidant, sharing the secrets of her private life while playing his protective role in public.

It was an ideal relationship for a married royal to have. Sergeant Cross could offer Anne all the support she needed without anyone having cause to ask questions, because they had a valid reason for being together. That meant that the press could never create a song and dance at their expense, which would not have been the case had Anne formed a close friendship with any male outside the Royal Household. Then, her detractors would have commented on the frequency with which she saw her special friend, thereby precipitating an avalanche of unfavourable comment, which would have buried Anne, the man in question and their relationship in a mountain of rubble.

Moreover, Anne is discreet. For all her supposed rebelliousness, she has never once rebelled against the true role of a traditional princess. She is as imperious, as aloof, as dignified and as discreet as was any one of Queen Victoria's daughters. The idea of behaving in a manner that would excite chatter was as alien to Anne the princess as it was to Anne the person.

There was yet another reason for discretion as far as the degree of Anne's friendship with Peter Cross was concerned. If the courtiers ever received confirmation that she was becoming too friendly with her private detective, they would move against the pair immediately. This she knew only too well. And this she was careful to avoid. Of course, every step that every royal takes is transmitted on the Palace bush telegraph, so there is no such thing as an unknown secret. There is, however, a big difference between unproven friendships and proven ones.

The best laid plans came a cropper, and so did Princess Anne. In September 1980, after she had failed to qualify for the Moscow Olympics, she discovered she was pregnant. She wanted the baby, but her condition put a new complexion on any relationship with any man other than her husband. To deflect potential gossip, Peter Cross was immediately transferred from the Royal Protection Department to a mundane uniformed police job in the suburbs of Croydon. The reason given was incredible. It was 'over-familiarity', which rather gave the game away at the very moment the Palace was trying to say it did not exist.

While Anne's pregnancy progressed, Charles became engaged to Diana, and Mark branched out into business in an even bigger way. This resulted in money-spinning projects such as the Captain Mark Phillips Equestrian Centre at the Gleneagles Hotel. He also took up travelling in a big way, giving equestrian courses in countries as diverse as Australia and Jamaica, New Zealand and Canada. For her part, Anne cut down on her engagements, sat back, and awaited the birth of her second child. She also remained in close touch with Peter Cross and telephoned him as soon as her daughter Zara was born to share the happy occasion with him.

By the time of Zara's birth, Cross was no longer a policeman. In January 1981 he left the police force and went to work for an insurance company. According to Cross, for the next two years he and Anne continued to enjoy their friendship in peace and secrecy. Her marriage was over in all but name, and his was faring no better. He seemed to have great difficulty in keeping his trousers on, for he began an affair with a young woman by the name of Gillian Nicholls while still with his wife Linda and friendly with Anne. Finally, this proved too much for Linda. She asked him to leave, and Cross moved in with his girlfriend. This development did not perturb Anne, who continued to telephone Cross whenever she wished to speak to him. According to Gillian Nicholls, who was present on innumerable occasions when Anne telephoned, she employed the witty alias Mrs Wallis whenever she asked for him.

Cross, however, made a move that ensured the end of the line. He approached the press in the shape of the *Sun* and the *Daily Star*. He offered them the story of his and Anne's friendship for the sum of £600,000. They declined, the news got back to Anne, and Peter Cross was out of her life.

CHAPTER TWENTY-THREE

Breaking New Ground

Apassionate woman at the peak of her sexual charms and desires who has neither a husband nor a lover paying close attention to her needs is a woman in an unenviable position. By the mid-eighties, Anne was in such a position. She and Mark Phillips now led totally separate personal lives and their professional lives overlapped only on the most necessary of occasions. He still accompanied her on some official trips, such as to the United Arab Emirates in 1984 or Switzerland in 1986, but even these were becoming increasingly rare events. Far more common were Anne's solo peregrinations to such places as Yugoslavia and the Indian sub-continent (1984), Germany, Zambia, Mozambique and other African states (1985), or Brazil, France, Canada and Belgium (1986). Mark accumulated a similar number of air miles flying from one part of the globe to another earning money at his equestrian clinics.

Anne and Mark's lives seemed to cross in the sky more than they did on earth. This was a state of affairs the press was calculated to notice. By this time, the media was full of stories about the marriage being under a severe strain. Anne and Mark were careful to deny or to dismiss all the claims, which rose to a crescendo when they both were in Los Angeles for the 1984 Olympics but stayed in separate parts of the city, then somehow never seemed to find the time to see one another. Such careless behaviour was the first indication the public had that the marriage might be in deep trouble, and all Anne and Mark's statements about being so busy with their Olympic commitments had a hollow ring.

Although the public did not yet know the full extent of the breakdown of relations between Anne and Mark, the marriage was over in all but name, and both partners were at liberty to do as they pleased. All that was required of them was that they do so discreetly. In this, Mark was as happy to oblige as Anne, for he is a thorough gentleman. Invariably, he thereafter conducted himself with the intention of avoiding embarrassment to his wife, family and in-laws.

Mark was a virile young man in his mid-thirties. No one expected him to deny himself the pleasures of female companionship, but equally, no one expected him to leave proof of satisfaction. But on the night of 19 November 1984, in the privacy of his suite at the Town House Hotel in Auckland, New Zealand, Mark Phillips left a marker of outstanding quality. Nine months later, Heather Tonkins, an art teacher whom Mark had first met when he gave her equestrian lessons, gave birth to a beautiful daughter whom she named Felicity Bridget, but called Bunny.

Bunny Tonkins's birth was the beginning of an incredible series of events, which would result in the end of Princess Anne's marriage. After the baby was born, her mother, who was no longer able to work now that she had an infant to care for, got in touch with Mark's Antipodean agents with a view to having him fulfil his financial obligations as a parent. Thereafter, James Erskine, International Management Group's managing director in Australia, acted as the go-between. The negotiations were tense, with much toing and froing, and Mark refusing, then as now, to admit paternity, but eventually agreed to pay Heather Tonkins the sum of £7400 per annum in quarterly instalments. Mark, however, is not a canny businessman for nothing. He knows the virtue of a denial as much as the danger of an admission, so the payments were disguised as 'acting as a consultant on equestrian matters for the International Management Group in New Zealand'.

Needless to say, the existence of this lovechild was a shattering blow to Mark Phillips, but he hoped that the course of conduct he had undertaken would bury the issue of public acknowledgement once and for all. Anne took a patrician view of the whole matter. Too many royal and aristocratic babies have been conceived accidentally for anyone but the most narrow-minded prig to make an issue of so slight a slip. However, little Bunny now hung like the sword of Damocles over Mark and Anne's heads. If word of her birth got out, the marriage would have to end in divorce, something the Queen hoped to avoid at all costs.

In yet another of those curious coincidences that seem to dog the Royal Family, while Bunny was being born the story of Anne's friendship with Peter Cross was about to surface in a limited way. Cross had still not found any takers for the wares he had been hawking around Fleet Street for years. Then in August 1985 he dumped Gillian Nicholls to marry a dental nurse named Angie Plant. Miss Nicholls knew just where she could go for a profitable dose of compassion. She headed straight for the offices of the *News of the World*, Britain's foremost Sunday tabloid, who ran a tame version of the truth. The trouble was, they hinted at it so delicately that only those who were already in the know could actually decipher what the paper was getting at. This nevertheless precipitated a week of media frenzy.

When Peter Cross had a chance to tell his tale, he did so in the *News of the World*, the following Sunday. When he did speak, his gentle hints about Anne had the ring of truth, but the readers would have had to possess acute hearing, plus an inside knowledge of what was really going on, to hear it, so carefully did the paper couch its claims. The result was that a story that was truly sensational died a death, and Anne emerged unscathed, with no one but the inner circle knowing who or what to believe.

The royals and the courtiers at Buckingham Palace all deplore scandal, so everyone breathed more easily once Anne was off the front pages of the newspapers. She and Mark resumed the pace of their life, shooting off in opposite directions. He still did not have a proper girlfriend, although he had fleeting flirtations, including one with the former Miss India and part-time call-girl Pamela Bordes. Nor did Anne have a proper boyfriend. The tabloids kept on linking her with the actor Anthony Andrews, much to the annoyance of Tony, his wife Georgina, her mother Heddy, Anne, Mark, the Queen and all the many other people connected to them. In one notorious incident of media manipulation, an intimate-looking photograph of Anne and Tony huddled in conversation was used to support the thesis of a torrid love affair being conducted behind the backs of their spouses. The only trouble was, the photograph, which was taken at a ball, was cropped. Georgina was sitting right at the table with her husband and her good friend Anne, though her presence was skilfully kept from the world at large.

Anne, however, did not have much longer to wait before love came into her life. In 11 October, 1986, Commander Timothy Laurence, RN, was appointed an equerry to the Queen. Although he and Anne did not strike up a romance immediately, she soon noticed the thirty-one-year-old bachelor who had so impressed her mother with his efficiency, discretion and courtliness when he was posted to the royal yacht *Britannia* that she had him attached to her personal staff. He was tall, slim, dark, good-looking and charming. He was athletic, with the taut body of a man who keeps himself fit, and tantalizing, for he was so confirmed in his status as a bachelor that he did not even have a history of girlfriends, much less one who had threatened to ensnare him in connubial bliss. This, of course, Anne did not know for quite a while, but she did soon discover how attractive she found the personable and agreeable royal servant.

The key to Tim's attraction was threefold. Apart from his obvious physical charms, he was quintessentially ordinary, and his position as equerry guaranteed that he would be strong and positive while being respectful. Having been married to a dominant man, Anne no longer had a taste for the more macho aspects of the male sex. What she wanted was support without challenge, or, as one wit has put it, 'a wife with a willie'. She wanted a relationship in which she called the shots, in which she was the dominant force, in which her desires took precedence. She was a leader. She wanted a follower.

The man who fitted Anne's bill so exemplarily was the second son of the second marriage of a former naval officer turned gunnery expert, Guy Laurence. The Laurence family had once had money, made from the silk, spice and tea trade with the Far East during the eighteenth century, though by the time Tim pitched up at the Palace neither much money nor much claim to the name existed. Indeed, but for a change of name, Tim would have been Commander Levy, for he was descended in a straight line from a Venetian money-lender named Zaccaria Levy. Zaccaria's son Joseph married the heiress granddaughter of the last of the Lawrences, as they then spelt their name.

Penelope Lawrence Jackson possessed a vast trading fortune and was the chatelaine of West Rainton Hall, a stately home bought from Queen Elizabeth the Queen Mother's family, the Earls of Strathmore. Shrewdly assessing that her granddaughters' progeny would never be able to assume their rightful place in a society that did not even allow Catholics to sit in parliament, Penelope Lawrence Jackson left her fortune to her namesake granddaughter with the proviso that the Levys change their name to Lawrence. This they did by Royal Licence in 1826, amending the spelling slightly, and Joseph Laurence went on to enjoy a successful career in the City of London, founding the respected firm Laurence Keen, which still exists in Bow Lane, Cheapside. He also embarked upon a successful venture as a Christian, to such an extent that his youngest son became the Reverend Percival Laurence.

Such an exotic ancestry had long been buried beneath a plethora of respectability by the time Guy Laurence married the 22-year-old Barbara Symons at Kensington Register Office on 15 February 1951. Timothy James Hamilton Laurence was therefore born into a family that was as relentlessly ordinary as it is possible to be. Even the place of his birth was a study in ordinariness: Camberwell, South London. So too was the small corner house in Ightham, Kent, where he lived with his parents and his elder brother Jonathan. Even his departure, at the usual age, for preparatory school at the New Beacon School in Sevenoaks stayed within the confines of the mould. However, Tim did have extraordinary virtues, chief of which were his intelligence and his application. He excelled at New Beacon School, gained a scholarship to the prestigious Sevenoaks School, went on to read geography at Durham University, left with a good degree and enlisted at Dartmouth Naval College. So impressive was he that he was soon serving on *Britannia*, catching the Queen's eye, then when he moved to Buckingham Palace, her daughter's in an altogether different capacity from the professional.

At first, Anne's friendship with Tim was not personal. She liked him; he liked her. He was good company; she liked being entertained. Only too soon, however, it changed gear, and she was seeing a great deal of him. He is bright, trustworthy and has a quiet but definite brand of nous to his credit. So she made him a trustee of one of her charities, and their relationship assumed a new dimension. She was actually sharing the official part of her work with a man with whom she was involved, which was a switch from her relationship with Mark.

In 1987, the Queen made Anne the Princess Royal. There had long been talk that Anne would never accept the title, but she did, partly because she recognized its weight would counterbalance the appeal of the two sisters-in-law, Diana and Sarah, and partly because it cut Mark Phillips out of her name. Previously, she had been officially known as Her Royal Highness The Princess Anne, Mrs Mark Phillips.

Armed with her new title, Anne continued touring the world and accepting so many official engagements that she was now the busiest member of the Royal Family. Publicly, she was revered for the outstanding work she did for the Save the Children Fund and other charities, while privately she had never been more fulfilled. Never before had Anne had a relationship such as the one she was now having with Tim. Its depth and scope were all encompassing. Theirs were compatible personalities, for they are both private but intense individuals who place great stress on personal achievement, on their personal lives and on athletic pursuits. All her life Anne had been an avid sailor like her father, and now she took up the sport of sailing with even greater vigour. To an extent this was a replacement, albeit a gradual one, for the sport of jockeying, which she had taken up in 1985 when she rode in a race at Epsom in aid of the Riding for the Disabled Association. Thereafter, she rode in a succession of races throughout the country, acquitting herself admirably, but it was a solitary sport, as well as a dangerous one, and the Queen was relieved when she gave it up in favour of the more sociable pastime of sailing.

With the passage of time, Anne's feelings for Tim deepened. She had never had an affair such as this. His intelligence made sharing the problems of her everyday life a joy, but it was not all heavy without being hot. Her passionate nature had unlocked something within him, and he was as obsessed with her as she was with him. Whenever they were apart, they wrote one another impassioned love letters, and when they were together the atmosphere surrounding them was electric.

Scandal, however, was around the corner. In March 1988, the press exposed Pamela Bordes as a call-girl. Up to that point, she had been better known as the girlfriend of Andrew Neil, editor of the *Sunday Times*, and as a former Miss India. While Neil tore into Donald Trelford, the editor of the *Observer*, as a result of that newspaper's reports arising out of the scandal, and treated Britain to the spectacle of one editor suing another, Pamela Bordes began singing like a bird in the pages of the tabloids. Her comments about the brillo-haired Neil were mildly entertaining, but what excited interest was her claim to have had a fling with Mark Phillips when she was taking riding lessons at his Gleneagles equestrian centre in Scotland. Buckingham Palace issued a denial, inferring that La Bordes had made the whole thing up, though those of us who knew what Mark's nickname was knew whom we believed.

Two weeks later, Kelvin Mackenzie, the editor of the *Sun*, received four love letters written by Tim Laurence to Anne. They had been posted anonymously. While he might have used them at another time, he had recently been put in the humiliating position of having to pay the Queen £100,000 for breach of copyright when he published a photograph of Princess Beatrice. So he handed the letters over to Scotland Yard and emblazoned the following headline over the next day's paper: PALACE THIEF STEALS ANNE'S LETTERS: *SUN* TO THE RESCUE. He did not reveal specifics about the letters, however, nor did he identify the writer. That was left to the Buckingham Palace Press Office to do, in what seemed like an own goal at the time. Commander Laurence was now out of the bag, and there was speculation that he would be sent packing. Instead, the Queen showed up in public with him behind her. It was as spectacular a display of solidarity as the sovereign could give, and to those who know how court circles function, it relayed the message that Tim Laurence was there to stay. The tabloids, however, were not sufficiently knowledgeable to pick up the message.

Commander Laurence was then taken off his royal duties, endowed with the Royal Victorian Order and entertained during the summer by the Queen at Balmoral. Significantly, Mark Phillips was not asked, not that or any other summer thereafter. Once more, the royal signals were clear.

By this time, Anne wanted a divorce. Mark, however, became reluctant after having initially agreed to a separation. He felt his son Peter and Zara would be destabilized by the break-up of their marriage. And of course being the husband of the Princess Royal was a great ace in the hole for a businessman of his calibre to have, especially now that he had started horse trials at Gatcombe. But Anne was adamant. She wanted to be free of the shackles of a dead marriage, and more importantly she wanted to be free to live her life with Tim Laurence. The matter was therefore turned over to the lawyers, the Queen's solicitor Sir Matthew Farrer acting for Anne and Lord Goodman for Mark.

As negotiations progressed, and Mark began to realize how tough the Royal Family can be when someone's interests are at variance with their own, a bitterness that had not existed until the letters were made public became exacerbated. Eventually, however, Anne and Mark struck a civilized agreement, whereby he would continue running the farms at Gatcombe; she would retain exclusive benefit of the trust that owned the property; she would have custody of the children, with him having generous visitation rights; he would undertake to uphold the confidentiality of their time together and of her family; and he would receive a settlement of £750,000.

On 13 August 1989, Buckingham Palace announced Anne and Mark's separation. The statement claimed that there was no intention to seek a divorce, but that assertion had been made at the time of Princess Margaret's separation and had subsequently proved to be as false as it was disingenuous, so no one in their right mind would have accepted it as true. Sure enough, two and a half years after the official separation, Anne and Mark were divorced.

If Anne's divorce was but one of the factors that contributed to the Queen's *annus horribilis* in 1992, her marriage to Tim Laurence was one of the few highlights. Lilibet liked Tim. He was everything a man should be, and while Anne's remarriage presented difficulties for the Queen, they were not insurmountable. She therefore gave her consent for the marriage to take place in Scotland, England being out of bounds due to the fact that the Church of England, unlike the Church of Scotland, does not allow divorced people to remarry in the church, and the Royal Family are forbidden to marry in an English Register Office.

Everyone was proving most obliging as Anne made plans to solemnize her union with Tim at Crathie Church near Balmoral. Even Queen Elizabeth the Queen Mother, who had made disapproval of remarriage into a principle, thereby preventing the Duke and Duchess of Windsor from ever enjoying anything approximating a normal family life, did a complete volte-face and stepped off the high moral ground she had occupied throughout the ninety-two years of her life. She accepted the invitation to attend the wedding, rearranging plans she had previously made to have lunch elsewhere. Anne was ecstatic about this marriage. Love had proved to be infinitely better the second time around, and this time her wedding was going to reflect her true self. It would be low-key, intimate and as private as possible under the circumstances.

With less than a week to go, Diana almost sabotaged Anne's big day. As recounted earlier, she informed Charles she would announce their separation on the day of the wedding itself unless he had the prime minister do so on the Wednesday before it. She very nearly succeeded in adulterating the pure joy somewhat. But, if a day in politics is long, three days in a family can be eternity, and by the time Anne's Range Rover swept up the road to the church for her wedding at three o'clock in the afternoon on Saturday, 12 December, Anne had better things on her mind.

The honeymoon was reflective of the new royal couple's attitude to fuss. There was none, except within the immediate family of the new Mrs Laurence. Zara was surly, churlish and rebellious. She hated having to share the mother whom she had had to herself with any man calling himself her stepfather. Anne had spoilt her from the moment of her birth in a way that she had never spoilt Peter. Up to the wedding, theirs had been a special and intense relationship, and though Anne did not withdraw from her daughter, Zara did feel threatened. She has still not made the adjustment, still acts up out of the fear that the mother she adores might love her just that little bit less than she did, now that she has a husband to love as well. This, however, is a problem that many stepchildren experience when they acquire step-parents, so even there Anne has headed towards the ordinary problems that divorcees face upon remarriage.

If Zara has been difficult, Peter Phillips has been exemplary. He gets along with his stepfather and gives his mother no trouble. Relations between Anne and Mark, however, are not cordial. There is not a great deal of contact between them, but such as there is, is polite. Too much heat and too much cold has been replaced by chilly civility.

And Anne and Tim are forging the life they want together. Unsurprisingly, its emphasis is on achievement, sport, satisfaction and ordinariness. She works hard at her job as the Princess Royal, he at his in the Ministry of Defence, where he earns £30,000 a year. They have very sensibly distanced themselves from the courtiers at Buckingham Palace. They know only too well how condescending many of the senior courtiers are, how fulsomely they disapprove of the marriage, and how happily they would wreck it if they could. In their snobbish eyes, Anne has married a servant of junior rank, and they snigger behind her back and Tim's. That is the reason why Anne has moved out of her suite of rooms in Buckingham Palace into a flat in Dolphin Square in Pimlico. She and Tim know only too well that the only way they can breathe pure air is to distance themselves from the pollution courtiers of a certain ilk will belch out at them. And they are determined they will remain pure and in love and as happy as they have been since their affair began.

The courtiers aside, Anne's move from Buckingham Palace has great significance because it is the first time a member of the Royal Family has opted for a bourgeois way of life. Anne's path is undoubtedly the direction in which the Royal Family will head in the future, for we live in increasingly egalitarian times, and if the monarchy is to survive – there is no more survival-orientated breed than the House of Windsor – they will have to make the adjustment from regal to more mundane.

Like many another couple who have married later in life, one spouse has children, while the other does not. Although Anne's views on motherhood are clear, she is nevertheless happy to indulge her new husband's desire for at least one child and preferably two children. Doubtless Anne will continue to tread the ordinary path and in the process provide the British nation with a respected and extraordinary Princess Royal. Already she is a figure of admiration, eventually she might become a figure of identification.

CHAPTER TWENTY-FOUR

Metamorphosis of the Monarchy

Royal marriages are not only unions of two people but also affairs of state. As we have seen, the emphasis used to be on the public aspects of partnership, which the royals felt must endure even after the personal dimension had altered. This has changed, partly because the Royal Family no longer have the privacy they used to. They can no longer pursue their private lives in the certainty that the public will never learn of their arrangements. This leaves them with a stark and unwelcome choice. Either they do without personal satisfaction once a marriage has outlived its personal purpose, or they get divorces like everyone else.

The rules governing royal marriages have changed, not because the deeply conventional royals have been inclined to alter their behaviour and attitudes, nor because they have been marrying commoners, but because society itself has been undergoing a profound metamorphosis. No longer does it respect appearances the way it did earlier this century. Private accommodations, which allowed the parties concerned to lead independent lives, are therefore no longer acceptable, primarily because such Victorian attitudes now seem hypocritical rather than admirable, and society has, to an ever increasing extent, been losing its tolerance of double standards ever since the end of the First World War.

Nevertheless, one tradition endures. The British public want the Royal Family to continue in their conventional role as symbols of the national identity. That identity, however, has been changing rapidly since the end of

239

the Second World War. The Empire has dissolved, and Britain is no longer the great power it once was. While it has lost much of its power and wealth, it has gained greatly in human terms, for it is now a more open, tolerant, multicultural society than it used to be.

Living in an alien world from the one his parents and grandparents knew, the average Briton reflects those changes by possessing different values from the ones they used to have. Neither marriage nor divorce is now the issue it once was. Society has merely altered its concerns, so that social consciousness, bettering the lot of the less fortunate, charity work and compassion for the infirm have replaced the old moral concerns of fire and brimstone, right and wrong.

There is also a national ethos of greater choice, and this is reflected not only in the way the average person lives and moves around in a previously unthought-of manner but also in the way the Royal Family conduct their lives. No one is expected to live in a strait-jacket any more, and while there is the general feeling that living up to one's duty is as admirable as ever it was, only the most unreasonable or narrow-minded Briton any longer expects the royals to sacrifice their personal fulfilment for a lifetime of sterile obligation.

There is no doubt that both the British and their Royal Family still have significant adjustments to make as they enter the third millennium. There are still residues of Empire, which will have to be sloughed off. For the royals, as for the citizens of the country, that will mean tailoring their standards to reflect a less grandiose ideal. The sacrifice of splendour, however, has not been such a bad thing to date. It has opened up society in a way that was inconceivable in the days when Britain was a powerful hierarchy. The result has been that even the Royal Family can now lead relatively normal private lives. The people no longer expect them to be perfect symbols, simply conscientious representatives of the national ethic. That, for both the royals and the country, can only be to the good, for an honest reflection is always preferable to a dishonest one.

This leads to one of the most fundamental changes taking place in British society at the moment. The people no longer wish to be 'led' by their leaders. Whether the leader in question is a politician or a royal, the people wish to be represented. At the beginning of the century, they were expected to follow the example of their 'betters'. Now, they do not regard politicians or royals as their betters. They are merely the people's representatives. This is a significant shift in attitude, and one which is reflective of power moving away from the rulers to the ruled. It means that the ruling class is more answerable to those they govern than ever before. It also signals significant changes in the style of governance, for people who are ruled by consent have the power to change their rulers in a way that those without such power cannot.

This is the reason why the Royal Family will have to modify its lifestyle. And, as they do so, divesting themselves of the trappings of greatness, they will also strip themselves of much that is presently regarded as regal. In doing so, they will be more visibly normal. And once they are more visibly normal, it will only be a matter of time before they do become more pedestrian. The Royal Family, like the British people, will undergo profound and fundamental adjustments by the time the twenty-first century dawns, but these should ultimately lead to a better if less glittering quality of life for all concerned.

INDEX

PICTURE CREDITS